FAITH
AND HUMAN REASON

SUPPLEMENTS TO
NOVUM TESTAMENTUM

VOLUME XL

LEIDEN
E. J. BRILL
1975

FAITH
AND HUMAN REASON

A STUDY OF PAUL'S METHOD OF PREACHING
AS ILLUSTRATED BY 1-2 THESSALONIANS
AND ACTS 17, 2-4

BY

DIETER WERNER KEMMLER

REGIS
BIBL. MAJ.
COLLEGE

LEIDEN
E. J. BRILL
1975

ISBN 90 04 04209 1

Copyright 1975 by E. J. Brill, Leiden, Netherlands

PRINTED IN BELGIUM

CONTENTS

PREFACE VII

ABBREVIATION IX

INTRODUCTION 1

CHAPTER ONE

ACTS 17, 2-4

Introduction 11

§ 1. *The "intellectual element" in Paul's method of preaching*
with respect to the sources : the "argument" from scripture   18

    Section 1 : Observations 18
        A) διαλέγεσθαι 18
        B) διανοίγειν 36
        C) παρατίθεσθαι 41
        D) καταγγέλλειν 42
        E) Correlation 43

    Section 2 : Interpretation of the findings 48
        A) The framework of interpretation : Paul's commission
            — action and suffering 49
        B) Interpretation : The connection between action and
            suffering with regard to the "intellectual element"
            in Paul's preaching 64

§ 2. *The "intellectual element" in Paul's method of preaching*
with respect to the aim : the "persuasion" of his hearers .   76

    Introduction 76

    Section 1 : Observations 78
        A) πείθειν in early Greek epic and lyric poetry . . . 78
        B) πείθειν in the major tragedians and comedians . . 91
        C) πείθειν in the major historians 104
        D) πείθειν in the Attic orators : Legal speeches . . 110
        E) πείθειν in the Attic orators : Other speeches . . . 117

Excursus I 134
Excursus II 137

Section 2 : Application of these observations with regard
to Acts 138

Conclusions : The reasons for and the significance and function
of the human reason in preaching 143

CHAPTER TWO

1 AND 2 THESSALONIANS

Introduction 147
§ 3. *1 Thessalonians* 149
Section 1 : 1 Th 1, 5 149
A) The Problem 149
B) Attempted solution 155
C) Conclusions 166

Section 2 : 1 Th 2, 2f. 168
A) The Problem 168
B) An attempted solution 173
C) Conclusions 177

§ 4. *2 Thessalonians 2* 178
Introduction 178
Section 1 : 2 Th 2, 2 179
A) σαλεύειν/σαλεύεσθαι 179
B) νοῦς 182
C) σαλεύεσθαι ἀπὸ τοῦ νοός 187

Section 2 : 2 Th 2, 13-15 190
A) The connection with 1 Th 1, 4f. 190
B) The relation of λόγος/διδάσκειν to the "coming of
the Gospel" 191
Conclusions : The reason for and the significance and function
of the human reason in preaching 206

BIBLIOGRAPHY 212

PREFACE

The material in this book was presented as a thesis for the degree of Doctor of Philosophy at the University of Cambridge (England) while I was a research student of Kings College, and was accepted in 1973. It appears here almost without alterations. Although it is decidedly a specialist essay, yet I believe that I have not indulged in theological "art for art's sake", and I hope that this book will ultimately serve the true end of all theology, namely the preaching of the Gospel.

I should like to record my appreciation of the guidance and encouragement that I received from my supervisor, Professor C. F. D. Moule of Clare College. I also thank Dr. A. J. M. Wedderburn who has helped me in the English presentation of this work, and Rev. C. Holladay who has helped in the typing of a difficult manuscript.

In dedicating it to my wife I pay tribute to her patience and companionship during our time in Cambridge.

Trinity College   D. W. KEMMLER
Legon, Ghana
January 1974

ABBREVIATIONS

A	Abbott, Johannine Grammar
A1/A2	Alexander, Acts
Ad	Adeney, Thessalonians
A-G	Arndt-Gingrich, N-T Lexicon
Alford	Alford, The Greek Testament
A-R	Auberlen-Riggenbach, Thessalonicherbriefe
A-S	Abbott-Smith, N-T Lexicon
Ba	Barclay, NT Words
Bar	Bartlet, Acts
Barn	Barnes, A., Thessalonians
Baur	Baur, Paulus
B-C	Baumgarten-Crusius, Thessalonicher
B-D-F	Blass-Debrunner-Funk, NT-Grammar
Be	Bengel, Gnomon
Beg	Jackson-Lake, Beginnings (Acts)
Ben	Benfey, Griechisches Wurzellexikon
Bens	Griechisch-Deutsches Wörterbuch
Bey	Beyer, Semitische Syntax
Bi	Bicknell, Thessalonians
Bis 1	Bisping, I. Thessalonicher
Bis 2	Bisping, II. Thessalonicher
Bjerkelund	Bjerkelund, Parakalo
Bl	Blaiklock, Acts
Blo	Bloomfield, I and II Thessalonians
Bo	Boisacq, Dictionnaire étymologique
Bor	Bornemann, Thessalonicherbriefe
Br 1	Bruce, Acts
Br 2	Bruce, Commentary on Acts
B-T	Brugmann, Griechische Grammatik
Bu	Buttmann, Grammatik des NT
Buck	Buck, Dictionary of Synonyms
Bur	Burton, Syntax
C	Cremer, Biblisch-theol. Wörterbuch
Ca	Calvin, Thessalonians
Ch	Chantraine, Dictionnaire étymologique
Ch Gr	Chantraine, Grammaire
Co	Conzelmann, Apostelgeschichte
Cu	Curtius, Grundzüge der griech. Etymologie
C-U	Cremer-Urwick, Biblico-Theological Lexicon
D	Deissmann, Light from the Ancient East
D B	Deissmann, Bible Studies
D NB	Deissmann, Neue Bibelstudien
De	Denniston, Greek Particles

Del	Delbrück, Vergleichende Syntax
Den	Denney, Thessalonians
Di	Dibelius, Thessalonicher I und II
Do	Dobschütz, v., Thessalonicherbriefe
Dr	Drummond, Thessalonians
E	Ebeling, NT Wörterbuch
Ea	Eadie, Thessalonians
Eg	Egenolf, II Thessalonians
El	Ellicott, Thessalonians
Ew	Ewald, Sendschreiben
F	Field, NT Notes
Fi	Fick, Vergleichendes Wörterbuch
Fin	Findlay, Thessalonians
Fo	Foakes-Jackson, Acts
Fr	Frisk, Griechisches Etym. Wörterbuch
Fra	Frame, Thessalonians
Fw	Preisigke, Fachwörter
G	Goodspeed, Problems of NT Transl.
Ga	Garrod, I. Thessalonians
Gl	Gloag, I., II. Thessalonians
Gr 1	Green, NT Grammar
Gr 2	Green, Critical Notes
Gra	Grayston, Thessalonians
G-T	Thayer, NT Lexicon
H	Heine, NT-Synonymik
vH	Hofmann, v., Thessalonicher
Ha	Haenchen, Apostelgeschichte
Han	Hanson, Acts
Har	Harris, The Writings of the Apostle Paul
He	Helbing, LXX-Grammatik
Hen	Hendriksen, I and II Thessalonians
Her	Hervey, The Acts
Ho	Hofmann, Etymologisches Wörterbuch
Hol 1	Holtzmann, Die Apostelgeschichte
Hol 2	Holtzmann, Thessalonicher
H-V	Hogg-Vine, Thessalonians
Hu	Hunter, Exploring the NT
J	Jannaris, An historical Greek Grammar
Jo	Jowett, Thessalonians
Joh	Johannessohn, Präpositionen
Ka	Kaltschmidt, Etymologisches Wörterbuch
K-B	Kühner-Blass, Grammatik
Ke	Kennedy, Sources of NT Greek
Kel	Kelly, Thessalonians
K-G	Kühner-Gerth, Grammatik
Ko	Koch, Thessalonischer
L	Lampe, Patristic Greek Lexicon
La	Lake, Earlier, Epistles

Lat	Lattey, St. Paul's Epistles
Li	Lightfoot, Notes
Lin	Lineberry, Word Studies in I Thess.
Lj	Ljungvik, Beiträge zur Syntax
Lu	Luther, NT-Wörterbuch
Lu 1	Lumby, The Acts (1904)
Lu 2	Lumby, The Acts (1893)
Lü	Lünemann, Thessalonicher
Lue	Lueken, I-II Thess.
M	Moule, Idiom Book
MI, II, III	Moulton/Howard/Turner, NT Grammar
Ma	Mayser, Grammatik
Mac	MacEvilly, Thessalonians
Mas	Mason, Thessalonians
Me	Meecham, Light from ancient letters
M-G Conc	Moulton-Milligan, Concordance
Meisterhans	Meisterhans, Grammatik
Mey	Meyer, L., Handbuch der griech. Etymologie
Meyer	Meyer, H. A. W., The Acts
Mi 1	Milligan, Selections
Mi 2	Milligan, Here and There
Mi 3	Milligan, Thessalonians
M-M	Moulton-Milligan, Vocabulary
Mo	Moore, Thessalonians
Mor 1	Morris, Thessalonians NLC
Mor 2	Morris, Thessalonians Tyn
Mu	Munck, Acts
Mü	Müller, Historische Grammatik
N	Nägeli, Wortschatz
Ne	Neil, Thessalonians
O	Oepke, Die kleineren Briefe
Ol	Olshausen, Thessalonians
P	Pape, Handwörterbuch
Pa	Parkhurst, NT Lexicon
Pal	Palmer, Grammar
P-C	Passow-Crönert, Handwörterbuch
P-K	Preisgke-Kiessling, Wörterbuch
Pl 1	Plummer, I Thess.
Pl 2	Plummer, II Thess.
Pl 3	Plummer, St. Luke
Po	Pokorny, Etymologisches Wörterbuch
Pr	Prellwitz, Etymologisches Wörterbuch
Pre	Preuschen, Apostelgeschichte
Ps	Passow, Handwörterbuch
R	Robinson, NT Lexicon
Ra	Radermacher, NT Grammatik
Rac	Rackham, Acts
Ro	Robertson, Word Pictures

Rob	Robertson, NT Grammar
Rö/Roe	Röhm, I. Thessalonicher
Ross	Rossberg, De praepositionum
S	Schwyzer, Grammatik
Sa	Sadler, Thessalonians
Sch	Schmidt, Synonymik der griech. Sprache
Scha	Schaefer, Thessalonicher
Schl	Schleusner, NT-Lexicon
Schla 1	Schlatter, Apostelgeschichte
Schla 2	Schlatter, Thessalonicher
Schm	Schmiedel, Thessalonicher
Schmi	Schmidt, Thessalonicher
Schü/Schue	Schürmann, I Thessalonicher
Si	Simcox, NT Language
So	Sophocles, Lexicon
Stä	Apostelgeschichte
T	Trench, Synonyms
TDNT	Kittel, Theological Dictionary (Engl. transl.)
Th	Thackeray, LXX-Grammar
ThBl	Coenen, Theologisches Begriffslexikon
Thr	Thrall, NT Greek particles
Thu	Thumb, Handbook
ThWB	Kittel, Theologisches Wörterbuch
Tu	Turner, Grammatical Insights
Ursprung	Meyer, E., Ursprung und Anfänge
V	Vincent, NT Word Studies
Va	Vanicek, Etymologisches Wörterbuch
van H	van Herwerden, Lexicon Graecum
W	Winer, NT-Grammatik
We	Wendt, Apostelgeschichte
Wet	Wette, de, Thessalonicher
Wh	Whiteley, Thessalonians
Wi	Williams, Acts
Wo	Wohlenberg, Thessalonicherbriefe
W-P	Walde-Pokorny, Wörterbuch
W-S	Winer-Schmiedel, NT-Grammatik
Wu 1	Wuest, Studies
Z	Zorell, NT-Lexicon
Zö/Zoe	Zöckler, Thessalonicher

INTRODUCTION

A. In the following work we are concerned with the question of what function and significance was attached to human reason in *Christians'* lives. We pose this question with regard to the *New Testament*. We hope to obtain our first insight into this problem by means of what we believe to be a representative example of the New Testament, namely the example of the *person of the apostle Paul.* Our interest, however, is not in the so-called psychology of the apostle; rather we are asking what role the human reason played in his *preaching* and, consequently, what significance he attached to it. Yet we will try to answer this question in our present investigation, not with regard to the content of his preaching, but solely, as a preliminary step, with regard to his *methods.* Thus the object of our investigation is not the methods of Paul's preaching as such but only in so far as it concerns the *"intellectual element"* which may be contained in it.

Therefore our two basic questions are :

Do Paul's preaching methods reflect his attitude to the *function* and *significance* of human reason in "preaching" ?

If they do, what exactly is it that, in the last analysis, *obliges* him and so us also to introduce human reason into our lives as Christ's witnesses ?

We must limit ourselves to the two Thessalonian letters together with the corresponding Thessalonica-pericope in Acts. Yet we hope that the results of the investigation will be representative.[1]

---

[1] We could only reach a really satisfactory answer to our question once we could gain a wider view of this whole complex of questions through other representative studies of the New Testament, quite apart from the examination of the content of the preaching itself (yet cf. p. 178, n. 7f.).

i)   Faith and human reason could, e.g., also be investigated through asking what role the latter plays in "knowing God's will".

ii) The same problem could be investigated by raising the question whether and how far the early Church saw itself also to have an intellectual responsibility towards its non-Christian environment.

iii) Again the problem of the relation of faith and human reason in Paul is raised, *prima facie,* when we concern ourselves with his missionary strategy. Here we would already find an interaction between the working of the Holy Spirit and Paul's deliberate planning.

iv) And this question raises itself too from the other end when we investigate the

B. The two Thessalonian letters are among the oldest, if not themselves the oldest, of the surviving letters of Paul.[2] In addition they are with A 17, 2 ff. a witness to the "first known Christian missionary to preach in Europe. This step ... set the course of Christianity westwards".[3] But apart from this very important but purely chronological and geographical [4] fact, the decisive reason for beginning with the two Thessalonian letters (and particularly in

---

spiritual background of Paul's hearers and ask how far Paul could find a "point of contact" and so how far he could reckon with hearers who were ready to listen to him. Although, strictly speaking, this is a question of the value of the human reason in non-Christians in hearing the gospel, yet it has its consequences for Paul's preaching methods (and in some cases the contents of his preaching) if his apologetic was not to be a pure farce. Did his hearers bring with them insights from their own age and situation which could give them help in understanding Paul's message? With regard to the persons mentioned in A 17, 4.11 f. at any rate the commentators have analysed the facts as follows :

a) the men ("a large number of minds" Fin xxv) in this typical Graeco-Roman city—"as in other places" (Mor 1, 18)—, "in various ranks of society, both within and without the range of Jewish influence" (Fin xxv), are depicted as "dissatisfied with the ... intellectual absurdity of polytheism" (Mor 1, 18; cf. also Mo 3), "weary of heathen ... philosophy" (Fin xvi)—"out of their native pagan darkness" (Ad 9).

b) they have already taken a step "towards the light" (Ad 9).

c) this step into the light made them "in a manner", as Gl (v) adds in qualification, into "congenial soil" (Fin xv), "soil specially fitted for the sowers of the Christian word" (La 66) : "the ground had long been prepared" (Bi xiii). If thus "der Stand der Gemüther empfänglich" (A-R 2; cf. also Wet 91), then they were really "a prepared people" (Fin xv) and "prepared for 'the good news of God' " (Fin xxv; xv), "for the reception of Christianity" (Gl v), to which they accordingly gave "a ready welcome" (Mor 1, 18).

d) and the "readiest hearers of the Gospel" (Fin xvi) are as such "ready to listen to reason" (Ad 9). Therefore the "readiest hearers of the Gospel" could only be "enquiring and thinking people" (Mo 3), "enlightened Gentiles" (Fin xvi), the "more refined and intelligent Greek women of the upper classes" (Fin xvii; cf. also Hen 9).

e) and, correspondingly, that which "Christianity offered" (Ne xi; Bi xii) to these men, i.e. this inclination to "reason" and as such to the gospel is "just (!) what they were seeking" (Bi xii), nothing else than the fulfilment of a "clearly felt want" (La 65) : "In Christianity they found a faith that satisfied" (Mor 2, 12; Mo 3; cf. also Mor 1, 18).

[2] Cf. New Testament introductions and commentaries on 1/2 Th.

[3] Mor 1, 15.

[4] B-C 122 remarks : "Merkwürdig ist, dass diese brieflichen Ansprachen des Apostles erst auf seinen europäischen Reisen begannen".

answering this question) is as follows : "No other writing of the great
apostle provides a greater insight into his missionary methods ...",[5]
into "the character of the Apostle's missionary preaching".[6] And "in
connection with the Acts" [7]..., "we can draw from the Epistles ... a
clear picture of the Apostle's manner of ... preaching at Thessalonica ...".[8] We do not need to concern ourselves in our investigations
of either A or 1/2 Th with all the data which they provide concerning
Paul's preaching methods. For the object of our investigation is, as
we have said, not the methods of Paul's preaching as such but only
in so far as they can throw light on the problem of the function and
significance of the human reason in the life of the first Christians.
But if *this* is the particular slant of our investigation then we must
ask again whether it really helps to take as our starting-point "the
Cinderellas of the recognized Pauline epistles ...".[9] For this is one's
evaluation of them if one holds that basically these letters "in force
of intellect ... do not rise to the height of some of the later Epistles ..." [10]
and thus show neither "constructive or dialectic skill ..." [11] as, e.g.,
Romans, nor "the logical dexterity of Galatians",[12] nor in short "the
more argumentative methods of the Epistles to the Galatians or
Romans".[13] In our study the centre of attention will not be the
content of 1/2 Th as such but only the allusions made there to Paul's
original missionary activity, so that this supposed "Cinderella-
character" of the letters does not really affect our question; but
quite apart from that it is worth mentioning in the interests of our
problem *how* scholars have tried to "explain" this apparent fact.

(1) On the one hand they cite the "infancy" of the Thessalonian
Christians as the reason for the "simple theology" [14] contained in
these two letters : "Babes in Christ, newly won over from idolatry,
need simple and pure religion rather than reasoned and systematized
theology".[15]

---

[5] Mor 2, 9.
[6] Mi 3, vii; so also Fin xxv.
[7] Cf. also Mi 3, xlii.
[8] El 77.
[9] Ne xxvii.
[10] Fin lviii.
[11] Mi 3, xliii.
[12] Ne xxvii.
[13] Mi 3, lxiv.
[14] *ibid.*
[15] Pl 1, xiv.

(2) On the other hand they "explain" the "plain, almost disappointingly straightforward, normal letter-writing" [16] not by the need in such early days for "simple religion" but by the "simple" character of its recipients in general : "This church was not troubled with any of the refined subtleties of thought that interested the more dreamy, speculative Christians of Ephesus and the Churches in the Lycus Valley, nor with the ambition of intellectuality in which the Greeks of Achaia indulged".[17] The last-named in particular "brought into their religion a shallow intellectualism, ... and a general instability ... They ... underrated ... sober moral qualities ...".[18]

In contrast, they go on to "explain", the first missionaries in Thessalonica were in a far more fortunate position. Here they had a "seltene schöne Zeit",[19] and the Thessalonians were "morally more promising material for missionaries to work upon".[20] Why ? Because they were "practical people",[21] "simple",[22] "solid, reliable, homely folk" [23] and as such had "a simple view of the teachings they had received".[24] Therefore they showed no interest in "doctrinal controversies" [25] or "theological refinements".[26]

All this, either the Thessalonian Christians' "infancy" or their "character" in general, is meant to explain the "fact" of the "disappointingly simple theology" contained in 1/2 Th with its "neither passionate nor argumentative" [27] theology. But has one here really "explained" a fact which actually exists ?

To (1) Quite apart from the fact that all congregations to which Paul writes were once "babes in Christ"—even the Corinthians—, we must leave aside here the extremely difficult question of what is *meant* by "simple and pure religion", and that in contrast to "reasoned theology".

i) We want here to recall the generally recognized "occasional

---

16 Ne xxvii.
17 Ad 13.
18 Bi xxiv.
19 Ew 40.
20 Pl 1, v.
21 Bi xxxv.
22 Ad 13.
23 Bi xxiv.
24 Ad 13.
25 Bi xxiv.
26 Bi xxxv; cf. also xxiii.
27 Fin lviii.

nature" of these letters : "they are especially adapted to the conditions
and needs of his correspondents in the special circumstances they are
designed to meet".[28] This certainly also goes some way to explain
the fact that the allegation of the "simple theology" of the two
"straightforward" Thessalonian letters continually comes up against
the glaring problems that the letters present for us [29] and the "obscurity that some people complain of when reading his epistles".[30]
What is the meaning of "simple theology", simple "religion" in the
light of the many "allusions to what the Thessalonians already know" [31]
—and the rule that "the more familiar the subjects with which they
deal were to their first readers, the more veiled they are from us ..." ? [32]
Can we really talk so sweepingly of "plain, almost disappointingly
straightforward, normal letter-writing" ?

ii) And if one "lays bare" the letters, one thing becomes plain, that
Paul "taught them—or at least expected them to understand—a
great many of the fundamental Christian convictions";[33] he "must
have taught a great deal of doctrine, so much is assumed as known ...".[34]
Therefore "to call the letter 'undogmatic' would be misleading".[35]
Rather the last two chapters of 1 Th and the whole of 2 Th are
nothing but "teaching and exhortation rendered necessary by his
converts' intellectual difficulties".[36]

To (2) The contrast that many commentators think that they see
between the "simple folk" at Thessalonica and the "shallow intellectualism" at Corinth and the connected contrast of "sober moral
qualities" and "moral instability" seem more artificial than real :
"Die Stadt trug durchaus griechisches Gepräge, wie denn überhaupt
der Unterschied zwischen den dort, im Herzen Makedoniens, sesshaften
Makedoniern, einem den Griechen verwandten Stamm, und den Süd-
hellenen um die Zeit, da das Christentum dort Wurzel schlug, nicht
mehr von Bedeutung war".[37] "Das sittliche Leben zu Thessalonich

---

[28] Ad 14; cf. Ne xxvi; Bi xxxv; etc.
[29] Cf. Ad 9.
[30] Ad 5.
[31] Mi 3, xli f.
[32] Mi 3, xlii; cf. also n. 1.
[33] Gra 51.
[34] Pl 1, xiv.
[35] *Ibid.*
[36] Ga 22.
[37] Wo 2; cf. Barn 4; Lat xiᴛ

wird zur Zeit Christi nicht besser und nicht schlechter gewesen sein als in jeder anderen bedeutenden und volkreichen, heidnischen Stadt des römischen Reiches".[38] The "fact" of the "Cinderella-character" of 1/2 Th with regard to the "intellect" is thus an extremely questionable matter in the light of both the references in the text and the existence of the text itself. Mostly, scholars have explained a "fact" which did not exist at all. The resultant inferences that one draws about Paul's first appearance at Thessalonica must therefore be drawn with the greatest caution, if at all.

In contrast it seems to me very important that we should constantly attend, in investigating this matter, to the following two points :

(1) We must always be aware of the dialectic which characterizes any letter : on the one hand we find in 1/2 Th a "Beschränkung auf Hauptsachen, die verhältnismässige Konzentration" and thus a "reflektierende ... Beurteilung" [39] that arises from the author's temporal and spatial detachment. That certainly applies also to the "insight into his missionary methods" [40] to be gained from these letters. But on the other hand we must at the same time note, as we have already remarked, that the letters were not written in order "to instruct us as to the character or the methods of St. Paul".[41]

This brings us to the important insight that, despite the "Beschränkung auf Hauptsachen" possible through his detachment, we can only learn anything about Paul's original missionary works in Thessalonica "gebrochen", refracted through the prism of the present and therefore quite specific situation in Thessalonica and the resultant purpose of Paul's letters to that place.

Positively that means that when Paul reminisces about his *former* visit he presumably does so more or less in the interests of his *present* purpose in writing the letters. Negatively that means that we cannot too quickly find "fundamental" truths in his words or allusions or deduce them from these. For we can only contact the missionary Paul through the letter-writer Paul.

(2) We must continually remain watchful and alert to the possibility of the content of Paul's preaching influencing his preaching

---

[38] Bor 10.

[39] *Op. cit.*, 24.

[40] Cf. p. 3.

[41] Pl 1, xv.

methods—and thus influencing his evaluation of the "intellectual element" as reflected in these methods.

Conclusions :

The absence of "reasoned theology" in 1/2 Th is too questionable a matter to count as a serious argument against our enquiry, which tries to discern the "intellectual element" above all through observing the way in which Paul originally encountered the Thessalonians.

Therefore there is no reason why we should not investigate the problem of the relation of faith and human reason to one another with regard to 1/2 Th (and A 17, 2ff.). For here we are not only very near to the "Herzschlag paulinischen Lebens" [42] and can thus "understand the personality and methods of St. Paul aright" [43] but also at the same time we can learn "something of the atmosphere and temper in which the primitive Church developed into the full flower of the Christian faith".[44] Both must be seen together. "A detailed study ... is essential, therefore, to a proper understanding of the Apostolic Age, and forms the best introduction to the more developed interpretation of Christian thought, which we are accustomed to describe as Paulinism".[45]

---

[42] Do 23.
[43] Ne xxvii.
[44] *Ibid.*
[45] Mi 3, vii.

CHAPTER ONE
ACTS 17, 2-4

INTRODUCTION

Because our chief concern is with the two Thessalonian letters—
and this can be no more than just a beginning for a comprehensive
study of the Pauline corpus—we must here elicit what Luke says in
his account of Paul's stay at Thessalonica which is relevant to our
question. We must therefore examine the "intellectual element" in
Acts 17, 2-4, as it is reflected in Paul's missionary methods.

i) First come some comments which attempt to show—however
cursorily—how this passage fits into the whole Pauline section of
Acts.
ii) Next we must show, again somewhat cursorily, how the Thessalonica
and Beroea pericopes hang together.
iii) Within the Beroea pericope we find evidence to suggest that it
would be helpful to treat both pericopes together for the purpose of
our investigation. From this will follow our procedure and methods
of investigation.

To i) Adeney's comment,[1] "The brief epitome of Paul's preaching
at Thessalonica in Acts sheds an interesting light on his method of
evangelizing", raises the question of what other information Acts
gives us on Paul's missionary methods.
a) Up to the end of ch. 16 there are hardly any detailed statements
on Paul's missionary methods. All the accounts of the first missionary
journey given to us in this respect are either characterized by the
absolute and all-embracing use of the word "preach" in various
formulae [2] or else attention is focused on some miracle and the preaching
is "tagged on" to that (13, 6-12; 14, 3.8-13; 15, 12).[3]

---

[1] 7.

[2] καταγγέλειν τὸν λόγον τοῦ θεοῦ 13, 5 ; κυρίου 15, 36 ; καταγγέλλεται ὑμῖν ἄφεσις ἁμαρτιῶν 13, 38 ; εὐαγγελίζεσθαι 14, 7.15.21 ; 16, 10 ; τὴν ἐπαγγελίαν 13, 32 ; ... διδάσκοντες
15, 35 ; λαλεῖν 14, 1.9 ; 16, 13 ; τὸν λόγον 14, 25 ; 16, 6 ; τὸν λόγον τοῦ θεοῦ 13, 46 ; 16, 32 ;
τὰ ῥήματα ταῦτα 13, 42 ; ὑπὸ Παύλου λαλουμένοις 13, 45 ; 16, 14.

[3] 13, 12 : miracle and teaching inseparably connected. There is no mention of
preaching in the account of the miracle. Faith follows because of the miracle, not
because of preaching. 14, 3 : miracles confirm the preaching. Full account of the miracle
and the reaction to it (v. 13). The sermon follows this.—14, 9.11 : miraculous healing
directly connected with his preaching. Division among the people because of the miracle

b) But from ch. 17 these references become more frequent and more regular. Now Paul's preaching comes more into the foreground and references to the manner of his preaching occur more often.[4] Correspondingly, miracles that occur are either no longer so directly related to the preaching or at least clearly play a secondary role compared to it (19, 12; 20, 10 f.), or else have nothing more to do with the preaching and occur completely separately and do not evoke faith (chs. 27, 28).

These general considerations lead us to conjecture that when Paul moved to the West his preaching methods changed. This change can also be summarized as follows : in 14, 3 Paul's preaching is confirmed by miracles, in 17, 11 Paul's hearers confirm his preaching after critical hearing.[5] In 14, 9.11 there is dissension among the people because of a miraculous healing, and in 17, 18.34 because of Paul's words. In other words, from ch. 17 on there appears to be in place of miracles real argument or exposition which appeals to the hearers' reason.[6] This *conjecture* needs fuller corroboration in the context of

---

and not really because of the message.—15, 12 : σημεῖα καὶ τέρατα.—16, 16ff. : central to this are two miracles : i) exorcizing of demons (vv. 18ff.), ii) earthquake pointing to hearing of prayer (vv. 25ff.). Paul's preaching is completely eclipsed. Faith is the result of the miraculous experience.

[4] διαλέγεσθαι 17, 17 ; 18, 19 ; 19, 9 ; 20, 7.9 ; 24, 25.
   διαλέγεσθαι διανοίγων 17, 2.
   διαλέγεσθαι παρατιθέμενος 17, 2.
   διαλέγεσθαι πείθειν 18, 4 ; 19, 8.
   ἐξετίθετο διαμαρτυρόμενος ... πείθων ... ἐπείθοντο 28, 23 f.
   ἐπείσθησαν 17, 4.
   ἐδέξαντο τὸν λόγον ... ἀνακρίνοντες ... 17, 11.
   διδάσκειν ... τὸν λόγον τοῦ θεοῦ 18, 1.
   ἀναγγέλλειν καὶ διδ. ... διαμαρτυρόμενος 20, 20 f.
   κηρύσσειν τὴν βασιλ. τοῦ θεοῦ καὶ διδάσκειν τὰ περὶ τοῦ κυρίου ... 28, 31.
   ὁμιλεῖν 20, 11 ; 24, 26.
   συνέβαλλον αὐτῷ ... 17, 18.
   συνείχετο τῷ λόγῳ ... 18, 5.

[5] When Fo writes that "These people listened to the arguments ... and verified them by daily examination" (162) then we could formulate it accordingly thus : in chs. 13-16 Paul's preaching is "verified" by signs and wonders.

[6] As far as I know, the only one to see here a shift of emphasis like this is Bi : "In the synagogue of the east *teaching* was the method of instruction ... and, the Christian evangelist accordingly taught and preached the word. But in the more critical atmosphere of the west dogmatic assertion was not sufficient and S. Paul had to adopt the method of *reasoning*, in which he was an adept" (295). A shift of emphasis of a rather different sort is described by O. Glombitza in his article "Der Schritt nach Europa : Erwägungen zu Act 16, 9-15" in *ZNW* 53, 1962, 77-82.

an investigation of the whole of Acts. Here it will serve us as a general hypothesis for our investigation.

To ii) There is no particularly clear connection with the Philippi pericope (16, 14-40). On the other hand the close connection with the following Beroea pericope is immediately revealed by the following points :

a) εὐγενέστεροι τῶν ἐν Θεσσαλονίκῃ (v. 11)

b) οἱ ἀπὸ τῆς Θεσσαλονίκης Ἰουδαῖοι → σαλεύοντες καὶ ταράσσοντες (v. 13 ; cf. v. 5)

c) τῶν τε σεβομένων Ἑλλήνων πλῆθος πολύ, γυναικῶν τε τῶν πρώτων οὐκ ὀλίγαι (v. 4)—τῶν Ἑλληνίδων γυναικῶν τῶν εὐσχημόνων καὶ ἀνδρῶν οὐκ ὀλίγοι (v. 12)

d) 10b-14

e) in both cases the use of the Scriptures is emphasized, in 17, 2 in the context of Paul's διαλέγεσθαι

in 17, 11 in the context of the hearers' ἀνακρίνειν

To iii)

a) ἀνακρίνειν τὰς γραφάς (17, 11) corresponds to διαλέγεσθαι ... ἀπὸ τῶν γραφῶν (17, 2).

b) When in v. 11 the Beroeans' reaction is described as that of those οἵτινες [7] ἐδέξαντο τὸν λόγον μετὰ πάσης προθυμίας,[8] [τὸ] καθ'ἡμέ-

---

[7] A lot depends on the correct rendering of this relative pronoun. Many translate it with "for they" (Br 1, 328; Han 175; Wi 196 et al.), "in that" (Rac 299; A 2, 140), "inasmuch as" (Gr 1, 123), "da" (Schla 1, 210 et al.), although M III (48) states that in "Ac 17, 11 they were not more noble *because* they received the message, but simply *who* received the message". Others avoid this difficulty by following Ha (447) in his assumption that "Mit οἵτινες beginnt praktisch ein neuer Satz" (so, e.g., Stä 225; Co 94). But a point raised in M 123f. must, it seems to me, be considered. After a discussion of M I (92) and H. J. Cadbury (in *JBL* 42, 1923, 150ff.), Moule remarks a propos of a distinction still to be made or no longer to be made in the New Testament between ὅς, ἥ, ὅ and ὅστις, ἥτις, ὅτι that in A 17, 11 "it is possible to argue that ... a distinction certainly improves the sense and may have been intended" (124). Moule thinks that the use of οἵτινες here is "essential" and has the meaning "*which by its very nature*" (following F. J. A. Hort, *The First Epistle of St. Peter*, I.1-II.17, London, 1898, p. 133). If applied to our passage that would then mean that the Beroeans were not εὐγενέστεροι because they showed προθυμία and because of this applied themselves to ἀνακρίνειν, but that they did these last two things because they were εὐγενέστεροι. Would their readiness (and capacity) for ἀνακρίνειν ultimately rest upon what is meant by εὐγενέστεροι? Apart from Moule, Rac (299) also seems to incline to this line of interpretation when he "argues

ραν [9] ἀνακρίνοντες τὰς γραφὰς εἰ [10] ἔχοι [11] ταῦτα οὕτως ... ἐπίστευσαν
then we have to bear this in mind when in v. 4 it was only briefly
said of the Thessalonian hearers' reaction that καί τινες ἐξ αὐτῶν
ἐπείσθησαν καὶ προσεκληρώθησαν ...

c) When it is remarked in passing in v. 13 ὅτι καὶ ἐν τῇ Βεροίᾳ
κατηγγέλη ὑπὸ τοῦ Παύλου ὁ λόγος τοῦ Θεοῦ, then behind this

that the Berean Jews were more open to conviction because of an aristocratic background, and presumably a better education" (so in Bl 130—quite apart from the fact
that Rac does not mention the first but doubtless intends the latter. According to A 2,
140 Luther and Calvin also assume an "aristocratic background"). The great majority
of interpreters, however, somewhat hastily reject this interpretation on the grounds
that "Luke ... does define his meaning, and it seems clear from the explanatory clause
that he calls the Bereans 'more noble' because their conduct contrasted with that of
the Thessalonian mob ..." (Bl 130 and many others, many of them writing years after
Moule's first ed. and Turner's grammar, but taking no notice at all of them). In contrast
to L 19, 12 and I C 1, 26 where in fact εὐγενῆς means "well-born, high-born" (A-G 319),
"well-born, noble" (L-S; M-M 259f.), it is here emphasized that "it (= εὐγενῆς) came
to denote those qualities which were expected in people so born" (Br 1, 328; so also
Lu 1, 303; Wi 198; A 2, 141). The emphasis is therefore on their disposition rather than
on their pedigree. This leads to translations like "noble-minded" (A-G 319), "von
edler Gesinnung" (Hol 109), or simply "edler" (Schla 1, 210), "von edlerem Charakter"
(We 361) and thus, thoroughly moralizing "anständiger" (Co 94; Ha 447; Stä 225;
Pre 106). But if Moule's proposal is right and we have to relate εὐγενέστεροι closely to
προθυμία and ἀνακρίνειν, then a translation like "more ingenuous or open-minded"
(Bar 297), "free from prejudice" (Fo 162), "more candid and impartial" (A 2, 141)
would be more appropriate.—Be as that may, it seems to be ultimately of secondary
importance for our question whether we are dealing here with a certain class of men
or with qualities which are characteristic of such a class of men. But what is important
for us is the idea suggested by Moule's proposal, namely that a certain intellectual
openness is here a prerequisite for an intelligent acceptance of the message. This idea
is the Beroean pericope's contribution to the Thessalonian pericope. This element was
not evident in the latter in its description of the Thessalonians' reaction. We should
certainly read it between the lines there, however.

[8] A stock formula; examples in *TDNT* VI 699, n. 13; cf. also D B 254f.; D NB 82;
Mi 1, 10 and comms. Its meaning is something like "willingness, readiness" (A-G 713;
L-S), "enthusiasm" (M-M 540), "zeal" (*TDNT* VI 699).

[9] As in L 11, 2; 19, 47; an adverb. Cf. Rob 487. Ha: "Paulus predigte ihnen also
täglich, ohne dass von täglichen Gottesdiensten die Rede wäre" (447).

[10] M III (127): "... clauses introduced by εἰ and dependent on a verb like ζητεῖν are
virtually indirect questions, a class. survival". Cf. also n. 7.

[11] M III (130): "Luke is fond of this opt. (in indirect questions)." Cf. also p. 131
for the possible consequences which Turner draws from this for the dating of L/A. Cf.
also Bur 11; Si 112; Rob 890, 1408, 1044: "the change is made from an indicative ..."
(cf. also 1021). The use of the opt. here throws an interesting light on the process of the
δέχεσθαι. Apparently the word was only accepted on the condition that one wanted
first to test the correctness of what Paul said.

general statement lies all that was described in so much more detail in 17, 2f. : διελέξατο αὐτοῖς ἀπὸ τῶν γραφῶν, διανοίγων καὶ παρατι-θέμενος ... καταγγέλλω ... The clearest difference within these two connected pericopes is thus that in the Thessalonian pericope the manner of *Paul's preaching* is in the foreground and in the Beroean one the manner of the *hearers' reaction* to his preaching, which is only mentioned here in passing; both are closely related to the "Scriptures". But that means that the manner of Paul's preaching is reflected in the manner of his hearers' reception of it, and *vice versa*.

These observations, especially the last, justify us, as we have said, in evaluating these two accounts together in our investigation into Paul's missionary methods in general and into the intellectual element within those methods in particular, and indeed they make it advisable that we thus proceed. In both accounts we have more or less the same situation and events, but one deals with this and the other with that element.

But how then can Acts 17, 2-4 and the Beroea pericope throw any light, perhaps even a particularly clear light, on our problem?

Procedure

Verses 17, 2 [12] .3 [13] .4 [14] use of Paul's preaching the terms διαλέγεσθαι, διανοίγειν, παρατίθεσθαι and καταγγέλλειν and of the hearers' reaction πείθεσθαι and προσκληροῦσθαι.

On the basis of the thesis that Paul's preaching methods are reflected in the way that his hearers react to his preaching this investigation of Acts will proceed along two paths :

§ 1.1

First we will make a general survey of the "intellectual element" in all the concepts with which L describes the manner—as opposed to the content—of Paul's preaching in 17, 2-4.

This is followed by a preliminary attempt at correlating the concepts investigated and their possible consequences for our investigation.

§ 1.2

Then we will try to think through in theological terms this intellectual

---

[12] On this verse in general cf. B-D-F 189, 1; Rob 408, 537; Bu 116; Si 196.

[13] On this verse in general cf. Bur 30.

[14] On this verse in general cf. Rob 224, 669, 1163; M III 282; W 234; Si 84.

element that we have detected and provisionally correlated; this will have to be done within the context of the understanding—at present still to be defined—which L has of the apostle's task.

§ 2.1

We will then investigate further that expression which above all also has in view the hearers of the preaching, and in particular their reaction to it—πείθεσθαι. But we will confine ourselves to the active form, since even here when paying more attention to the hearers' reaction our principal concern is for the methods of Paul's preaching.

§ 2.2

Using our investigation of this concept in classical Greek we must then try to interpret theologically the concept conveyed by this word in Acts.

But the procedure and argument of the Acts section of our investigation will only become fully apparent when it is noted that the division previously mentioned (between § 1 and § 2) coincides with another division which also characterizes the whole investigation :

The first main section (§ 1) is rather like the observation of the tips of various icebergs. The survey of interrelated ideas (διαλέγεσθαι, ἀνακρίνειν, διανοίγειν, παρατίθεσθαι, καταγγέλλειν) which only deals with what is above water level is presented solely for what it can offer for the clarification of relations and the answering of our specific question, namely what is the function and significance of the human reason in the life of Christians, as it is reflected in the example— fragmentary though it is—of Paul's method of preaching. In the second major section (§ 2) a considerable part of the underwater mass of *one* iceberg (πείθειν) receives closer examination. This will enable us to subject the result obtained through the survey, which would be open to the charge of arbitrariness, to an additional control, that of a study in depth of a concept belonging to the same circle of ideas.

This union of two interrelated investigations seems to me to be justified on two grounds :
i)   such a two-pronged attack is invited by the text itself;
ii) it provides the easiest way of guaranteeing that, despite the fact that this study is limited to such a narrow field, we yet obtain a relatively assured *and* representative insight into the function and significance of the human reason in the life of the first Christians.

With regard to the New Testament the following rule holds good, that we shall, in investigating Acts 17, 2-4, stick as closely as possible to the immediate context. We do not want to throw away the chance of gleaning valuable knowledge from this text by precipitately reading the two Thessalonian letters into it.

§ 1. The "Intellectual Element" in Paul's Method of Preaching with Respect to the Sources : the "Argument" from Scripture

Section 1 : Observations

A) διαλέγεσθαι [1]

I) Survey of the problem

Acts uses this word almost [2] exclusively of Paul's missionary activities. Yet [3] it has been understood in various different ways. [4] Two considerations are in place with regard to this varying under-

---

[1] Occurs in all 13 times in the New Testament, once in Mk (9, 34), once in Hb (12, 5), once in Jud (9) and 10 times in Acts (17, 2.17; 18, 4.19; 19, 8.9; 20, 7.9; 24, 12.25).

[2] Cf. A 20, 7.

[3] On its *etymology*, cf. Bo 563f.; Buck 1253ff.; Fr II 94-6; Ho 175; Ka II 10; Mey IV 496ff.; Po 658; Pr 263; W-P II 422; also vanH 204; *op. cit.* App. 50.

[4] While none of the NT lexicons, grammars or exegetes go so far as to apply to the New Testament the meaning of διαλέγεσθαι as "gewandt seyn im Reden" which is found in P I 586 and Ps I 1, 645 and which arises naturally from the idea of dialectical procedure, yet many agree with the other, more general meaning of "... sich unterreden, unterhalten ... im Wechselgespräch etwas ins Klare bringen ..." (P and Ps, *op. cit.*). So we find "discuss, conduct a discussion ... of lectures which were likely to end in disputations" (A-G 184; E 99; Ma II 1, 93.106.117); "sich besprechen" (P-K I 353; Schla 1, 208); "Wechselgespräche" (Hol 1, 109; We 358 = dialogue form); then "to reason" (Wi 196) and/or "discourse" (Pa 128; Bar 295) or "to argue" (Rac 295; Han 173; Beg IV 203); "reasoning in friendly intercourse" (Mi 3, xxvi); "he conducted discussions" (O'Neill, J. C., *The Theology of Acts in its historical setting*, London, 1961, 120); "διαλέγομαι bedeutet die Diskussion" (H 138, who on p. 159 lumps ὁμιλέω, διαλέγομαι and διατρίβω together); Her (60) thinks that " 'Disputed' gives the force of διαλέγεσθαι better than 'reasoned' " (cf. also M-M 150; Schl I 586; Z 127; Sch 1, 53.60; Ma II 1, 255.313; II 3, 46; He 95, 99; Th 21, 4.6). On the other hand Schrenk (in *TDNT* II 94) rejects "disputation" categorically ("no reference") and decides in favour of "delivering of religious lectures or sermons". Similarly categorical are Dibelius (Dibelius, M., *Studies in the Acts of the Apostles*, London, 1956, 74); Co (96); Pre (105), while Ha (445, n. 7) and Fürst (in *ThBl* 181f.) choose the middle way and say that this word comes very near the meaning of "eine Ansprache halten, predigen" (also A-G, *ibid.*, considers this possible). Referring to it, Br (1, 372) emphasizes that it is "A conversation rather than an address ..." (cf. also 349) and Fo holds that it is "... arguing, not necessarily preaching ... The verb διελέξατο ... has the same meaning as our word dialogue, and instruction was carried on ... by question and answer".

standing of διαλέγεσθαι, which chiefly concern those who understand it to mean preaching (cf. n. 4).

1) If διαλέγεσθαι really means "preach", how can we explain the fact that this word only appears from ch. 17 onwards? If by διαλέγεσθαι L really meant "preaching" here (as earlier), why did he not use for it the rich vocabulary that he had at his disposal and which he had used up till now?

2) Let us assume for the moment that L really meant "preach" here. Do we not then have to go on to ask what is the *significance* of L's being able to use διαλέγεσθαι for "preach" here and apparently having to use it here and in many subsequent passages? Why does he speak of διαλέγεσθαι when he means to say "preach"? What does that tell us about "preaching"?

Now it seems to me that those who either simply assume that διαλέγεσθαι here means "preach", or else come to the same conclusion either arguing from this word's *origins* or its *destined use*, cannot answer this question. Should we not rather, at least for the time being, ignore the use of this word in past and future and form our judgments on the basis of its *present* meaning in this context?

But let us linger awhile with a representative example of those scholars who argue from the origins of the word.

Schrenk (cf. n. 4) traces its usage in classical and Hellenistic Greek, and in Polybius, Epictetus, the LXX, Josephus and Philo. He then concludes with regard to the διαλέγεσθαι passages in Acts that the "only relevant parallels are in Hellenistic Judaism rather than Greek philosophy". And again, "Linguistic parallels may be found in Polyb. ..., Diod. S., Jos. ...".[5] Thus Schrenk plumps for "preach, give an address", its meaning in Hellenistic-Jewish literature, as opposed to "dispute", its meaning in philosophical writings, where it refers to an eliciting of the truth.

Two things need to be said here:

1) a check on the authors and passages cited by Schrenk shows that διαλέγεσθαι in the Hellenistic-Jewish literature adduced mostly means official, political or military negotiations or, above all, an address given to the people by a king, a general or some other important person. That immediately shows that there is no opportunity in such a context to ἀνακρίνειν εἰ ἔχοι ταῦτα οὕτως ...

---

[5] *TDNT* II 94f.

2) on the other hand, when Fürst,[6] describing the διαλέγεσθαι of the Greek philosophers, says that "man debattiert und gewinnt so im Gesprächsablauf Erkenntnisse", or when Schrenk shows that in classical and Hellenistic Greek διαλέγεσθαι mostly means "converse, discussion",[7] and that for Socrates, Plato and Aristotle it means "the art of persuasion and demonstration ... in the form of question and answer",[8] then in our immediate context (διανοίγειν, παρατίθεσθαι, ἀνακρίνειν, πείθεσθαι) we are nearer to this usage than to the military speeches and political negotiations in Josephus and Polybius. Thus one cannot assume from the mere fact that in Hellenistic-Jewish literature διαλέγεσθαι can occur with the meaning "make a speech" that it means that in A 17, 2 without first examining the immediate context of A 17, 2. And this context clearly indicates a situation of seeking the truth, through ἀγάπη τῆς ἀληθείας (II Th 2, 10), and accepting it, rather than of an official address. The very fact that the Thessalonian Jews are unfavourably contrasted with the Beroean ones because they did not so eagerly join in the search for the truth also shows us that we are nearer to philosophical Greek than to the military speeches of Polybius, etc.

But what led Schrenk, who used the same evidence as we have, to deny categorically the influence of the philosophical usage of διαλέγεσθαι here? This categorical denial is itself a pointer to a weakness in his argument. For here a false alternative lurks in the background, which treats everything Greek as bad, except when it has passed through the filter of Judaism. This is clearly shown by his reasons for his conclusion : "In the New Testament there is no instance of the classical use of διαλέγομαι in the philosophical sense. In the sphere of revelation there is no question of reaching the idea through dialectic. What is at issue is the obedient and percipient acceptance of the Word spoken by God, which is not an idea, but the comprehensive declaration of the divine will which sets all life in the light of divine truth".[9] But is that *the* alternative which is also justified by the New Testament passages in which διαλέγεσθαι occurs? If the word διαλέγεσθαι is of such "central importance"[10] for Greek philos-

---

[6] *ThBl* 181.

[7] *TDNT* II 93.

[8] *Ibid.*

[9] *TDNT* II 94.

[10] *Ibid.* 93.

ophy, why could L use this "dangerous" word, even in a context of discovering the truth? For ἀνακρίνειν εἰ ἔχοι ταῦτα οὕτως and "to open their minds to love of the truth" are inseparably connected with διαλέγεσθαι.

Let us also pause briefly to consider the case of those who argue from the future use of the word. They point out how διαλέγεσθαι later meant "preach". L [11] points that out too, but he also points out that this is only one meaning among others. The primary one is still "to hold converse with".

But what does it mean when one says that διαλέγεσθαι *comes very near* to the meaning of "make a speech, preach" (Fürst)? This word's meaning, therefore, is in flux. That in itself is not surprising. And one also says *where* it is going, namely in the direction of "preach". But what is surprising is that we are not told whence, i.e. from what range of meanings, it has come. And that is just as important—also for the understanding of its destination! So the statement that διαλέγεσθαι shows here "schon den Übergang zur späteren Bedeutung 'predigen' " (Haenchen) seems to me to give no answer to the question of the significance of the fact that an L can despatch a word like διαλέγεσθαι on its way (to keep our metaphor) or can use a word that is already on the way, so that at its journey's end it will have taken on the meaning "preach". And if one then adds "Sachlich handelt es sich um Lesung und Auslegung des AT" (Fürst), then that is correct but does not answer the question *why* L has used διαλέγεσθαι here and what *new* idea is introduced here (apart from that expressed by other words for "preach" like κηρύσσειν, καταγγέλλειν, εὐαγγελίζεσθαι, λαλεῖν, λέγειν). Have we not too quickly docketed this word under the heading "preaching" without taking the time to consider the particular meaning conveyed by this word—perhaps even in contrast or in relation to καταγγέλλειν. Perhaps the decisive factor is whether and how one relates διαλέγεσθαι to "preaching" or "making a speech".

We can only fully grasp the exact meaning of διαλέγεσθαι within Paul's preaching activity when:

1) we have carried out a thorough investigation of this word and its meaning within and outside the New Testament, and

2) we have information from other sources on the function of διαλέγεσθαι within the synagogue. For if Foakes-Jackson is correct when he writes: "a synagogue was not so much a preaching-house

[11] 355.

as a school, in which education was carried on by discussion",[12] then
that is of immediate relevance for our enquiry. Unfortunately we
cannot do either of these here, and so we must content ourselves
with our verse and its context; yet, I think, two observations can
already be made here which help us better to understand what is
meant by διαλέγεσθαι.

II) Towards a solution

(1)   διαλέγεσθαι + dative and accusative

διαλέγεσθαι can be followed either by a dative [13] or by πρός + the
accusative.[14] In the following section we will put forward some considerations, not in order to show that a thorough investigation of this
word and its meaning is unnecessary, but rather to show first that
one is necessary; these considerations arise mainly from these two
possible constructions and the opinions of the foremost grammarians
on them. The question is, what significance has it for the possible
meaning of διαλέγεσθαι + the dative that it can also be followed by
πρός + the accusative ?

i)   The grammatical data

a)   A look at grammars obscures the matter rather than clarifies it.
Three factors are responsible for the problem :

aa)   already in classical Greek both constructions are found
together.[15]

bb)   in MGr the dative disappears and is replaced by the
accusative and the genitive or also by prepositional phrases.[16]

cc)   on the other hand, in the New Testament the dative "is still
retained ... in a wide range of usages".[17] Yet we can already find
"traces of the process which ended in the complete disappearance of
the simple dat. in MGr".[18]

---

[12] 159; so also Pl 3, 117.

[13] A 17, 2.

[14] A 17, 17; cf. Mk 9, 34.

[15] Cf. B-D-F 193, 4; B-T 467 etc.

[16] Including πρός + acc.

[17] B-D-F 120 (with literature on this whole problem).

[18] M III 236.

How are we to explain the occurrence and the meaning of the two constructions in the New Testament in the light of these three basic facts?

On aa): Should we explain it primarily with respect to the basic fact aa)? Those representing this view interpret the prepositional construction as *contrasted* with the dative construction and try to define the *difference*: the "simple dative" refers to "nur ganz allgemeine" [19] relations, i.e. to an "an sich weiten und vagen Bereich".[20] The use of prepositional constructions is the inevitable result of the fact that "der menschliche Geist tiefer in die Beziehungsverhältnisse der Dinge einzudringen anfing" [21] and this means that they had a defining function: in contrast to the simple dative they indicate "bestimmtere Verhältnisse",[22] at first only spatially more definite; they express "die mannigfaltigen Beziehungen ... bestimmter und schärfer",[23] indeed "logisch bestimmter".[24] "Die Präpositionen konnten ... auch gedankliche Schattierungen ausdrücken, die für die blossen Kasus unerreichbar waren ...".[25]

On bb): Or should we explain this primarily with reference to fact bb)? Those representing this view interpret the prepositional construction as a *substitute* for the dative construction and thus presuppose considerable *synonymity*. They base their argument on the disappearance of the dative [26] in MGr and therefore treat the alternative construction [27] from the viewpoint of the competition between the two constructions and the final successful dispossessing of the dative by the prepositional construction: "... das im Ngr fertig vorliegende Ausgehen des Dativs (hängt zusammen) ..." [28] with their "encroachment" [29] and the successful "Eindringen von Prä-

---

[19] K.-G II 1, 448.

[20] S II 432.

[21] K.-G II 1, 449.

[22] *Ibid.* 448.

[23] *Ibid.* 449.

[24] *Ibid.* 450.

[25] S II 432.

[26] F. Krebs, *Zur Rection der Casus in der späteren historischen Gräcität,* 1887-90, investigates the literary koine more thoroughly; cf. also S II 170f.

[27] Dat. and πρός + acc.

[28] B.-D-F 120.

[29] *Ibid.*

positionen" [30] which had the task in the Koine "of supplanting the
disappearing dative".[31] So we have :

α) a *basic thesis* also for the New Testament data : "Für die
Entwicklung der κοινή und des Neugriech. kommt vor allem der
Ersatz des Dativs durch den Akkusativ ... und durch präpositionale
Wendungen ... in Betracht".[32]

β) The *presupposition* for this thesis is that originally the simple
dative was in no way general or ill-defined; rather it then possessed
the whole "Kraft" [33] and "Schärfe und Reinheit".[34] The loss of this
original "Schärfe und Reinheit" is a sign of the decay of the case.
Correspondingly, the prepositional constructions which spring up "in
Stellvertretung" [35] of and as "Ersatz" [36] for the dative to restore its
original "Kraft", "Schärfe und Reinheit" are "*nichts weiter* [37] als
Alterserscheinungen der Sprache",[38] and so not a sign of the deeper
penetration of the human spirit into the relations of things. Thus one
has here no sense of added meaning in the prepositional constructions;
rather they merely fill up gaps arising from the "decay" [39] of the
dative : "Präpositionen dringen an Stelle der alten Casus ein, weil
diese an ursprünglicher Kraft mehr und mehr verlieren".[40]

γ) The *consequence* of this thesis is that the prepositional constructions could have no other meaning than their function of replacing
the simple dative. "Verschiebungen auf dem Gebiet der Bedeutungen
kommen dabei weniger in Frage".[41] The corresponding

δ) *rule* is that : "Da der Accusativ in Verbindung mit εἰς oder
πρός den Dativ vertreten kann, so dürfen alle Wörter, welche den
Dativ regieren, auch mit dem Accusativ in Verbindung mit εἰς oder
πρός construiert werden".[42]

---

[30] Ra 127; cf. 128; μετά, εἰς, πρός and περί.
[31] Rob 626.
[32] B-T 430.
[33] Ra 137.
[34] Bu 124.
[35] Mü 188.
[36] Ra 131.
[37] My italizing.
[38] Ra 131.
[39] M I 63.
[40] Ra 137.
[41] *Ibid.*
[42] Mü 195.

On aa) and bb) : Or should we try to explain it by taking both facts into account ? The contradiction is then even clearer.

For example, Buttmann says on the one hand that the prepositional construction expresses "die mannigfachen inneren ... Beziehungen" better than the simple dative.[43] On the other hand, such prepositional constructions are in the New Testament merely "Umschreibungen",[44] "anstatt oder im Sinne des Dativs",[45] "statt des Dativs",[46] which here "ebenso gut stehen könnte".[47] It is not used because—and the two reasons that he gives contain the same contradiction—

α) "die adverb. Umschreibung lebendiger, bildlicher, der orientalischen Anschauungsweise angemessener (ist)".[48] Similarly, W [49] says : "Den N.T. Schriftstellern legte sich die Construction mit Präposition wohl auch durch die expressivere und anschaulichere Redeweise der vaterländischen Sprache nahe";

β) "mit dem Verfall einer Nation in der Regel auch ein Verfall in sprachlicher Hinsicht einzutreten pflegt", or, in more concrete terms, "es wird die mehr auflösende und zersetzende Sprache der Späteren oft schon Präpositionen mit ihren Casus da gebrauchen, wo die ältere noch mit den blossen Casus ausreichte".[50]

b) The fundamental question remains how διαλέγεσθαι + the dative and πρός + the accusative are affected by this problem. Do both constructions have the same meaning, expressed in different forms, or not ? K-G [51] assumes that the meaning changes but "rein räumlich", but gives no further clue as to what figurative sense "rein räumlich" has in the case of διαλέγεσθαι and πρός + the accusative; S [52] also only states that changes of construction can occur with or without change of meaning.

c) At any rate, two facts must not be overlooked :
aa) the "intensified free use of prepositions" in Hellenistic Greek,

---

[43] Bu 150.
[44] 149f.; cf. also the detailed excursus in § 132, 2 and § 293.
[45] 150.
[46] 153.
[47] 150.
[48] *Ibid.*
[49] 191.
[50] Bu 124.
[51] II 1, 431 A 1.
[52] II 73.

"where we are perpetually finding prepositional phrases used to express relations which in classical Greek would have been adequately given by a case alone",[53] should not blind us to the fact that already in classical Greek the parallelism of διαλέγεσθαι + the dative and πρός + the accusative is characteristic. So we have to ask whether διαλέγεσθαι + the dative was used synonymously with διαλέγεσθαι + the accusative in classical Greek or not. If not, then can we find, as the language develops, cases of the construction with πρός being used where earlier the dative would have been used ?

bb) on the other hand, we should not forget the New Testament data to which M III [54] refers : "the process has scarcely begun ..." and "the dat. does sometimes oust the class. accus. ... and in NT the dat. is still retained in a large range of meanings, notwithstanding the constant tendency to add ἐν".[55]

ii) διαλέγεσθαι αὐτοῖς and πρός and the accusative

With reference to our passage A 17, 2 we merely note the following :

a)   what is meant by διαλέγεσθαι + the dative is characterized by two things :

aa) διά :

α) Preposition.[56] The basic meaning is "entzwei, auseinander, zer-".[57] "The etymology of the word is 'two', δύο ... But the preposition has advanced a step further ... to the idea of by-twain, be-tween, in two, in twain. This is the groundmeaning in actual usage".[58] "Durch", "through", i.e. "passing between two objects or parts of objects" [59] is thus not the original meaning of διά [60] but it is "being evolved from the idea of duality or 'betweenness' ",[61] "of interval between".[62] So "erhielt durch eine Bedeutungsverschiebung ... das idg. dis- im Griechischen die Bedeutung 'durch' ".[63]

---

[53] M I 61; III 251, 274.
[54] 236.
[55] Cf. also 249.
[56] Literature is given in *TDNT* II 65; M III 267 A 1; S II 448-54.
[57] S II 449.
[58] Rob 580; so also M 54.
[59] Rob 581.
[60] Over against : A-G 178; W 337; cf. B-T 520.
[61] M 54.
[62] Rob 581; cf. K-G II 1, 480; M II 300; M III 267; Si 139; Bu 287; B-D-F-222f.
[63] S II 449.

β) διά in compounds.[64] It is well known that in the New Testament, where we find in all 79 διά compounds, L uses them the most :[65] 200 out of 343 occurrences are to be reckoned to him. But whereas the basic meaning of διά, "asunder, from another, apart", is only preserved in a relatively pure form in Latin and Gothic, it exists in Greek only as a verbal prefix. Thus we find διά "als Präverb noch überwiegend in der Bedeutung 'auseinander' ".[66] "Der Begriff der ... Trennung, der im lat. *dis* gegeben ist, erscheint nur im Präverbium".[67] So, too, M II states [68] that : "The survey of the whole field (i.e. of διά-compounds) shows us that the etymological connexion with two justifies itself by usage". This clearly shows what meaning is conveyed by διά in διαλέγεσθαι : it shows this verb to be basically a *relational* word : "To represent it graphically, we have two points or areas (A) (B) set over against one another, and the preposition (= διά) is concerned with their relations and their interval between them".[69] διά in the sense of *dis* (not *per*, *trans*, or *inter*) "emphatically dwells on the interval as a gulf fixed between them".[70] "Trennung von Verschiedenartigem bedeutet *Ordnung* ... Trennung bringt *Verschiedenheit, Hervorhebung* ... so auch nachhom. von *konkurrierender Tätigkeit mehrerer* : 'um die Wette' (διαγωνίζομαι) ..." [71] Correspondingly, the "mutual relation of the A and B" indicated in the case of διαλέγεσθαι [72] by the "mediating διά" is best translated by "between, or to and fro" [73] and thus "im Wechsel"; by means of this, "die Sonderung des Verschiedenen *Klarheit, Genauigkeit* erzielt".[74] The διά in διαλέγεσθαι is thus the sign of "des Verkehrs zwischen Personen",[75] the διά "recall(s) the two parties in a conversation".[76]

---

[64] Literature given in B-D-F 318, 5.

[65] A good list—still valuable but needing updating—in Winer, G. B. *De verborum cum praep. compos. in NT usu*, 1834-43 pt. 3 and 5.

[66] S II 449.

[67] B-T 520.

[68] 300.

[69] M II 300.

[70] *Ibid.* 301.

[71] S II 450.

[72] As also διαλαλέω, διαλογίζομαι, διερωτάω etc.

[73] M II 302.

[74] S II 450; cf. also 353, 398, 522, 531.

[75] B-T 521.

[76] M II 302.

bb) αὐτοῖς. We have only got as far as the statement that the διά
in διαλέγεσθαι shows this verb to be a relational concept. How can
we advance beyond this basic description to describe this mutual
relation? That is made possible by the definition of the αὐτοῖς as a
dat. sociativus/comitativus,[77] a dative "der Gemeinschaft".[78] What
relevance has this for our question?

It is well-known that Greek had three cases with which it could
express objective relations: accusative, genitive and dative. Amongst
these, "die Hauptfunktion des echten Dativs ..." is "die Bezeichnung
der persönlichen Beteiligung an der Verbalhandlung oder die Stellung-
nahme derselben".[79] So the dative's meaning can be called that of
"personal interest", so that the dative "has a distinctive personal
touch not true of the others (= accusative and genitive)".[80] In other
languages we find, besides these three cases which mostly serve to
express purely grammatical relations, three further local cases, i.e.
once used in the first place of spatial relations, the ablative to indicate
whence, the locative to indicate where, and the instrumental, which as
a true instrumental case expresses the means by which and as a
comitative expresses that together with which an action is performed.
Greek originally also possessed these three cases but later, apart from
a few traces,[81] lost them when the relations expressed thereby were
taken over by the dative and genitive.[82] The dative and genitive can
be described in this respect as mixed cases [83] or syncretistic cases.[84]
From this arise two fundamentally important points for the definition
of διαλέγεσθαι + the dative:

a) The instrumental dative as comitative indicates the person (or
thing, or object) "mit der zusammen der Träger der Handlung diese
vollzieht" [85]—"together with" means here "unter deren Mitwirkung,
Gegenwirkung oder Begleitung".[86] Thus there appears scattered
throughout the whole of Greek literature the preposition-less but

---

[77] B-D-F 193b.
[78] W 187f.; Ra 127f.; Bu 149; Rob 528f.
[79] S II 139.
[80] Rob 536.
[81] Cf. K-G II 1, 405 A 1.
[82] Ra 126; S II 138.
[83] K-G II 1, 404.
[84] B-T 428.
[85] Ibid. 428; cf. also 466; K-G II 1, 292; 430.
[86] K-G II 1, 405.

"meist persönliche" [87] comitative in conjunction with verbs "die ein gemeinsames Sein oder Tun ausdrücken, also schon an sich komitativ-soziative Bedeutung haben ...",[88] or, alternatively, "die durch sich selbst eine Vereinigung oder eine Zusammenwirkung ausdrücken",[89] indeed, Ra [90] points out that they occur with both persons and things.[91] "Erst griechisch ist gewohnheitsmässige Verbindung eines Komitativs mit αὐτῷ ... αὐτοῖς ..., wobei der pronominale Bestandteil des Syntagmas zur Stütze oder gar zum (Haupt-)Träger der komitativen Bedeutung zu werden scheint".[92] Such verbs are an expression "für die Gemeinschaft, die jemand mit einem anderen eingeht" [93] and thus are "Verben der Gemeinschaft, der Vereinigung, des Verkehrs",[94] both friendly :[95] ὁμιλεῖν, μιγνύναι, συμ-, προς, μίγνυσθαι, κεραννύναι, κοινοῦν, (ἀνα)κοινοῦσθαι, κοινωνεῖν, διαλλάττειν, συμφωνεῖν etc. and also hostile : ἀγωνίζεσθαι, ἐρίζειν, πολεμεῖν etc.; this goes for διαλέγεσθαι,[96] too.

In contrast, in the "echten Dativ" [97] there appears "die Person oder Gesamtheit, die bei der Handlung eines Verbs beteiligt ist, ohne von ihr unmittelbar erfasst zu werden ... Zuweilen ist sie nichts weiter als das Ziel, auf das die Aktion gerichtet ist : ... λέγειν τινί".[98]

β) The boundaries between the sociative/comitative and the instrumental dative in the narrower sense are fluid; "denn das, in dessen Gesellschaft man eine Handlung ausführt, ist oft nur das Mittel oder Werkzeug".[99] K-G [100] formulates this fully but precisely : "Als Vertreter des Instrumentalis bezeichnet der Dativ teils im Sinne des Komitativs die Person oder Sache, mit der zusammen ... eine Handlung vollzogen wird, teils im Sinne des eigentlichen Instrumentalis

---

[87] S II 159.

[88] *Ibid.*

[89] B-T 467.

[90] 127.

[91] E.g. χρῆσθαί τινι, ἐγγίζειν τινί ...

[92] S II 164.

[93] Ra 126.

[94] K-G II 1, 430.

[95] B-D-F 193, 4

[96] Cf. for the whole S II 160.

[97] S II 138.

[98] Ra 126; cf. also n. 1.

[99] Ra 127.

[100] II 1, 405.

das Mittel, die Ursache, das Mass usw ...". [101] M III [102] regards the
two as no longer distinguishable and states that the "dativus sociativus" or "comitativus" "expresses the 'means by which', but with
strong emphasis on physical accompaniment or nearness".

b)   A 17, 17 has the dative and accusative together.

aa)   Apart from the question whether the two usages mean the
same or not, the preposition πρός [103] belongs, through its meaning of
a spatial relation, to that group of prepositions "welche räumliche
Gegensätze ausdrücken". [104] Its basic Indo-Germanic meaning [105] is
"entgegen, gegenüber, gegen", [106] "over against": [107] "The idea seems
to be 'facing', German *gegen*". [108] Since "jede Präposition ... eine
Grundbedeutung (hat), die sie überall festhält", [109] πρός + the accusative with verbs of speaking conveys the figurative sense of "die
Richtung des Geistes auf etwas" [110] and thus "motion to", [111] "direction", [112] "Richtung" [113] and in such a way that "sich der Redende
gegen einen wendet", [114] either "zu Personen hin (eig. 'gegenüber,
gegen')", [115] "tending towards ... with reference to (almost against)", [116]
or "im Hinblick auf ... angesichts", [117] "concerning ... in view of", [118]
or "betreffend, angehend, interessierend", [119] "in Beziehung auf
(sprechend auf sie hindeutend)". [120]

A comparison of this last statement with ii) a) bb) clearly shows

---

[101] So similarly S II 159.
[102] 240f.
[103] Literature given in M III 273; S II 508, n. 3.
[104] K-G II 1, 451.
[105] On its etymology cf. K-B I 2, 249.
[106] B-T 515; S II 509.
[107] M II 323.
[108] Rob 623; cf. 624, 626.
[109] K-G II 1, 451.
[110] W 360.
[111] M 52.
[112] M II 323.
[113] K-G II 1, 518.
[114] *Ibid.* 519.
[115] S II 510.
[116] M 53.
[117] S II 511.
[118] M 53.
[119] S II 511.
[120] W 360.

the great difference that could lie in the fact that in the one case (διαλέγεσθαι + the dative) the αὐτοί in the process of διαλέγεσθαι could be, by virtue of the close connection of dat. sociativus and dat. instrumentalis in the true sense, as it were the axe which someone (the apostle) has in his hand to fell a tree, whereas in the other case (διαλέγεσθαι with πρός and the accusative) the αὐτοί [121] are simply the passive object *against* which the blows are directed. In the first case one speaks (together) *with* them, in the second one simply speaks *to* them.

bb) M I [122] seems to make a correct observation, which should be quoted here in full because it is of immediate relevance for our question : "We should not assume ... that the old distinctions of case-meaning have vanished, or that we may treat as mere equivalents those constructions which are found in common with the same word. The very fact that in Jn 4, 23 προσκυνεῖν is found with dat. and then with acc. is enough to prove the existence of a difference, subtle no doubt but real, between the two, unless the writer is guilty of a most improbable slovenliness. The fact that the maintenance of an old and well-known distinction between the acc. and the gen. with acc. saves the author of Ac 9, 7 and 22, 9 from a patent self-contradiction, should by itself be enough to make us recognise it for Luke ... until it is proved wrong". Should not this also apply to the two uses of διαλέγεσθαι in A 17, 17 ? "It depends upon the character of the word itself. If its content be limited, it may well happen that hardly any appreciable difference is made by placing it in one or another of certain nearly equivalent relations to a noun. But if it is a word of large content and extensive use, we naturally expect to find these alternative expressions made use of to define the different ideas connected with the word they qualify ... In such a case we should expect to see the original force of these expressions, obsolete in contexts where there was nothing to quicken it, brought out vividly where the need of a distinction stimulated it into new life". M gives an example of this observation by citing the case of πιστεύειν + the dative, with εἰς and ἐπί and ἐν. This needs to be done in the case of διαλέγεσθαι + the dative and πρός + the accusative.

---

[121] For translation cf. M 103; also M III 151.
[122] 66f.

iii) Conclusions

A 17, 17 indicates that in all probability διαλέγεσθαι could certainly have the sense "make a speech", but when it was constructed with the dative it could *not* have this sense. Then the αὐτοί are not just objects at which Paul's address is directed but are those "mit denen zusammen der Träger der Handlung diese vollzieht". The αὐτοι bear the same relationship to διαλέγεσθαι as the αὐτοί to χρηματίζειν.[123]

(2) ἀνακρίνειν

Our statement that the διά in διαλέγεσθαι represented the "intercourse between persons" is confirmed, from the other end so to speak, by the ἀνακρίνειν connected with it. What can the mention of the use of ἀνακρίνειν [124] on the part of the hearers tell us about the meaning of διαλέγεσθαι?

i) The original local-adverbial meaning of ἀνά [125] seems to have been "auf" = "(an einer schrägen Fläche und senkrecht) empor",[126] "an—hin, auf—hin",[127] "upwards, up" [128] "denoting motion from a lower place to a higher",[129] although "the NT usage is not easy to connect with such a sense, except when ἀνά is compounded with verbs...".[130]

ii) But the ἀνά of the compound ἀνακρίνειν [131] does not retain the

---

[123] S II 160, 4.

[124] On the etymology cf. Bo 318f., Ch 584f., Fr II 20f., Ho 161, Ka I 474, Mey II 407f., Po 946, Pr 245, W-P II 584; also vH 64, Ch Gr I 404 (with literature).

[125] According to Del III 734 a "proethnic" preposition, in later Greek—including papyri and inscriptions (Ra 115)—"stark reduziert" as a separate word (B-D-F 203; also Ra 138, M III 249, Si 137) and in the New Testament the rarest preposition (13 times; contrasted with 10 pp. of ἀνά—compounds in M-G Conc.; many further compounds according to Ma II 2, 486 in papyri; according to J 366 it then completely disappears as a separate word in MGr, yet not completely eliminated (like, e.g., ἀμφί) because of its "distributive use" (M I 100) already found "im Altattischen" (Ra 20) and then often found in the papyri (M-M 29).

[126] S II 440; cf. K-G II 1, 473.

[127] W 355.

[128] A-S 27, while according to M II 295—and S II 440—"over, of space covered, on ..., and up to, of a goal attained, are developments reached in other languages than Greek".

[129] G-T 34.

[130] M 66; cf. also B 98f., A-G 49, Ra 140, 143-5, Rob 571f., Bu 285, B-D-F 204.

[131] Cf. A-S 27, G-T 35, H 40.

original local meaning of ἀνά used separately.[132] Rather the ἀνά[133] here has an "intensifying" force.[134] On the other hand, the expression "perfective force" seems to be problematic in the case of the ἀνά of ἀνακρίνειν [135] in view of the criticism of it.[136] (Cf. also [137] "looking through a series (ἀνά) of objects or particulars to distinguish (κρίνω) or search after".) The intensifying function of ἀνά in ἀνακρίνειν seems to me to be most clearly expressed if the original local meaning "from bottom to top",[138] "to sift up and down",[139] "von unten bis oben" [140] is used figuratively "für 'deutlich, genau' ".[141]

iii) If ἀνά "intensifies", what does the uncompounded stem mean? The basic meaning of κρίνειν is "die Tätigkeit des Richters von der *logischen* Seite aus, nach der er das Für und Wider erwägt und hernach seinen Spruch abgibt".[142] This projects in the first place "die Erwägung der Umstände, die prüfende Tätigkeit", the "genaue Prüfung des Sachverhaltes" and of the "Tatsachen" "in den Vordergrund", something "was nur unter Ruhe geschehen kann".[143]

iv) The "intensified" meaning of ἀνακρίνειν is therefore "to examine closely",[144] "to examine well, search carefully",[145] "implying a thorough examination",[146] "make careful and exact research",[147] while simply "to examine, investigate, question",[148] "befragen, aus-

---

[132] In only 13 cases does ἀνά still have a local sense in compounds in the New Testament.

[133] As also, e.g., in ἀναζητέω, ἀναθεωρέω, ἀνετάζω, ἀνευρίσκω etc.

[134] M 88.

[135] M II 296.

[136] S II 268.

[137] G-T 39.

[138] V I 428.

[139] Ro III 274f.

[140] S II 440.

[141] *Ibid.*, as also. e.g., in ἀνείρομαι, ἀνειρωτάω, ἀνπυνθάνομαι etc.

[142] Sch I 357.

[143] *Op. cit.* 358.

[144] L-S; L 107.

[145] R 47.

[146] V I 428.

[147] Ro III 275.

[148] A-S 31, A-G 56, G-T 39.

fragen, untersuchen" [149] does not do justice to the "intensifying"
aspect of ἀνακρίνειν.[150]

v) The ἀνακρίνειν here is thus an expression of what Be 488 calls
"character verae religionis, quod se dijudicari patitur" and so implies
three things :

a) Classical Greek used this word of a "preliminary investigation"
and L generally uses it of "holding an enquiry".[151] It is thus a matter
of eliciting the truth from the one examined by putting the right
questions. Thus ἀνακρίνειν implies both "the ability to sift the facts",[152]
or "sifting evidence" [153] and objectivity, "unbiased equanimity" and
"open to conviction" [154]—in contrast to "pride and prejudice".[155]
Referring to προθυμία Be 488 comments : "promta voluntas et
scrutinium accuratum bene conveniunt".

b) The Beroeans are represented as such : they "verhörten" the
Scriptures "um nämlich zu prüfen εἰ ...". [156] "Here we have a noteworthy instance of the right of private judgment. Even an Apostle's
word is not to be taken for granted".[157]

c) This "right of private judgment" must, however, be taken
with the ἀνά and καθ'ἡμέραν. For not only the ἀνά but also the
καθ'ἡμέραν [158] point to an "offenbar intensives"[159] study and examination of the scriptural passages cited by Paul περὶ Χριστοῦ [160] and so
of the arguments [161] and method of argumentation; in short of the
hermeneutics by means of which Paul was able to adduce these
passages at all.

---

[149] P-K I 92, Ma I 3, 207; preferable is "aus-, durch-, nachforschen" P I 193;
Ps I 1, 179; E 30; TDNT III 945, or simply "forschen" ThBl 511.
[150] Cf. also M-M 35; Schl; Z 42; F 120 f.; H 174; N 22, 68; Pal 147.
[151] L 23, 14; A 4, 9; 12, 19; 24, 8; 28, 18.
[152] Li 182.
[153] Lu 1, 303.
[154] A 2, 141.
[155] Rac 300; Br 2, 347; Fo 162.
[156] We 361.
[157] Lu 1, 303.
[158] Cf. ἀνακρινόμενος καθ'ἡμέραν περὶ σοῦ quoted in P-K I 92.
[159] Stä 226.
[160] Using "testimonia" as his thesis or producing them himself ? Cf. Wi 198; Han 175.
[161] Rac 300.

vi) Conclusion

ἀνακρίνειν τὰς γραφάς ... describes from the other end what is involved in the process of διαλέγεσθαι [162] ἀπό [163] τῶν γραφῶν. According to this the ἀνακρίνειν, characterized by understanding (as a result of one's own careful scrutiny of the arguments and facts) is perhaps in contrast to the ἐκπλήσσεσθαι [164] which is marked by lack of understanding. What helped to stimulate the Christians to faith were not inexplicable mighty "signs and wonders" but the apostles' διαλέγεσθαι which was meant to be examined carefully afterwards.

III) Conclusions from II 1 and 2 together

(1) διαλέγεσθαι and ἀνακρίνειν imply that the hearers were not surrendered helpless and without resources to the mercy of "signs and wonders". Rather Paul surrenders himself and what he is commissioned to say to the mercy of διαλέγεσθαι and its concomitant ἀνακρίνειν : what Paul has to say has to be proved and made good in the arena of argument and counter-argument.

Correspondingly the chief emphasis in the verification of what he has said, both on Paul's side and on that of his hearers, lies in the argumentation carried on by the presenter of the arguments as well as by those accepting them and in no way on the additional signs and wonders (14, 3). This process, designated by the two poles of διαλέγεσθαι and ἀνακρίνειν, is, whether διαλέγεσθαι means here "discuss" or "preach", essentially bound up" ... with the idea of intellectual stimulus".[165] This clearly shows that the decision on the meaning of διαλέγεσθαι in the sense of an either-or is ultimately of secondary importance—as long as we can grasp what in essence was meant by it in that situation.

It seems to me that the best short description of the process described by διαλέγεσθαι (and ἀνακρίνειν) is this : "Reasoned, or discoursed

---

[162] G-T : "To think different things with one's self, mingle thought with thought ... revolve in mind" (139).

[163] ἀπό here : "The notion of source is the real idea" (Rob 576) and W (333) : "ausgehend (bei seinen Unterredungen) von der heil. Schrift oder von ihr seine Beweise entlehnend ..."

[164] A 13, 12.

[165] Ro III 267.

argumentatively, either in the way of dialogue ... or in that of formal and continuous discourse".[166]

(2)   But, leaving behind the more fundamental meanings of διαλέγεσθαι and ἀνακρίνειν and the process which they indicate, we discover an interesting and important fact, when we examine these expressions in their relation to what is meant by καταγγέλλειν and draw that into our interpretation. We will attend to that in E). But here we can already see in our correlation of these ideas their striking *proximity* to one another. For the way in which διαλέγεσθαι and ἀνακρίνειν are introduced in the text in no way gives the impression that they refer to something additional or something secondary to the real "gospel-event" constituted by κηρύσσειν on the one hand and πιστεύειν on the other, perhaps in the form of a clearing up of *preliminary* questions or of a *subsequently* deepened intellectual understanding. In relation to καταγγέλλειν, διαλέγεσθαι and ἀνακρίνειν at any rate do not seem to refer to something which is only *additional* or an *afterthought* which is ultimately of no importance. No, if the gospel means a "salvation-event" then it is not achieved in isolation from the process referred to by διαλέγεσθαι and ἀνακρίνειν. How and how closely διαλέγεσθαι/ἀνακρίνειν on the one hand and καταγγέλλειν on the other are to be co-ordinated—so as not to err in a too speedy identification of them—will be considered, as we have said, in E).

B)   διανοίγειν [167]

I)   Apart from Mk 7, 34 διανοίγειν only occurs in L.[168] Our starting-

---

[166] A 2, 135.

[167] "Explain, interpret" (A-G 186); "eröffnen, auslegen, erklären" (Ha 446); "Aufschluss geben" (Hol 1, 109; We 358); "expounding" (Beg IV 203; Mu 164; G-T 140); "explaining" (Han 174; O'Neill, *op. cit.* 120); "opening up so as to connect" (Wi 197); "opening up their meaning" (Bar 295); "making plain what before was not understood" (Lu 1, 300).

With regard to the grammatical structure, I would follow Beg IV 203, who takes ἀπὸ τῶν γραφῶν with the following participles, but then goes on: "But Luke is accustomed to place clauses in ambiguous positions perhaps with the intention of not attaching them exclusively either to what precedes or to what follows". Cf. also Pl 3, s.v. Amphibolous constructions.

[168] 4 times in L, 3 in A. It has as object
the eyes : L 24, 31—ἐπιγινώσκειν
the Scriptures : L 24, 32
the understanding : L 24, 45—συνιέναι
the heart : A 16, 18—προσέχειν.

point must be the recognition that διανοίγειν in A 17, 3 is parallel to Jesus' διανοίγειν in L 24, 31.32.45. The meaning and function of διανοίγειν here can only become clear to us when we consider briefly the context of this verb in L 24.

We can describe this context in which διανοίγειν appears in ch. 24 as one of the identification of the resurrected Jesus. For apparently there are obstacles to this identification. That is clear on the one hand in the encounters with the risen Jesus : in the case of the Emmaus disciples they cannot recognize him and in the case of the main body of disciples they think that they are seeing a ghost. On the other hand, it is shown by the rich vocabulary in ch. 24, which reflects well the confused situation which reigns in that chapter.[169] How could this situation have arisen? The text gives two reasons :

1) that they had forgotten Jesus' own words and teachings and indeed had not properly understood them even in his lifetime (24, 6.44; cf. 9, 45).

2) they had also, however, been too slow of understanding "to believe all that the prophets had spoken" (v. 25).

For these reasons Jesus called them not "unbelieving", but "slow of understanding"; not unbelieving, because their love and loyalty to Jesus is largely only the reason for their present sorrow, but slow of understanding because "Unverstand und Langsamkeit des Herzens (sie) am Glauben (hindern), den sie auf Grund dessen ..., was durch Prophetenmund verkündet ist, hätten fassen können".[170] This difficulty in identifying him, this lack of understanding, thus have "in ihren falschen Erwartungen ihren Grund".[171] "Ihr Zweifel beruht einfach auf ihrer Unwissenheit über den Verheissenen. Sie haben ihr Bild von ihm weniger der Schrift entnommen, wie sie es hätten tun sollen, als es durch die eigenen Wünsche prägen lassen".[172] The identification problem is therefore based not on any defect in their

---

[169] ἀπορεῖσθαι v. 4; ἀπιστεῖν vv. 11, 41; ὁμιλεῖν, συζητεῖν v. 15; μὴ ἐπιγνῶναι v. 16; ἐξίστημι v. 22; ἀνόητοι καὶ βραδεῖς τῇ καρδίᾳ v. 25; πτοηθέντες ... καὶ ἔμφοβοι v. 37; τεταραγμένοι ... διαλογισμοί ... v. 38.

[170] Grundmann, W., Das Evangelium nach Lukas, Berlin 1961², 446.

[171] Op. cit. 446.

[172] Rengstorf, K. H., Das Evangelium nach Lukas, Göttingen 1958, 283; cf. also Zahn, Th., Das Evangelium des Lucas, Leipzig 1913, 724 : "Er tadelt sie ... wegen ihres Mangels an Schriftverständnis".

love for Jesus, but is the result of "slowness of thought and perception" [173] and is thus a matter of the "intellectual side" of man.[174]

How does Jesus tackle this identification problem? How does he
prove that ἐγώ εἰμι αὐτός (v. 39)? Essentially there seem to be two
possible ways:

1) Jesus could by a supernatural event prove himself *directly* to
be the resurrected One. In other words, Jesus would be "recognized"
as such in a moment of the suspension of the normal laws of perception.
There are in fact indications, but only indications, of such a supernatural event in our passage:

i)   his mysterious coming and going (24, 31.36), and
ii) his belonging to a different form of reality (24, 37-39).

But these supernatural signs seem rather peripheral to the account
and are related to their "recognition" of him not so much as answers
to their question, as posing new questions and increasing their confusion. This brings us to the second possibility:

2) Jesus could show himself to be the resurrected One *indirectly*,
i.e. with the help of normal human means of perception. And in fact
these are more prominent in L: Jesus identifies himself as the risen
One by making himself open to proof, indeed inviting this (39b; 41b).
This proof takes a threefold form:

i)   a cosmological proof: the empty tomb (24, 3)
ii) a proof through the senses: touching Jesus (24, 40) and his
eating (24, 41-43), and
iii) an intellectual proof: the "opening" of their understanding so
that they can understand the Scriptures concerning himself (24,
45.27.32, the διερμηνεύειν).

It is within *this* context that we must understand διανοίγειν and its
allied concepts.[175] Ultimately one thing is involved, a coming to terms

---

[173] Adeney, W. F., *St. Luke*, Edinburgh and London, n.d., 392.

[174] Ragg, L., *St. Luke*, London 1922, 315.

[175] L 24, 45 : τότε διήνοιξεν αὐτῶν τὸν νοῦν τοῦ συνιέναι τὰς γραφάς = διήνοιγεν ἡμῖν
τὰς γραφάς (v. 32) = διηρμήνευσεν αὐτοῖς ἐν πάσαις ταῖς γραφαῖς τὰ περὶ ἑαυτοῦ (v. 27).
διανοίγειν is thus synonymous with διερμηνεύειν and συνιέναι and has the human
νοῦς as its object. συνιέναι here means "verstehen, einsehen, begreifen, zur Einsicht
kommen" (E 564); "to perceive, understand" (G-T 605; M-M 607f.) and really goes
back to the literal meaning "to bring together, to set together" (M-M *ibid.*), i.e. "to set

with the reality of the risen Jesus. In other words, just as Jesus made himself available that he might be recognized as the risen One, not by his unusual nature or by an unusual miraculous event, but by normal means, and thus that he might be recognized not through the suspension of the usual organs of perception but through their help, so he invited recognition by means of the human νοῦς. Thus we do not perceive Christ directly, e.g. in a direct vision or flash of insight, but indirectly through the human organs of perception. Self-authentication is clearly replaced here by the various forms of authentication which can, so to speak, be called in to help from outside. The authentication here takes concrete forms which can only be called "human".

We will not be wrong in suspecting an apologetic interest to lie behind this. Jesus counters in two ways a problem of identification caused by a misunderstanding (v. 21): firstly he starts from the present. On the empirical level he shows himself to be the risen One through the senses (vv. 36-43). Then he turns to the past, to the Scriptures : on the intellectual level he shows himself to be the risen One through the reason (vv. 44-46). To Ed. Meyer's comment that "Lukas kommt alles darauf an, jeden Zweifel an der Realität der Auferstehung niederzuschlagen und die Einwände, welche der christlichen Mission immer wieder gegen die Möglichkeit einer Auferstehung des Fleisches ... gemacht wurden ... durch die völlig gesicherte geschichtliche Tatsache zu entkräften",[176] we must add that L does not only put all the emphasis on the empirical proofs of the historical fact of the resurrection but also, to the same end, he places as much emphasis as possible on the idea that, as far as the reason (νοῦς) is concerned, there is no reason for ἀπορεῖσθαι and ἐξίστημι with regard to the resurrection. Proofs for the historical fact come from the empirical. Proofs for the rationality of this historical fact come from the "Scriptures". From them the disciples' defective knowledge of Jesus as a prophet is supplemented by a new vision of his Messiahship : the Messiah must suffer and die and only thus attain to his glory. Thus it is the Easter-event which makes it possible for the disciples also to share the understanding which Jesus had from the Scriptures. The risen One stands up to the scrutiny of the human senses, but he also stands up to that of the human reason.—Un-

---

or join together in the mind" (G-T op. cit.). It is synonymous with νοεῖν (Mk 8, 17), just as ἀνόητος (L 24, 25) and ἀσύνετος are synonymous (Mt 15, 16f.).

[176] Ursprung I 24.

mistakable is the *special* significance attached here to a correct understanding of the Scriptures, in contrast perhaps to proof through the
senses. We can agree with Ed. Meyer when he writes : "der Schrift-
steller will dies fundamentale Moment so nachdrücklich wie möglich
einprägen, welches das Rätsel der Passion löst und die Realität der
Auferstehung des Messias dadurch, dass sie vorausverkündet ist, über
jeden Zweifel erhebt".[177] Thus the motif of the explanation and
understanding of the Old Testament runs like a constant refrain
through the whole chapter (vv. 6 f.; 27; 45 f.). On each occasion this
"opening" arises from lack of understanding and aims at understanding:

v. 4 ἀπορεῖσθαι

v. 25 ἀνόητοι

v. 45 τὸν νοῦν τοῦ συνιέναι

And it is Jesus himself who leads them to "understanding" : on the
one hand 39.41b, on the other 26.44-46. In both it is ultimately a
matter of identifying him, of verifying that ἐγώ εἰμι αὐτός. The miracle
of the resurrection of the crucified One must be understood—*as a
wonder.*

II) What does this exegesis contribute to our understanding of
A 17, 3 ? We were struck how much significance was attached to
understanding the wonder of Jesus' resurrection in L 24—and attached
to it by the risen Jesus himself ! This, one would think, would have
been a situation in which an appeal to the reason would really have
been unnecessary. We also noticed that διανοίγειν is used in L 24 in
the context of identifying the risen Jesus : ἐγώ εἰμι αὐτός. Transferring
this to our passage we find that διανοίγειν serves to identify him who
is proclaimed and indeed is present in Paul's καταγγέλλω. διανοίγειν
refers to the identification of the Lord present in the proclamation—
on the level of the understanding and reason. Just as the authentication
of ἐγώ εἰμι αὐτός was not possible without empirical and intellectual
identification, so καταγγέλλειν is not possible without such an identification. Naturally the story of the historical Jesus on the one hand
and the testimony to the risen Jesus on the other replaces the empirical
identification. Just as the ἐγώ εἰμι αὐτός could in theory have been
an illusion, so the καταγγέλλειν, in which the risen Jesus is present,
could be a phantom—unless supported by the νοῦς. Just as the
presence of the risen Jesus was not self-evident but could only be

---

[177] *Op. cit.* 28.

indirectly *grasped* as his presence, so the Lord present in the καταγγέλλειν must be mediated. And no more than the presence of the risen Jesus could be grasped without the assistance of the normal organs of perception could the "proclamation", representing the presence of the risen Jesus, avail without the νοῦς. Here διανοίγειν is not, so to speak, a technical procedure, a means which could be completely detached from its purpose. For, as we learn in L 24, 31f., the "opening" of the Scriptures, however "human" an activity it may be, at the same time opens their eyes to the present activity of the Lord.

C) παρατίθεσθαι [178]

If in the investigation of the concept of διανοίγειν we asserted that this first part of διαλέγεσθαι meant above all the "opening" of the νοῦς for a new understanding of the Messiah based on the Scriptures, so παρατίθεσθαι with its following "declarative" ὅτι,[179] which also goes with the preceding διανοίγων,[180] is above all concerned with man's understanding. In this, the second part of διαλέγεσθαι, so to speak, the emphasis is above all on the idea of "putting forward" [181] proofs "in addition to" (= παρά[182]) the new understanding of scripture presented by Paul. We can but agree with Wendt [183] when he regards the difference between διανοίγειν and παρατίθεσθαι as that between the "Merkmal der Neuheit" and the "Merkmal der beweisen-

---

[178] On the etymology cf. Bo 969f.; Fr II 897f.; Ho 365; Ka II 457; Mey II 743; Po 235ff.; Pr 461; W-P I 826ff.; cf. also vanH 628; *id.* App. 164; S I 492, 686ff., 722, 725, 741, 761f., 774f., 782.

[179] Cf. Rob 1034.

[180] Cf. *op. cit.* 1035.

[181] "To bring forward, quote as evidence" (A-S 343; Br 1, 324); "to cite as evidence" (L-S; Beg IV 203); "bring forward by way of proof" (M-M 490; cf. the examples quoted here); "prove by citations from writers" (Pa 464); "adducing in proof" (Bar 295; Han 174); "als Zeugen, als Beweis für sich anführen, bes. Beweisstellen für sich u. seine Meinung citieren" (P II 503); "lehrend darlegen, auseinandersetzen" (Maurer in *TDNT* VIII 164); "daneben stellen um zu vergleichen, dah. auseinanderhalten, dagegen halten, vergleichen" (Ps II 1); "vor-, darlegend" (E 319); "demonstrate, point out" (A-G 628; O'Neill, *op. cit.* 120) etc. Cf. also Be 487; C 1013; P-K II 258f.; Schl II 429; Sch 18, 8; 104, 3; Z 430; Me 124; Ma II 1, 103.314; 3, 46.

[182] Literature on παρά in M III 272, n. 2; παρά as a verbal prefix—cf. M II 318-20; cf. also H 45; S II 493; Rob 561.

[183] 358.

den Ausführlichkeit". "Explaining" [184] and "expounding" [185] are
really too weak as expressions for what is meant here if we do not
include therein the element of "presenting proofs".[186] The extent to
which this concept too is essentially part of man's "understanding"
is clear from the following quotation : "... he expounded the OT
scriptures ... bringing forward as evidence of their fulfilment the
historic facts accomplished in the ministry, death and exaltation of
Jesus, setting the fulfilment alongside the predictions in order that
the force of his argument might be readily grasped".[187]

D) καταγγέλλειν [188]

In coming to this concept we pass from the sphere of teaching,
explaining and understanding and of giving proofs into that of
"proclaiming "and "preaching". According to Schniewind [189] this
word "always" has a "sacral" meaning and "the thought of *solemn
proclamation* is uppermost".[190] Its sense is "that of the proclamation
or declaration of a completed happening ... the expectation of the
ἀνάστασις νεκρῶν has become a reality 'in Jesus' and is now declared
(A 4, 2).[191] Similarly ... in 17, 3 ... the expected Messiah is now
present. In both cases the expectation is fulfilled in the name of
Jesus". This καταγγέλλειν is an expression of Paul's personal
testimony.

---

[184] Mu 164; G-T 486.

[185] Wi 197.

[186] Ha 446. Similarly Ro III 268 : "Paul was not only 'expounding' the Scripture,
he was also 'propounding' (the old meaning of 'allege') his doctrine ... quoting the
Scripture to prove his contention ..."

[187] Br 2, 343.

[188] Occurs only in A and P. Synonymous with κηρύσσειν, εὐαγγελίζεσθαι τὸν Ἰησοῦν
(twice each in A : 9, 20; 19, 13 and 5, 42; 8, 35). Only once κηρύσσειν τὸν Χριστόν 8, 5
and once εὐαγγελίζεσθαι τὸν κύριον Ἰησοῦν 11, 20. In P : τὸν Χριστὸν καταγγέλλειν Ph 1,
17; Col 1, 28; Χριστὸς καταγγέλλεται Ph 1, 18. Synonymous with this are Χριστὸν
κηρύσσειν Ph 1, 15 etc. and εὐαγγελίζεσθαι Gal 1, 16ff. Similarly τὸ εὐαγγέλιον καταγγέλλειν
1 C 9, 14 τὸν λόγον τοῦ θεοῦ A 13, 5; 17, 13; τοῦ κυρίου 15, 36; synonymous with this
is τὸ μαρτύριον (= synonym of εὐαγγέλιον) τοῦ θεοῦ 1 C 2, 1.

[189] In *TDNT* I 71.

[190] So also A-G 410 and M-M "make proclamation with authority" (324); Westcott, B. F., *The Epistles of St. John*, Cambridge 1909⁴, 15 : "to proclaim with authority".

[191] Westcott, *ibid.* : "in καταγγέλλειν the relation of the bearer and hearer of the
message (is) ... most prominent".

E) *Correlation*

I) Thus far our survey. After making all these observations we must ask what indications we have found for the correct co-ordinating of the concepts investigated and their associated ideas. This can only be provisional despite the fact that we shall adopt certain individual insights from the preceding study (particularly from B).

It is important to attend to the correct correlation of these since no word and an attendant concept leads an isolated existence, but— over and above its basic meaning—it leads something like a second life within its context. The specific nature of a word's meaning, and with it its concrete, actual use and life, can only be elicited from the context within which such a word and its concept live and breathe.

Thus it makes a fundamental difference for our understanding, whether the correlation of words and concepts demanded by the context is understood as fitting them *together* or setting them *apart*, as standing either in *relation to one another* or in *contrast to one another*.

In the first case (and here we must note the structure of the text and the direction in which it moves) one understands a word when one recognizes it *in its relation to* other words and concepts (with all that such a relation may imply) and thus accordingly asks why they are so related.—The reason must be something like a unity of an event or a reality, which binds them both together but is also prior to both of them. This would be too extensive, too diverse, too rich and thus too vital to be adequately expressed simply by one word. Rather this reality which is prior to all its explications is unfolded and develops different emphases and nuances with the help of different words and concepts. If the use of different words was evoked by the basic unity of a reality, then the relation in which we see one word standing to another can only be properly understood in the light of this prior reality. Thus it is false to disregard this actual function which these words have when we define their meaning. But this can happen easily when, for whatever reason, through isolated investigations of different terms and ideas, the presupposed unity of a reality is rapidly lost to view. This reality, which it was the original function of these various terms to explain, has therefore no longer an adequate bearing on the interpretation of the text. Then a feeling for nuances or aspects of meaning gives way to a preoccupation with differences and finally perhaps even with contrasts.

In the second case, correspondingly, the key to understanding lies in "separating" the words from one another, not in finding their "closeness" to one another.

II) Since διανοίγειν and παρατίθεσθαι spell out more fully what is involved in διαλέγεσθαι [192] we have to co-ordinate the following :

διαλέγεσθαι - λέγειν - λόγος
καταγγέλλειν - ἀγγέλλειν - εὐαγγέλιον

These two seem to form the basic co-ordinates of Paul's preaching. The study of our text clearly showed that the correlation of these two is to be defined in terms of their relation to one another and not in terms of their contrast. These words and their associated ideas are related to one another and are not opposites. So, if we want to arrive at an adequate interpretation of L's witness, we, with the above principle in view, must ask this further question : why do these words stick together and, as it were, sympathize with one another and support one another ? What or who is the *one* common factor which is prior to both of them and always anticipates them and so also forms their basis, with reference to which they are related to one another ?

Thus it is not the separation of the words and their ideas from one another but their *nearness* to one another and, above all, that which first forms the basis of that nearness, which must be regulative for the definition of their relation —with all that that implies.

This is directly relevant to our specific question. For the intellectual element attracted our attention especially in our investigation of the διαλέγεσθαι-group (together with ἀνακρίνειν). Therefore we must suppose that only by a correct definition of the relation of these two basic terms (καταγγέλλειν and διαλέγεσθαι) to one another can we gain a deeper insight into the understanding which the Lukan Paul had of the relation of faith and intellectual activity within his own preaching activity. The relation of faith and intellectual activity thus takes part in the question of the relation of καταγγέλλειν and διαλέγεσθαι, of εὐαγγέλιον and λόγος. The hermeneutic key to the correct understanding of διαλέγεσθαι and thereby of the intellectual element in its relation to καταγγέλλειν is thus this relationship itself— and that with reference to that reality which first makes this relationship possible. In other words, it means, negatively, that the intellectual element—as L wanted us to understand it—cannot

---

[192] B-D-F 327.

adequately be defined as such, and, positively, that we can actually achieve an adequate understanding of the function and significance of the human reason within this relationship. We must in our interpretation reckon just as much with the reality of this relationship as with the reality that precedes it and thus forms the basis for it.

But what is this reality which always precedes and anticipates both καταγγέλλειν and διαλέγεσθαι and the intellectual element within it alike? When we say that διαλέγεσθαι and καταγγέλλειν are related, then that implies that the intellectual element expressed by διαλέγεσθαι is related to the object of the καταγγέλλειν. But if the "object" of καταγγέλλειν is none other than the resurrection of Jesus from the dead and his being alive and present, then the intellectual element, represented by διαλέγεσθαι, "is related" to the presence of the risen Jesus. *This appears to be the reality which always precedes both the καταγγέλλειν and the διαλέγεσθαι—and will continue to do so.* This conclusion is in essence nothing but the statement that the "methods" of Paul's preaching, within which we are trying to trace the intellectual element, cannot be separated from its "contents". Here perhaps the influence of the contents of his preaching on his methods is detectable. That fact we must give its due attention.

But if the necessity for the employment of human reason within proclamation arises from its relation to the presence of Christ and the presence of the risen Christ itself is somehow the determinative cause of the involvement of the human reason in "matters of faith", then there arise two important questions :

(1) in what sense is the intellectual element related to the presence of the risen Christ ? In other words, in what way can Christ's presence be determinative for the employment of the powers of reason ?

(2) what influence does the presence of the risen Christ have on the intellectual element and so on our understanding of it ?

On (1) Two observations help us here :

i) we should first note the twofold distinction which seems to hold these two aspects apart :
  a) indirect speech after διαλέγεσθαι,
     direct speech [193] after καταγγέλλειν, and

---

[193] Cf. Rob 442, 1034; Bu 330 : "Es ist nicht zu verkennen, dass vor allen Lukas

b)   an emphasis on the γραφαί in connection with διαλέγεσθαι,
     an emphasis on the ἐγώ [194] in connection with καταγγέλλειν.

Thus in connection with διαλέγεσθαι "the Scriptures" take first
place, and with καταγγέλλειν Paul himself.

A second observation may further show how this distinction in
fact assists in the definition of the relationship rather than of the
difference.

ii)   We should remember that in L 24 the recognition of the presence
of the risen Christ stood so emphatically in the centre of attention
because without this recognition there is no possibility of an encounter
with him. Thus the risen Christ is present with his disciples long
before they identify him, i.e. recognize him as the One who is present
and so encounter him. Encounter can thus only take place in and
after recognition of his presence. Quite apart from L 24, passages
like Mt 18, 20 and 28, 20, and also 25, 31-46, which one could call
the parable of the perceived and unperceived presence of Christ,
show that the recognition of the presence of Christ was already a real
problem for the earliest Christians. In the case of L 24, recognition
of his presence and so encounter with the ἐγώ εἰμι αὐτός comes about
not through the disciples' leaving behind or ascending away from
what was familiar to them, or at any rate leaving it, e.g. by entering
into a vision that bypassed the normal organs of perception, or into
inward contemplation. Recognition rather comes about by referring
to what is "to hand"; ultimately one was only conscious of his presence
because Christ, even as the risen One, presented proofs, whether
perceptible or intellectual, appropriate to the different human organs
of perception. Jesus was grasped and seen to be the present and risen
One by reference to and use of the normal means of recognition.
Thus encounter as recognition of his presence "happened" not only
through "touching" him (24, 40) and his "eating before their eyes"
(24, 41-3; cf. also vv. 30f.) but also through the tradition about the
"empty tomb" (24, 3) and through the "opening" (of their minds and)
of the Scriptures (24, 27.32.45). διανοίγειν thus plays a fundamental
part in identifying the risen Jesus and so in meeting with him as

---

sich diese echt griechische Ausdrucksweise am meisten zu eigen gemacht hat". Transition
from indirect to direct speech also in 1, 4; 14, 22; 23, 22; 25, 5. Stä 224 : "Der persönliche Charakter dieses zweiten Teils der Botschaft ist von Lukas durch den Übergang aus der indirekten in die direkte Rede zum Ausdruck gebracht".

[194] Cf. Br 2, 325.

present. The "employment" of the human reason understood in this way thus leads into the presence and so into the sphere of the work and influence of the risen Jesus.

Applied to A 17, 2-4 this means that the personal ἐγώ εἰμι αὐτός found its expression in the emphatically personal testimony of the apostle. The presence of the risen Christ accredited itself in Paul's personal testimony. But this is not simply the same as saying that one also really recognizes the presence of the risen Christ proclaimed in the apostle's testimony and encounters him himself. According to L 24 διανοίγειν is a means contributing to the encounter with the present and risen Christ. διανοίγειν in our passage is used in a similar, if not in an identical, sense to that of L 24, 27.32.45. In addition, this term is here an explication of διαλέγεσθαι. What does that tell us about the meaning of διαλέγεσθαι? One could perhaps formulate it in general terms thus—and, to avoid possible misunderstanding, this must be qualified later : καταγγέλλειν τὸν Χριστόν is accomplished by the use of διαλέγεσθαι. This formulation has the advantage that proper scope is given for the element of *simultaneity*. Thus we protect ourselves from regarding one element as prior to the other;[195] there is nothing here like an (essentially less important) human part, let us say a technical part which would comply with the laws of human logic, and a separate second part (which is ultimately all-important) which could only be understood as a "solemn appeal". πείθεσθαι [196] and προσκληροῦσθαι [197] in v. 4 complement one another in a similar way. But we must not reach our understanding of this simultaneity at the expense of a correct definition of their relation; we must not therefore understand it as an identity. We must rather hold fast to the simultaneity and also do justice to the distinction indicated by the terms διαλέγεσθαι and καταγγέλλειν. Thus just as the reality *and* presence of the ἐγώ εἰμι αὐτός is revealed only by means of an effective tackling of the problem of identification, so the "proclaimed" present Lord, announced in the apostle's personal testimony, is only revealed through tackling the διαλέγεσθαι. This search for identification certainly made use not only of "the Scriptures" but also of accounts of the facts about the historical Jesus.[198] The "simultaneity" of καταγγέλλειν and διαλέγεσθαι of which we spoke must thus be qualified

195 Cf., e.g., Stä 224.
196 Cf. § 2 of this thesis.
197 Cf. dictionaries and comms.
198 Cf. οὗτος in 17, 3.

by saying that διαλέγεσθαι and the intellectual element contained in it have in relation to καταγγέλλειν the function of assisting in the identification of the risen Jesus proclaimed as present in the apostle's personal testimony and thus bringing about encounter with him. But this implies that the relation of faith and the intellectual element to one another is as close and intimate as the approach of Christ himself to his disciples can be intimate—so close that they can touch him and thus identify him. Faith and the intellectual element, as reflected in Paul's method of preaching are together like two peas in a pod—but no closer. Neither merges with the other at the expense of its own identity.

On 2) What consequences has this insight into the function and importance of διαλέγεσθαι and thus of the intellectual element for our understanding of διαλέγεσθαι itself? The relation in which faith and the intellectual element stand to one another is not just one which of necessity arises from the presence of the risen Christ; but also this relation—and thus also διαλέγεσθαι—is itself characterized by this presence :

i) if identification is the way by which the encounter with the already present Christ is mediated, then the practice of διαλέγεσθαι (with all which that may involve in terms of form and content) as a means to this identification is nothing but an expression of the actual encounter with the present Christ proclaimed in the apostle's personal testimony. But then is διαλέγεσθαι not also preaching and proclamation—but only with respect to the One encountered ?

ii) if the activity referred to as διαλέγεσθαι, embracing speaker and hearer (ἀνακρίνειν), is the basis for the production of literary materials, then can such products be anything other than testimonies to actual encounters with the risen Christ—and *as such* also proclamation, εὐαγγέλιον? Seen in this way, διαλέγεσθαι would have the character of proclamation, without ceasing also to be real διαλέγεσθαι !

Section 2 : Interpretation of the findings

In the preceding first sub-section we tried to discern the relation between faith and intellectual activity by noting Paul's methods of preaching in respect of the intellectual element in them.

In doing this what we *described* in our observations more and more crystallized around the question of the relation of the intellectual element to the presence of the risen Jesus.

In the following second sub-section we must try to *interpret* this closeness of the intellectual element to the presence of Christ in the light of the task given to Paul theologically or christologically, i.e. with regard to the doctrine of the presence of Christ within Paul's testimony.

A) *The framework of the interpretation :*
Paul's commission—action and suffering

I) Paul's action—God's action

(1) Paul's action

What Paul *is* does not come from himself. Rather it was the "Holy Spirit" or "God" who προσκέκληται (13, 2; 16, 10), or "the Lord" who τέθεικεν (13, 47); "for him" therefore he is a σκεῦος ἐκλογῆς (9, 15). And since God προεχειρίσατο him (22, 14; 26, 16), he will τάσσεται him (22, 10).

Correspondingly, he *does* what he does, not on his own initiative, but he has "received" (λαμβάνειν 20, 24) a ministry, he ἀφορίζεται to it and is παραδιδομένος through the "Holy Spirit" in the Church (13, 2; 14, 26); he is sent (ἀποστέλλεται, ἐξαποστέλλεται (26, 17; 22, 21). He himself does not say what he has to "do", but λαλήσεται σοι ... (9, 6; 22, 10). For εἰς τοῦτο ... ὤφθην σοι ... (26, 16).

Both of these elements are often expressed simply through the use of the word δεῖ : Paul is under a *necessity* (9, 6; 23, 11; 27, 24).

There are two basic characteristics of Paul's commission :

i) the carrying out of his commission implies a *going* : 22, 21 (18, 6); 28, 26; 16, 7.16; 17, 14; 19, 1.21; 20, 1.22; 21, 5 etc. Its execution is significantly compared to a δρόμος which one runs and "finishes" (20, 24).

ii) Paul's basic commission involves doing (ποιεῖν : 9, 6; 22, 10) something (... ὅ τί 9, 6; ... περὶ πάντων ὧν ... 22, 10), being called εἰς τὸ ἔργον (13, 2; 14, 26; 15, 38), to which he ἔρχεται (15, 38) and which he πληροῖ (14, 26).—And this "doing" is really essentially a λαλεῖν (18, 9), a λέγειν (17, 18; 28, 26), for this particular "work" cannot be "fulfilled" or done through σιωπᾶν (18, 9)—even though he runs the risk of being mocked as a σπερμολόγος (17, 18). And through this "speaking" Paul is to carry out the βαστάζειν τὸ ὄνομά μου (9, 15). And τὸ ὄνομά μου stands for ἄφεσιν ἁμαρτιῶν λαμβάνειν (10, 43);

ἀπολούειν τὰς ἁμαρτίας (22, 16); δύναμις : ἴασις, σημεῖα, τέρατα (3, 16; 4, 30; 16, 18; 19, 13.17); σώζεσθαι (2, 21; 4, 12); σωτηρία (4, 12). βαστάζειν τὸ ὄνομά μου thus involves a καταγγέλλειν ... ὁδὸν σωτηρίας (16, 17). So Paul is set "to bring salvation". In short, Paul must εὐαγγελίσασθαι (16, 10). But this εὐαγγελίσασθαι is achieved essentially by means of "bearing witness" : the apostle should be a μάρτυς "for him" (22, 15; cf. 13, 31 and 13, 2—ἀφορίζειν δή μοι), or a ὑπηρέτης καὶ μάρτυς (26, 16), with his μαρτυρία περὶ ἐμοῦ (22, 18). Therefore he "received the ministry" of διαμαρτυρεῖσθαι τὸ εὐαγγέλιον τῆς χάριτος τοῦ θεοῦ (20, 24), or simply of διαμαρτυρεῖσθαι (μαρτυρεῖν) τὰ περὶ ἐμοῦ (23, 11).

This is to take place ἐνώπιον ἐθνῶν τε καὶ βασιλέων υἱῶν τε 'Ισραήλ (9, 15) or, putting it geographically, ἕως ἐσχάτου τῆς γῆς (13, 47) or also εἰς 'Ιερουσαλήμ ... εἰς 'Ρώμην ... (23, 11). Thus Paul is ecumenical (this squares with the accusations levelled at him : 16, 20; 17, 6; 18, 13; 19, 26; 24, 5). And just because of the Jews' rejection has he become "only" a φῶς ἐθνῶν (13, 47) and ἐξαποστέλλεται ... εἰς ἔθνη μακράν (22, 21).

(2) God's action

Yet Acts does not only make statements about Paul's "doings" but also about those of God. Or, more accurately, when the apostles speak of their action they speak of God's action. This can happen in different ways :

i)   ὅσα ἐποίησεν ὁ θεὸς μετ'αὐτῶν ...[199] 14, 27 ; 15, 4
      ὅσα ἐποίησεν ὁ θεὸς ... δι'αὐτῶν ... 15, 12
      ὧν ἐποίησεν ὁ θεὸς ... 21, 19
ii)   Correspondingly, in the context in which the Holy Spirit separates the apostles εἰς τὸ ἔργον (13, 2; cf. 14, 26; 15, 38) God speaks : ἴδετε ... ὅτι ἔργον ἐργάζομαι ἐγὼ ... ἔργον ... (13, 41).
iii) 14, 3 : ὁ κύριος ὁ μαρτυρῶν τῷ λόγῳ τῆς χάριτος αὐτοῦ

The action of the apostles and the action of God are thus not two different actions but in some respects *one* action—though we must

---

[199] M (61) : "... association with ... Acts 14, 27 ... may well mean 'all that God had done in fellowship (or co-operation) with them' "—and therefore need not be a Semitism (so also Rob 609; M-M 401). Cf. also M III (269) : "of mutual participation ... In contrast to σύν, the meaning of μετά is never 'in addition to' ".

not deny the concreteness and reality of the apostles' activity. The interplay of God's action and the apostles' is interestingly balanced in the summaries about the growth of the word or of the Church (9, 31; 13, 49; 16, 5; 19, 10; 19, 20 etc.). God's action and the apostles' are not simply identical with one another, any more than God and the apostles are. Rather they are ἄνθρωποι and as such δοῦλοι τοῦ θεοῦ (16, 17); they ὁμοιοπαθεῖς εἰσιν ὑμῖν ἄνθρωποι and as such εὐαγγελιζόμενοι (14, 15). Or the same thing can be put thus in respect of their activity by means of the word διακονία: what God "did" among the Gentiles he could do διὰ τῆς διακονίας αὐτοῦ (21, 19), or simply μετ' αὐτῶν (14, 27; 15, 4) and δι'αὐτῶν (15, 12), since Paul received his διακονία παρὰ τοῦ κυρίου Ἰησοῦ (20, 24). God "does his work in your days" through and by means of the actions, i.e. the preaching, of the apostles. Thus he can only really do this when he serves him (20, 19: δουλεύων τῷ κυρίῳ; 24, 14: λατρεύω τῷ πατρῴῳ θεῷ ...).

This is an essential and fundamental statement which we must constantly remember in all that concerns the manner of the carrying out of this ministry if we are to understand the individual statements aright.

(3) Conclusions

We have shown that the apostles' action, for all its difference, expressed in the idea of διακονία, at the same time can be called God's action. Both are bound together through the διακονία which characterizes the apostle's activity; it is thus not an activity on the same level, so to speak, as if it were completely identified with it, but an activity in God's service in obedience and subordination. Here we showed that the ποιεῖν entrusted to Paul is essentially his λαλεῖν, i.e. βαστάζειν τὸ ὄνομά μου = εὐαγγελίζεσθαι. It is no argument against this that Paul from time to time also performs signs and wonders and miracles of healing. These are only occasional outward signs or testimonies—in contrast perhaps to the inward signs which consist in the belief or unbelief "worked" by this λαλεῖν (e.g. opening of the heart: 16, 14 or 14, 27)—of the power and effectiveness of the revelation of God declaring itself in this λαλεῖν. These outward and inward signs are one in that they—both of them— are the proof, the evidence, of the wonderful power and effectiveness of the preaching of the word of grace.

II) Paul's suffering—Christ's suffering

(1) Paul's suffering

Till now in our description of the terms of the commission given to Paul of something to *do* we have passed over the fact that the *necessity of suffering* was also part of these terms. We must now try to fit this motif into the framework of Paul's commission and interpret it aright. For only thus will we be in a position to understand correctly the role of the human reason within his preaching. The best way into the problem is the programmatic passage, 9, 15 f., which marks the beginning of Paul's Christian "career": εἶπεν δὲ πρὸς αὐτὸν ὁ κύριος· πορεύου, ὅτι σκεῦος ἐκλογῆς ἐστίν μοι οὗτος τοῦ βαστάσαι τὸ ὄνομά μου ἐνώπιον [τῶν] ἐθνῶν τε καὶ βασιλέων υἱῶν τε Ἰσραήλ· (16) ἐγὼ γὰρ ὑποδείξω αὐτῷ ὅσα δεῖ αὐτὸν ὑπὲρ τοῦ ὀνόματός μου παθεῖν.

It is generally [200] recognized [201] that the "bearing my name" and "suffering for my name" go inseparably together. Their connection is usually understood by supposing that the passage is speaking of Paul's preaching on the one hand and of the bodily/physical sufferings and dangers that he underwent as a consequence of his preaching [202] on the other. The former is thus related to his activity and the latter to his personal existence, his condition. His sufferings are mainly related to his everyday experiences,[203] or the ὑποδείξω is taken to refer above all to the testimony of the Holy Spirit (which begins in 20, 23 [204]) to his future sufferings in Jerusalem. Now certainly one can adduce many immediately compelling reasons for these two variations of the one basic thesis that the sufferings mentioned in 9, 16 are physical and arise out of his preaching. And these immediately compelling

---

[200] Yet cf. Pre (59): "Dass der Verf. ... die Berufung des Apostels nur unter dem auch in der Schilderung der paulinischen Mission festgehaltenen Gesichtspunkt der Leiden betrachtet hat, zeigt, wie wenig er in den Geist der Berufsauffassung des historischen Paulus eingedrungen ist".

[201] Yet Beg IV 104 and Wi 124 at least find the mention of future sufferings to say the least of it "(a little) unexpected".

[202] A 1, 367: "There is an exquisite mixture of ... severity in sentencing this 'chosen vessel' to endure as well as labour"; and many others.

[203] Lu 1, 196: "The truth of this is borne out by that long list of the Apostle's sufferings which he enumerates in his letter to the Corinthians (2 Cor 11, 23-28) and ... 6, 4f.". So also Ha 273; Hol 1, 69; We 255 etc.

[204] So A 1, 368; Bar 221; Mu 82 et al.

reasons are certainly so compelling partly because they can be fitted so smoothly into a universally recognized schema which was developed above all in the martyr tradition.

In support of the first variation one can point to all the passages where the threat of suffering or death and actual individual experiences of suffering result more or less directly from Paul's preaching : continual threats (συμβουλεύεσθαι, etc.) and attempts (ἐπιβουλή 9, 24; 20, 19; 23, 30)—both on the part of the Jews and of the Ἑλληνισταί (9,29)— to ἀναιρεῖν (9, 23f., 29; 23, 15.21.27; 25, 3), θνήσκειν (14, 19), ἀποθνήσκειν (21, 13) or διαχειρίζεσθαι (26, 21) him. Correspondingly, he is prepared to die (15, 26; 21, 13). Further apart from threats, there are actual διωγμός and ἐκβάλλειν (13, 50), ὑβρίζειν and λιθοβολεῖν (14, 5) or λιθάζειν (14, 19), as well as ῥαβδίζειν and βάλλειν εἰς φυλακήν (16, 22; cf. v. 37), δεῖν (21, 11), δεῖν ἁλύσεσι δυσί (21, 33; cf. 22, 30), δέσμα καὶ θλίψεις (20, 23), παραδιδέναι εἰς χεῖρας ἐθνῶν (21, 11), τύπτειν (21, 32), τηρεῖσθαι (24, 23; 25, 4.21). Along with this go the sufferings affecting his nation and the Church, e.g. θορυβεῖν (17, 15), ταράσσειν (17, 8), τάραχος (19, 23), σαλεύειν καὶ ταράσσειν (17, 13) etc. Here too we must add the sorts of sufferings which Paul himself before his conversion inflicted on the Christian community : ἀπειλή (9, 1; cf. also 4, 17.29), φόνος (9, 1), θάνατος (22, 4), as well as πολλὰ ἐναντία πράσσειν (26, 9), κακὰ ποιεῖν (9, 13); δεῖν (9, 2.14.21; 22, 5), δεσμεύειν (22, 4), δέρειν (22, 19; cf. 5, 40; 16, 37; 2 C 11, 20); παραδιδόναι εἰς φυλακάς ... (22, 4), κατακλείειν ἐν φυλακαῖς (26, 10), φυλακίζειν (22, 19), ἀναιρεῖν (26, 10) and also πορθεῖν (9, 21; cf. Gal 1, 13.23).

In support of the second variation one can of course refer to the special revelations through the Holy Spirit emphasized from ch. 20 onwards and Paul's corresponding readiness for death.

(2) Christ's suffering

i) The problem

The fact that Paul personally experienced suffering in his own body and as a result of his preaching (cf., e.g., 26, 20 f.) cannot and therefore should not be doubted. Yet, despite the close connection of 9, 13 and 16 on the one hand and 9, 22 f. and 29 on the other, the contents of chs 9-28 as a whole present certain problems which make the usual interpretation of the sufferings in their relation to the preaching, as L is understood in 9, 16 and also in the whole Pauline section of Acts, at least doubtful.

Four observations :

a) Does the usual interpretation take seriously enough the two ideas which dominate chs 9-28, namely that

aa) Paul's whole being, his existence, is as it were absorbed in his actions, and so in his preaching? Paul's life is his being a witness, his testifying. Paul has, so to speak, no real self apart from the carrying out of his commission. His personal success or failure is thus at the same time the success or failure of his preaching. If we think this through, could it not mean that the sufferings which apparently only affect his personal existence are above all to be seen as the sufferings of the preacher—and that more comprehensively than is usually the case, when the sufferings resulting from the preaching are seen as themselves a form of preaching.[205] This is contradicted by the second basic idea, that

bb) his personal suffering endured in his own body as a result of his preaching has no importance in itself as, for instance, possessing "proclamatory" or "persuasive/convicting" power. It is indeed striking that in the Pauline part of Acts Paul's individual experiences of suffering never serve as "testimony to Christ" like the isolated miracles of Paul through which one can come to faith.

Both ideas (aa and bb) ultimately condition one another. For if Paul's existence is completely absorbed in his preaching, we could scarcely expect that any particular weight should suddenly be attached to his personal sufferings, which only affect his existence. But if Paul's being is wholly absorbed in his activity of preaching and if, correspondingly, we find no sign in the Pauline part of Acts that Paul's own bodily sufferings serve for proclamation/testimony, how can we then understand the sufferings which Paul encounters through his preaching as a divine necessity? Should we not at least ask, on the basis of this connection of being and action, whether such suffering must not indeed affect the process of his "bearing my name" itself— and not only its consequences? Could it not be that the preaching too, or even in the first place, has to do with suffering and not just the preacher? If Paul's whole existence is shaped by "suffering", must not above all else the "preaching" itself, in which Paul's existence

---

[205] Cf. e.g. Stä (137) : "Darum will Lukas … zeigen, … dass … für ihn leiden für ihn wirken heisst … wie denn auch Paulus selbst das apostolische 'Christusleiden' immer als eine seiner höchsten Aufgaben angesehen hat, die der Ausbreitung des Evangeliums unmittelbar dient …"

is absorbed and on the basis of which he lives and exists, be shaped by suffering? And must one not go on to ask whether the personal sufferings actually experienced by Paul are ultimately only the consequences of the suffering which characterizes the preaching? As we have noted, the commentators usually regard the preacher's suffering as chiefly or even entirely consisting in his personal painful experiences in the service of his preaching. But what is to preclude us from seeing the sufferings of the preacher as essentially in the process of preaching itself? If the event of the cross and resurrection shapes Paul's whole life, must not this double event also shape the preaching and thus the "bearing my name" itself? Can "preaching" tell of that event without being at the same time itself an expression of it?

In passing, we should also note the interesting fact that again and again we come across passages which give the impression that the preaching must be helped along and that a weakness attaches to it which one tries to remove with particular arguments, as, e.g.,

17, 28 ... ὡς καί τινες τῶν καθ'ὑμᾶς ποιητῶν εἰρήκασιν ...

26, 22 ... οὐδὲν ἐκτὸς λέγων ὧν τε οἱ προφῆται ἐλάλησαν ...

26, 25 ... ἀλλὰ ἀληθείας καὶ σωφροσύνης ῥήματα ἀποφθέγγομαι ...

26, 26 ... οὐ γάρ ἐστιν ἐν γωνίᾳ πεπραγμένον τοῦτο.

etc.

b) If we assume that L in fact in 9, 15f. gives us a programmatic preface to his account of Paul's work, then we must also assume that in the following account he wanted to show these two fundamental items in the programme to be "fulfilled". In fact that is true of the first point :[206] chs 9-28 show a singular development and implementation of the programme of "bearing my name before Gentiles and kings and the sons of Israel". But when we come to the second aspect of the missionary existence in store for Paul we cannot avoid the impression that this item is not implemented to the same degree— at least not according to the usual interpretation of it. For

aa) the bodily sufferings *actually* experienced by Paul can only be described as rather minor in relation to the whole account and do not appear quite to justify such a radical assertion.

bb) Most of the sufferings are *possible* ones, i.e. threats, which are, however, avoided by the adroit action of Paul and the disciples.

---

[206] Cf. Co (59) : "Das hier entworfene Programm wird Punkt für Punkt durchgeführt".

Indeed the whole range of experiences of "sufferings personally
encountered and also evaded" in the Pauline section of Acts could, if
there really was this supposed connection between 9, 16 and the later
accounts of situations full of suffering, be used as a copy-book example
of the problem of the relationship one to another of faith and the
exercise of human reason. For on the one side there is the *divine
inevitability* of suffering. On the other hand, what *human conditions*,
one must ask, does one attach to this inevitable-sounding divine
necessity (cf. only as an example 25, 11)? In other words, how does
one *understand* this necessity of suffering? How is the human initiative
related to this divine necessity? How does one live with this necessity
if one does not want to hasten to death at one's first encounter with
danger? Or is only the acceptance of bodily suffering an act of
obedience and not the avoidance of it? And so how does one live in
the face of possible sufferings and affliction? Here the text certainly
gives enough hints: looking at it in quite general terms, one could
perhaps allude to Paul's different policies with regard to his right
understanding, and also his practice, of living with and under this
promise of the divine necessity of suffering up to ch. 20 and again
from ch. 20 onwards. Up to ch. 20 it is mostly disciples and brethren
who deal with this question (e.g. 9, 25.30; 17, 10.14; 19, 30 f.) and
Paul submits to their decisions (particularly striking in 19, 30 f.).
While Paul seems to have felt himself more impelled to suffering,
the disciples and churches hold him back from it. Yet from ch. 20
onwards Paul develops such an independent policy with regard to
the suffering ordained for him that he no longer submits to the
Church, but ignores their proposals and advice (cf., e.g., 21, 4.11-14).
Yet there underlies both sections the strong consciousness that the
"necessity" of the sufferings ordained by God for Paul are under no
circumstances to be accepted as an unalterable blind fate into which
one runs heedlessly. Rather one seeks to avoid these sufferings to
the best of one's human ability (e.g. 20, 3) to the extent of adroit
manipulation (e.g. 9, 25) and even betrayal (cf., e.g., 23, 16)—and if
all else fails one runs away from them. Suffering, even in the sense of
a divine δεῖ, thus does not mean simply a pious self-surrender to
every situation of danger, without seeking the counsel of human
reason, but implies a weighing it up in the light of God's other promises.
In the first part one could mention in addition

    a) the frequent mention that a dangerous situation has been recognized (e.g. 9, 24 : ἐγνώσθη ... 9, 30 : ἐπιγνόντες ... 14, 6 : συνιδόντες)

β)   the corresponding reactions to these, especially the mention of "speedy" action (e.g. 17, 10.14 etc.), and

γ)   Paul's asserting of his rights : the suffering ὑπὲρ τοῦ ὀνόματός μου (if this connection were right) should not take place at the expense of the right common to all Romans (16, 35-40).

In the second part one could mention

a)   Paul's intelligent and shrewd speech with the declared purpose of averting the danger of death by provoking dissension among his hearers (23, 6 f.),

β)   his appeal to what is ἔξεστιν (22, 25 etc.); this also marks the limits of his readiness to die (25, 11; cf. 21, 13),

γ)   his stubborn appeal to Caesar in order to avoid death in Jerusalem (25, 11, etc.), and

δ)   the precautions taken for the journey to Caesarea (23, 12 ff.).

These hints can only confirm us in our suspicion that most of the sufferings are only possibilities which are avoided as far as possible. To put it polemically, one uses every resource at one's disposal so as *not* to have to suffer the apparently necessary sufferings ordained by God. Or, to be more true to scripture, chs 9-28 are rather a testimony to the promise "and I will rescue you [207] from the people and from the Gentiles" (26, 17). Thus one can describe the principal theme of chs 9-28 in respect of sufferings as a strikingly skilful and by and large successful attempt to avoid sufferings; in no way do we see Paul willingly accepting the sufferings destined for him by God; here there is no inclination towards suffering but a flight from it. The deep seriousness of the necessity of suffering which confronts us in 9, 16 leaves no trace in the largely successful attempts to avoid suffering. Must not a form of suffering have been meant here which

aa)   is really ordained by God as *necessary* (and not to be avoided as far as possible), and

bb)   so cannot and *must* not be avoided ? This suffering must be as necessary as the preaching itself.

---

[207] ἐξαιρεῖσθαι can certainly mean "erwählen, für sich aussondern", but here, as in Jer. 1, 7f., it should mean "erretten", since this is the sense in 7, 10.34; 12, 10; 23, 27 (so most comms.; undecided are A-S 158; Rob III 449).

We see, according to the usual interpretation, the disparity in the fulfilment of the two items governed by the divine δεῖ (1. preaching, 2. suffering) in the following chapters : in the one case there is a willing submission, in the other a continual resistance.

The necessity of sufferings, interpreted as bodily sufferings, therefore finds in these chapters no "necessary" echo, as the "necessity" of preaching does—even to the very last verse ! So we at least have to ask whether *this* understanding of suffering as something separate from the preaching and following after it was in L's mind in 9, 16. If L had thought that these sufferings promised in 9, 16 would in his description have been related only or at least primarily to this kind of suffering, and if he had regarded these as ordained and willed by God through the divine δεῖ, then the life of Paul described in 9, 16 ff. would have been a remarkable witness, not to his obedient submission to God's will (as in fact it was in the case of the preaching) but of his "struggle against God" (5, 39).

c)   To this we may add a further observation : however the three different accounts of Paul's conversion are related to one another, we must yet somehow see them together since all three are trying to describe the one event of Paul's conversion or call. All three (9, 15 f. ; 22, 14 f. ; 26, 16-18) are thus dealing with Paul's commission. It is striking that in the two parallel passages, 22, 14 f. and 26, 16-18, which are also trying to set out the commission given to Paul, there is absolutely no mention of πάσχειν in the sense of bodily suffering— on the contrary, in 26, 17 Paul is promised as part of his commission that he will be rescued from suffering at the hands of Jews and Gentiles.[208] But how can we do justice to the δεῖ πάσχειν of 9, 16 without running into difficulties in 26, 17 ? Admittedly there does not need to be a contradiction here. For the fact that Paul is rescued from suffering indeed presupposes that sufferings are bound up with the preaching.[209] It is quite possible, therefore, that both were promised Paul in his call, sufferings and deliverance from them. But we cannot help feeling that somehow this conflicts with the δεῖ, in that it implies a weakening of its seriousness.[210] So must we perhaps take

---

[208] Only Bar 221 contrasts 26, 17 with 9, 16.

[209] Mu 82 speaks of a "weak parallel to the prediction of Paul's suffering" in 26, 17.

[210] But cf. Stä (309) : "Zeugesein aber ist untrennbar von Gefahr und Leiden ...; darum wird zugleich mit, ja vor der Sendung ... die Rettung ... verheisen ..."

the πάσχειν of 9, 16 in a way which allows the δεῖ its full weight and seriousness and yet leaves room for 26, 17 rather than rule it out? Is not the usual interpretation of 9, 15 f. from this point of view too at least questionable?

d) But the setback that Paul really experienced—and indeed daily—is fundamentally the opposition (ἀντιλέγειν, ἀντιτάσσεσθαι) to his preaching, and this in various forms, including mockery (χλευάζειν) and even abuse and slander (13, 45; 18, 6; 19, 9), whereas the attempts to kill him which often resulted from this could be avoided through "circumspect" dealing. Thus we must suppose that if in 9, 16 L really *meant* sufferings, we should see those cases where they simply could *not* be avoided. So, we ask, must we not understand the daily fact of this contradiction of being just as much or even more the suffering of which L spoke in connection with preaching in 9, 16? [211] And how far and why should such a suffering be *necessary*?

As a result of these observations we must ask anew what L could have meant by the mention of sufferings in such close connection with preaching if the usual interpretation conflicts so much with the Pauline part of Acts as a whole and if this interpretation thus does not seem to square with L's real concerns.

ii) An attempt at a solution

In the following section we shall try to find a possible answer to this question posed by the contents of chs 9-28 as a whole by investigating more carefully the two ends of this section, i.e. 9, 15 f.; 28, 26 f.

a) *9, 15 f.* :[212] this passage is rather like a prologue to the life and work of Paul described in the following chapters. So we must try to understand it aright. Two things seem to me important:

aa)   the connection of v. 15 and v. 16 by γάρ.[213] This has received

---

[211] Only Schla 1, 117 seems to point in this direction, even if it is no more than a hint: "Weil er nicht überall Glauben sondern auch Feindschaft erregt und nicht nur zur Rechtfertigung sondern auch zum Gericht den Menschen verkündigt wird, hängen sich Leiden an die Arbeit des Paulus ..."

[212] A critique of Chr. Burchhard, *Der dreizehnte Zeuge*, Göttingen, 1970, 100ff. would really be in place here, but is unfortunately not possible within the scope of this work.

[213] γάρ (cf. K-G II 2, 330ff.; Ma II 3, 121ff.) is a "causal co-ordinating conjunction", whose "use in the NT conforms to the classical" (B-D-F 452; so also Rob 1190; M III

almost [214] no attention from exegetes.[215] Yet one cannot simply ignore the fact that γάρ gives the "reason" or simply the "explanation" for something. In both cases that would mean in respect of the connection between vv. 15 and 16 that the fact that sufferings are ordained for Paul ὑπὲρ τοῦ ὀνόματός μου ... would then be the "reason" or the "explanation" for the βαστάζειν τὸ ὄνομά μου also ordained for him. The reason or the explanation for the "bearing my name" would thus lie somewhere in the "suffering ὑπέρ ...". That Paul has to suffer ὑπὲρ τοῦ ὀνόματός μου explains (or is the reason for) the fact that he preaches or that he must preach.[216] The "suffering" would then be the basic, the broader category from which the preaching would somehow be derived. Thus the preaching would not be, as generally supposed, the reason for the (bodily/physical) suffering, but the suffering ὑπὲρ τοῦ ὀνόματός μου is the reason or explanation for the preaching. Whatever that means, one thing is clear : it would not exclude Paul's bodily sufferings but would simply fit them differently into the whole complex event of preaching. Naturally this immediately raises the questions (1) whether we have not put too much weight on v. 15 in this interpretation and (2) what *sort* of suffering this suffering ὑπὲρ τοῦ ὀνόματος is, if it is somehow to be the "reason" or "explanation" for the preaching. It seems to me that both of these can only be answered if we rightly grasp the meaning of ὑπέρ + the genitive [217] n our passage.

---

331). γάρ serves "zur Einführung von Erläuterungssätzen ... Erläuterung im weitern Sinn ist aber auch jede Begründung oder Beweisführung ..." (W 395). So similarly De (58) : "I. Confirmatory and causal, giving the ground for belief, or the motive for action ... II. Explanatory. This usage ... is nearly related to the confirmatory". Cf. also Thr 41-50;

[214] Yet cf. as exceptions A 1, 367; Hol 1, 69 etc.

[215] Cf. the comms.

[216] The γάρ connects the two verbs mentioned in immediate contact with ὄνομα, βαστάζειν and πάσχειν, as their proximity suggests.

[217] ὑπέρ has the basic meaning "oberhalb", "over", "upper". With the gen. (or abl., cf. Rob 629f.) it has the following meanings :

(1) "for one's benefit, in behalf of" (the latter in Rob 630 and A-G 846; in contrast to "on behalf of" this implies "the loss of an important distinction". "On behalf of" means "on the part of another, in the name of, as the agent or representative of, on account of, for, instead of", whereas "in behalf of" simply means "in the interest of, as a friend or defender of, for the benefit of"; yet Rob 630-2 discusses at length the "notion of substitution" and "notion of instead" in "in behalf of", by which he again comes near to the meaning) "on behalf of", "für, zum Besten" or "zum Vorteil von Jmdn", "für Jmdn sein, auf Jmds. Seite stehen".

(2) "for the sake of, with a view to"

bb) ὑπὲρ τοῦ ὀνόματός μου παθεῖν in our passage is understood
wholly in the sense of "for my name's sake" in the grammars and
correspondingly in the dictionaries and commentaries. To test whether
this is correct we will do three things :

(α) find out whether L can also use ἕνεκεν/ἕνεκα[218] if he wants to
say "for the sake of",
(β) look at the other uses of ὑπέρ + the genitive in Acts and
(γ) consider also the content of 9, 15 f.

On α) : when L wants to say "for the sake of" in his Gospel he uses
ἕνεκεν/ἕνεκα

L 6, 22 ... ἐκβάλωσιν τὸ ὄνομα ὑμῶν ὡς πονηρὸν ἕνεκα τοῦ υἱοῦ
τοῦ ἀνθρώπου.

9, 24 ὃς δ'ἂν ἀπολέσῃ τὴν ψυχὴν αὐτοῦ ἕνεκεν ἐμοῦ ...

21, 12 ... διώξουσιν ... ἕνεκεν τοῦ ὀνόματός μου ·

The use of ἕνεκεν/ἕνεκα in the context of these ideas and motifs
(but cf. Acts 19, 32; 26, 12; 28, 20) is not continued in Acts. In place
of it we find ὑπέρ + the genitive :

Acts 9, 16 : ὅσα δεῖ αὐτὸν ὑπὲρ τοῦ ὀνόματός μου παθεῖν (cf. L 21,
12 and A 9, 5).

15, 26 : παραδεδωκόσι τὰς ψυχὰς αὐτῶν ὑπὲρ τοῦ ὀνόματος τοῦ
κυρίου ἡμῶν Ἰησοῦ Χριστοῦ [219]

21, 13 : ... καὶ ἀποθανεῖν εἰς Ἰερουσαλὴμ ἑτοίμως ἔχω ὑπὲρ τοῦ
ὀνόματος τοῦ κυρίου Ἰησοῦ.

Apparently L wants to express more in Acts than he did in his
Gospel : "for the Son of man's sake, for my name's sake, for my sake,
to be despised, persecuted and killed". If he wanted to say this in
Acts too (as all commentators assume) then he could simply have
continued to use ἕνεκεν/ἕνεκα in Acts as he did in his Gospel. That
he has not done so shows that he wanted to say something other than

---

(3) "in the place of, instead of; anstelle von, anstatt"
(4) "about, concerning, as regards"
(5) "because of, for the sake of; wegen, um ... willen, für"
Cf. Ra 126, 139f.; Rob 628-32; M 63-5; M III 270f.; W 342f; Si 155-7 (B-D-F 231
mentions only "for, on behalf of", "zugunsten"; Bu 288 is likewise cursory); cf. also
A-G 846f.; G-T 638f.; M-M 651; T 290-2; H 47, 201; Gr 1, 221; F 225; D 120, 166,
331, 335; Mi 1, 8.6; M I 105.
[218] ἕνεκεν/ἕνεκα wegen, causa and propter.
[219] Cf. L 9, 24.

"for the sake of". Thus, if we attend to L alone, we cannot here take ὑπέρ + the genitive to mean "for the sake of" (even if that is possible and indeed is the case *elsewhere*). L himself prevents us. But if he wants to say more, then the only possible meaning is "on behalf of, instead of".[220] Applied to our passage that means that Paul's suffering is a suffering "on behalf of my name", "instead of my name". Paul vicariously assumes Christ's suffering just as, e.g., he vicariously presents a sacrifice ὑπὲρ ἑνὸς ἑκάστου αὐτῶν (21, 26). What another really had to suffer (do), Paul suffers (does). Before we draw any conclusions from this, we must first deal with the other two tests.

On β): ὑπέρ + the genitive is used at least once more (21, 26) but probably also in a further passage (8, 24—in connection with v. 22; yet here the idea of intercession may also be conveyed but at least not exclusively [221]) with the meaning "on behalf of", "instead of" and thus with the idea of representative or vicarious substitution.

On γ): The suffering which Paul inflicted on the Christians is comprehensively described by the word διώκειν (22, 4; 26, 11). But the particular way in which this word is used also shows that in persecuting the Church Paul had really persecuted Jesus himself (9, 4f.; 22, 7f.; 26, 14f.). In other words, in "persecuting" those (= οἱ μαθηταὶ τοῦ κυρίου 9, 1; οἱ ἅγιοι 9, 13; οἱ ἀδελφοί 22, 5; οἱ πιστεύοντες 22, 19) who called on τὸ ὄνομά σου (9, 14), τὸ ὄνομα τοῦτο (9, 21), he had "committed πολλὰ ἐναντία against τὸ ὄνομα Ἰησοῦ τοῦ Ναζωραίου himself" (26, 9). 9, 5; 22, 8 and 26, 14 thus also lead us to suppose that in 9, 16, etc., we are to see the idea of "representative" suffering: in the persecution (cf. L 21, 12 but here in contrast ἕνεκεν τοῦ ὀνόματός μου) and suffering of the Church, at first instigated by Paul but then with Paul as one of its victims, Jesus himself suffers and is persecuted, "of whom Paul says that he lives" (25, 19). This also supports the sense of "as representative of", "as a substitute for" (cf. likewise 5, 39: to struggle against the Church is to struggle against God!).

If these observations are correct, then that would mean that the

---

[220] When Si (156) says that "It is a question how near ὑπέρ in this sense, 'on behalf of', approximates to the meaning of ἀντί 'instead of' ", W (342) has already stated before then that "In den meisten Fällen tritt der, welcher zum Besten Jem. handelt, für ihn ein ... daher streift ὑπέρ zuw. an ἀντί statt, loco". Therefore the idea of representation or substitution is here contained in the ὑπέρ. Rob 630-2, M 64 and M III 271 take up this insight: "The boundary between ἀντί and ὑπέρ c. gen. is very narrow (substitution), necessarily so because what is done 'on behalf of one' is often done 'in one's stead' "

[221] Differently Rob 630; M 65; M III 270.

"name of Jesus" is represented on earth by "suffering". The office of representing "Jesus' name"—and this "name" stands for "salvation", "power" and "forgiveness of sins"—is essentially an office of weakness and suffering. Jesus' "salvation" and "power" is "represented" on earth in the form of suffering. And it is the apostle Paul who represents "the name of Jesus" in the form of suffering; the way in which "the name of Jesus" is represented is by the suffering which Paul endures. But does this idea of "representation" imply that we must also understand the "suffering" differently?

What then is the concrete form of this suffering and what is the "place" where Paul experiences this suffering representatively for Christ? Here we must take up again the discovery that the γάρ in v. 16 binds together the two phrases βαστάζειν τὸ ὄνομά μου and πάσχειν ὑπὲρ τοῦ ὀνόματός μου in such a way that the latter is the "reason" or "explanation" for the former. In other words, the concrete form, the place of this suffering is nothing but the "bearing my name". Apostolic preaching in the broadest sense would then be the form of suffering and the place of suffering ordained (δεῖ) by God, where the "name of Jesus" is represented here on earth, in the world between his resurrection and his return. "Suffering in the place of my name" was Paul's experience in his preaching and is a basic element in preaching in general. Where ἄφεσις ἁμαρτιῶν 10, 43/ἀπολούεσθαι τὰς ἁμαρτίας 22, 16 δύναμις : ἴασις, σημεῖα, τέρατα 3, 16; 4, 30; 16, 18; 19, 13.17 σώζεσθαι 2, 21; 4, 12/σωτηρία 4, 12 are involved, there is Paul's suffering which he bears representatively for Christ in his βαστάζειν, εὐαγγελίσασθαι. But if it is primarily here a matter of Christ's sufferings, we must also ask what this suffering of Christ is in concrete terms which Paul experiences and must bear representatively for Christ while carrying out his preaching.

But before answering this question, we want to point out that 22, 14f. and 26, 16-18 mention, as we have already shown, no sufferings in the sense of bodily sufferings as part of Paul's apostolic commission, as one generally supposes 9, 16 to state. But what we do not find in 9, 16f. but do find in both the parallel passages is that Paul's commission is referred to by the word μάρτυς (22, 15; 26, 16). In view of the fact that this word does not occur in 9, 15f. and that the two parallel accounts know of no bodily suffering of Paul as a constitutive part of his commission, could it not then be that this word (μάρτυς) comprehends what the two verses 9, 15f. together are trying to express, i.e. the definition of Paul's preaching in the sense of "being a witness"? To repeat, what is that suffering in concrete terms which Paul undergoes in carrying out his preaching?

b) At the start we stated that we wanted to try to answer the questions posed by the contents of chs 9-28 by means of a more careful examination of the framework within which L apparently set his description of Paul's life and work. We seem to have found a prologue in 9, 15 f. that looks towards the future. It seems to say that the "name of Jesus" is represented on earth by sufferings which Paul endures on earth in his "bearing Jesus' name". But the prologue does not show what this suffering is in concrete terms. Possibly we can deduce this from the contents of chs 9-28 as a whole, but perhaps also—and in a more concise form—from the other end of this section. So here we must briefly attend to 28, 26 f. And here we do well to remember that we could trace the execution and "fulfilment" of the first basic point in the programme (preaching) right up to the last verse of Acts, whereas we could not say the same of the second (suffering)—at least as usually interpreted. The epilogue that corresponds to the prologue of 9, 15 f. is doubtless to be found in the résumé which Paul gives at the (supposed) end of his career looking back over his whole activity, in his citation of Is 6, 9 f. in 28, 26 f. But that is the conclusion of one who despairs of all his efforts to bear the "name of Jesus" before the Gentiles, kings and the sons of Israel and suffers most bitterly—though we hear nothing in this epilogue of suffering in the sense of personal sufferings. Here is one who suffers deeply, not from his bodily pains, but from and with the preaching itself. We can see what sufferings are meant here when we recall that 28, 26 f. not only marks the other end of the frame which L seems to have given his description of Paul's work but at the same time it is the last passage where Paul turns away from the Jews to the Gentiles and in doing so pronounces judgment on the former—because of their blasphemy against Christ. The other passages are : 13, 46 ; 18, 6 f. ; 19, 9.

Thus we have sketched out the framework necessary for the following interpretation.

B) *Interpretation : the connection between action and suffering with regard to the "intellectual element" in Paul's preaching*

I) The apostolic suffering which Paul undergoes representatively in carrying out the work of preaching primarily concerns the carrying out of this preaching itself, i.e. the βαστάζειν τὸ ὄνομά μου in the sense of λαλεῖν (18, 9). Basically it is the "contradiction" which is brought against Christ, who is present in this preaching, and which takes the form of a continual attempt to ἀποστρέφειν ... ἀπὸ τῆς πίστεως (13, 8), whereas the stoning, imprisonment, blows and even threats of death are only derivative and secondary sufferings. Thus what was expressed in connection with the action by the word διακονία is expressed in connection with the suffering by the word "representation". Just as the sufferings ordained for Christ reached their deepest point in his crucifixion, so the suffering which is inflicted on the Christ who has entered into the apostolic kerygma is at its deepest and bitterest where Christ is, despite Paul's most earnest and intellectually exhausting efforts, again "put to death" and "crucified", by blasphemy. One should not here try to separate the glorious task of preaching on the one hand from the apostle's suffering as a result of his preaching on the other. The "cross" rather finds its primary expression in the preaching itself. We cannot only connect the weakness and suffering with the communicator of the gospel but primarily it must refer to the communication of the gospel itself.

It seems to me that only this interpretation of the connection between preaching and suffering can explain

(1) why Paul only when he experiences blasphemy against Christ and not when he experiences bodily suffering, even stoning, reacts so sharply by
i) turning away from the Jews and
ii) actually carrying out judgment and not only proclaiming it, and

(2) why L on the one hand lays such emphasis on the unconditional necessity of representative sufferings and on the other could lay so little on the bodily/physical sufferings of the apostle and apparently did not find it necessary somehow to connect the apostle's bodily/physical sufferings with such a divine necessity. For these bodily sufferings have in no way anything like a divine compulsion about them.

When these sufferings are mentioned L does not regard them as particularly serious. They reflect nothing of the divine necessity of 9, 16; rather they happen accidentally when one can no longer avoid them. The insistent and emphatic "must" of 9, 16 finds its corresponding echo, not in these scattered and random, rather than pre-ordained, events, but rather in the rejection of Christ underlying the whole of Acts and permeating it from beginning to end. When L speaks of this then he attaches great seriousness and emphasis to it with language reminiscent of 9, 15 f.; here, but not in the case of individual bodily sufferings, he speaks of an ἀναγκαῖον (13, 46) and of the unalterable destiny of preaching as preaching (28, 26 f.) which echoes both 9, 15 and 16 : the necessity of preaching and the necessity of the rejection of the Christ present in the preaching is "fulfilled" here.

II)   But what, we must go on to ask, is it in the preaching which evokes or indeed provokes this suffering of Christ in the form of blasphemy ?

(1)   Let us stick to the Pauline section of Acts. Before Paul experienced his call, he had, in persecuting the Church, persecuted Christ himself and, in compelling the Church to blaspheme against Christ (26, 11), he blasphemed against Christ himself (cf. also I Tim. 1, 13). And then came the moment when Christ encountered him personally in an epiphany and spoke to him in a direct revelation. And then a blasphemer of Christ was turned into a disciple of Jesus. But that means that it is a fact that preaching is no direct revelatory speech, but can only point to the revelation of God, that apparently invites blasphemy, the sufferings of Christ. Similarly, Paul later could only point to his experience of a direct word of revelation. Thus preaching as the mediating of God's promise is not the handing on of a revelation but it is a pointing to the event of revelation. We can also say now (which comes to the same thing but yet uses a term which Acts itself uses) that the element in the preaching which makes the Christ who has entered into the preaching "vulnerable" to suffering in the sense of blasphemy is the element of "testimony". Since there is no preaching that takes the form of a direct word of divine revelation (as Paul had experienced it; but cf. also God's words to Moses in Acts 7, 30 ff.; Exod 3) which only leaves room for "prostration", adoration and obedience, but it always wears the cloak of witness, therefore the witness-character of preaching is ultimately the element which evokes and makes possible contradiction, blasphemy and thus the suffering of Christ.

But what exactly is it in witness which makes it "vulnerable" to the sufferings of Christ in the sense of blasphemy ?

2)   But this element of testimony within preaching is, as we have

already indicated, not just *one* element among others but refers to the basic characteristic of preaching as such and is thus not separate from it or only a part of it. Purely superficially this can be seen from the fact that Paul's status can be summed up with the word "witness" (22, 15; 26, 16) and his commission likewise with the word "witnessing" (23, 11).

III)   Since both these insights seem to depend on each other and we seem to have reached the point where the Christological significance of the human reason within preaching becomes visible, we now want to investigate a further question. What significance has it for preaching that "witness" is the form in which this preaching, inasmuch as it is meant to be and to remain Christian preaching, can only take place when "witness" at the same time constitutes that element in the preaching which makes possible the suffering of Christ in the sense of blasphemy which Paul must representatively bear ?

(1)   That there can only be preaching in the form of witness means *positively* that the verificatory element which characterizes witness is built into the process of preaching itself. Therefore preaching as preaching has a necessarily verifying aspect to it.

Preaching can only take the form of witness or there is no preaching at all. One does not therefore preach first and then tag on a supporting testimony. Witness is thus not something which may be added to preaching (or not, as the case may be), as if the preaching were a separate entity which could be attested in the same sense as the legitimacy of an institution may be "attested" by a divine word (13, 22), or the truth of preaching may be "attested" by divine signs and wonders (14, 3), or the truth of a promise may be "attested" by the outpouring of the divine Spirit (15, 8), or other people may "attest" the conduct and statements of a man (16, 2; 22, 5.12; 26, 5). In contrast to all these examples, in the relation between "preaching" and "witness" the act of witnessing is so very much drawn into the process of preaching itself that preaching is always witness to something (23, 11). The difference from the other examples mentioned is that when Paul bears witness for someone he does that not as something secondary or additional to the real thing but so that the primary, the real thing only ever takes place in the form of witness. But that does not mean that what elsewhere forms the essential nature of witness is lost through being "wedded" to preaching. Rather it means that the basic

characteristics which apply by nature to witness are therefore also
characteristic of preaching as such. But what characterizes "witness" ?
This word is a legal one and has the primary meaning of verifying a
statement or an assertion or also a person. The witness therefore
wants on the one hand only to attest or point to the truth of a fact
before men; but, on the other hand, he will do this in a way which
makes the truth attested intelligible as truth to other men. In other
words "witnessing to" must also, if it is to be effective, at the same
time be "witnessing for".

And in fact this is what we find in Acts. In 23, 11 it is promised
Paul that he will also "attest" τὰ περὶ ἐμοῦ in Rome. In Rome the
Jews come and ask Paul: ἀξιοῦμεν δὲ παρὰ σοῦ ἀκοῦσαι ἃ φρονεῖς ...
(28, 22), and in v. 31 we read: ... καὶ διδάσκων τὰ περὶ τοῦ κυρίου
Ἰησοῦ Χριστοῦ. We can already infer three things from this:

i)   The μαρτύριον is based on the ability to φρονεῖν (= think, judge,
form opinions : 23, 11→28, 22f.31) and is nothing but the right use of
this. It is not a matter of an introverted φρονεῖν but it has its place
in the service (διακονία) of a "helper" (26, 16), whose sights are set
on "being a witness to" and "being a witness for".

ii) The μαρτύριον aims at "understanding", "recognition". This is
shown *firstly* by all the passages where the goal of speaking and
witnessing "concerning something" (18, 25; 23, 15; 24, 10; 24, 22;
28, 31) is given as

   a) διαγινώσκειν (23, 15), οἶδα (24, 22) and
   b) doing so ἀκριβῶς, or ἀκριβέστερον (18, 25; 23, 15; 24, 22)
and *secondly* by 15, 7f., where the words ἐπίστασθαι (= know, be
known) and μαρτυρεῖν are identical as regards their epistemological
character and their power to bestow recognition : ἐπίστασθαι is the
expression of such a "knowledge-situation" as μαρτυρεῖν aims to create.

iii) If μαρτύριον is based on φρονεῖν and aims at ἐπίστασθαι, it also
uses appropriate methods :

   a) διδάσκειν (15, 35; 18, 11; 20, 20; 21, 21; 28, 31)
   b) συμβιβάζειν (9, 22)
   c) συνζητεῖν (9, 29)
   d) πείθειν (13, 43; 18, 4; 19, 8; 28, 31)

e) διαλέγεσθαι (17, 2.17; 18, 4; 18, 19; 19, 8; 20, 7.9)

f) διανοίγειν (17, 3)

g) παρατίθεσθαι (17, 3) ἐκτίθεσθαι (28, 23)

h) διαμαρτυρεῖσθαι (18, 5; 20, 21.24; 28, 23)

i) ὁμιλεῖν (20, 11)

j) νουθετεῖν (20, 31)

Even the mere listing of these expressions which mark preaching as witness may reflect the intellectual effort that marks the process of preaching. This is in striking contrast to the working of miracles in connection with preaching the gospel. If this is chiefly characterized by the demonstration of power, the other rather gives the impression of labours, of continual effort, of failures. Whereas miracles produce quick results, the words describing Paul's method of preaching depict a long process of dealing with the questions and doubts of his hearers. "Miracle" aims at astonishing the spectators, διαλέγεσθαι etc. at the hearers' understanding.

The meaning and purpose of being a witness is—in whatever way this may take place—to verify a fact, i.e. to make it certain and thus intelligible, i.e. "worthy of full acceptance". The basic category of μαρτύριον is therefore the correct functioning of φρονεῖν which is realized in different ways (διδάσκειν, συμβιβάζειν ...) and thus aims at recognition of the truth. If we must say on the basis of the New Testament text that preaching only exists in the form of witness, then we must infer that the preaching always contains the element of verification and, since it is witness to something and for someone, is specifically orientated towards the understanding. Or, to put it differently, since preaching is not direct divine revelation but can only point to it and thus is witness to something, it has, if it is really going to be able to be witness for someone, already *qua* preaching a verificatory aspect to it, taken in the widest sense.

One would have to turn one's back on this insight if one were still to try to separate preaching and witness from one another. This would be something like a substitute solution for the desired identification of preaching and divine revelation, but this is difficult to sustain on the basis of the New Testament itself. In theory the verificatory aspect, the element of verification in preaching, could be partly taken on by signs and wonders, or by the apostle's conduct, or even by his sufferings. These could all have value as witness and so as verification. And that could, we may add here, be welcomed by its advocates as a justification of a holy "language of Zion", insulated

from the problems of verification. It is correct to say that μάρτυς/
μαρτυρεῖσθαι are indeed concepts which embrace the apostle's entire
existence. But since in A the apostle's existence is entirely absorbed
by the act of preaching, it follows that the idea of μαρτυρεῖσθαι in
Paul's case is used in A exclusively of the process of preaching itself
(and thus does not describe his life and sufferings). The whole emphasis
in being a witness (= verification) is thus not distributed among
different levels which would then together make up the whole meaning
and on which preaching as a separate entity could then be, as it were,
securely based; rather the whole emphasis is laid completely on the
process of preaching itself and is concentrated on this. One could of
course think that if a part of the verification came from "signs and
wonders" or an upright life, the preaching itself would not need so
much to give its undivided attention to the business of verification,
if it could, as it were, vicariously introduce that "from outside" either
entirely or in part. But that must have the result that, since the
preaching itself does not need so much to give its undivided attention
to the understanding, the character of coming to faith is also different.
In fact we find a hint of this, but only a hint, in ch 13, where a
"mighty act" is an independent entity over against the preaching.
Here the "teaching of the Lord" is primarily an exhibition of power
which produces not an understanding, but a bewildered faith (v. 12 :
ἐκπλήσσεσθαι = "be beside oneself, be astonished").

In this way, by separating the human element of verification from
the process of preaching itself and distributing it amongst various
other objects, one seeks to come near to identifying preaching with
the divine word of revelation itself, but this attempt founders on the
text of A itself. For there "making certain" as the aim of convincing
preaching is achieved not by exemplary conduct accompanying this
preaching (together with or perhaps instead of absent signs and
wonders), but is achieved simultaneously in the process of preaching
itself. The element of "making certain" is thus not added "from
outside" but is entirely part of the process of preaching itself. But if
that is the case, then in L's conception of Paul's preaching, its character as witness and thus its verificatory aspect are essential and
can and may not be delegated to other levels (e.g. in the sense that
one says that, even if preaching itself is not verifiable, yet we will
prove it true through our life/suffering/conduct or perhaps even
through miracles).

(2)   That there can only be preaching in the form of witness means *negatively* that the verificatory element which characterizes witness is also—and precisely in the context of the preaching of the gospel—no more than a human witness which shares in the inadequacy, weakness and ambiguity of human speech and ideas—and all the more so in respect of *this* object of witness. There would be no "contradiction" and so no sufferings of Christ if Paul's preaching were identical with God's revelation itself, i.e. if in his preaching, naked, sheer deity were to burst in all its immediacy upon the world and human understanding and if the apostles really were "gods, who have become like men and descended to them" (14, 11). But there are "contradictions" and thus sufferings of Christ because the apostles are "men of like nature with you" and *as such* "bring you good news" (14, 15). But that implies two things :

i)   "men of like nature with you" means that with their human speech they share in the ambiguity and thus the vulnerability of all human speech. The apostles can neither claim for themselves a so-called biblical "language of Zion" nor appeal to a so-called simple or even cultured language as a "self-authenticating authority" and as the medium that suits the object in question. They cannot and must not force the identification of God's revelation with preaching by moving towards a magical understanding of the word of preaching. They cannot thus either eliminate the ambiguity or conjure up clarity.

ii)   "As such we bring you good news" means that it is a case of the problem of theological language not only in the sense that it can be no other language than that of the world, but also in the specifically Christian sense that this language, despite this general handicap, at whatever cost must, and believes that it can, speak of God's revelation *in* this language as *theological* language in constant *defiance* of the natural capacities of this language. Preaching even of this "Treasure", i.e. the gospel as the "power of God", can only exist in the "earthen vessels" of human concepts and speech (cf. 2 C 4, 7).

Both points (i and ii) can be illustrated by a historical note : Lutheran orthodoxy had a doctrine, formulated polemically against the Calvinists, the Schwenckfeldians, the Quakers, and others, of the "efficacia Verbi divini etiam ante et extra usum": to the preached and written word belongs a divine power quite apart from its effect upon the hearer or reader. There takes place in the Bible and in the sermon a divine *actus primus*, irrespective of the *actus secundus* in men's hearts (so Quenstedt and Hollaz). Inasmuch as this doctrine was concerned to show that the truth of the belief that the Bible and preaching are God's word is entirely independent of subjective experience and superior to it, it was certainly right. But it tried to say more than that and with this "more" we cannot agree. Quenstedt flatly denied that the Bible is an *instrumentum* which is in need of "novo motu et elevatione nova ad effectum novum ultra propriam suam naturalem virtutem producendum". The Bible and the sermon are rather *media* in which dwell, naturally and permanently, "summa vis et efficacia" (*ib.*). The Bible is, Hollaz thinks, the saving word of God, just as the sun pours forth its warmth even behind the clouds or a seed retains its powers even in unfruitful soil or the hand of sleeping man is still a living hand. Again Hollaz bluntly explains that God's word is no *actio* but a *vis*, a *potentia* which as such has *efficacia* also *extra usum*, namely a *vis hyperphysica analoga efficaciae physicae* i.e. *vera et realis*. It is as if the theological criterion of what is true and real must and may be its analogy to the physical! Granted this presupposition, the theory is at any rate logical and impressive. A power comparable to sunshine and the potency of a seed needs no *nova elevatio* anyway. It is there, just as natural powers are there. But is God's word there like that? If it really is a word? And if it is the word of God who is a person? One has to choose between the ideas "word of God" and "*vis hyperphysica*". And A is here unequivocal: if the "suffering instead of my name" is such as happens quite concretely through the "bearing my name" in witness, then the preaching as such knows of no sort of hidden *vis hyperphysica* which would swallow up the element of "witness" and would turn the "suffering instead of my name" into an illusory suffering. Paul is as really "only" a witness as he really suffers.

(3)   Conclusions: the fact that the witnessing is not added to preaching as a separate process but belongs to the process of preaching itself has two necessary consequences:

i)   the idea of verification which is most intimately bound up with the concept of witnessing is not separate from preaching itself but is an integral part of it;

ii)   the idea of suffering which is most intimately bound up with the concept of witnessing is not separate from preaching itself but is part of it.

IV) Summary

We should attend briefly to both of these, for this seems to be the decisive point where the correct place and understanding of the intellectual element within Paul's preaching becomes visible. Witness is that element in preaching which makes the sufferings of Christ in the sense of blasphemy possible. At the same time, preaching can only be Christian preaching when it takes the form of witness. Witness is thus not something which one could leave out, e.g., in order to avoid the sufferings of Christ. For, if preaching must take place and if preaching can only take place in the form of witness, preaching leads inevitably to the suffering of Christ which is borne representatively by the apostle. This character of preaching as testimony and thus verification is thus essential, just as is the suffering which results from it. Inasmuch as faith in preaching enters into association with the human reason it thereby associates itself with suffering

To undertake this representative suffering thus means for Paul, in L's eyes, to bear witness through the different forms of φρονεῖν and thus to bring about the situation where belief and disbelief take place. The place where Paul enters into the representative sufferings of Christ, the platform where Paul representatively encounters the sufferings of Christ and must bear these is, according to A, not his life which bears witness through suffering and death, but his φρονεῖν, through which he bears witness and thus has laid upon him and bears the suffering of the rejection of Christ. The place of the representative sufferings of Christ is not his back, beaten because of his preaching, nor his hands, bound in the service of bearing witness (c.f. διὰ τῶν χειρῶν 14, 3), but his intellectual efforts suffering "contradiction" in his carrying out of preaching as witness. And it is this form of suffering in the ἀντέλεγον τοῖς ὑπὸ τοῦ Παύλου λαλουμένοις βλασφημοῦντες (13, 45) that is followed by the other form of suffering in the ἐπήγειραν διωγμὸν ἐπὶ τὸν Παῦλον ... (13, 50). We have grown accustomed to thinking of the Christian's role as a witness primarily in categories of bodily suffering extending even to a martyr's death. And here we have to ask whether we have listened enough to the New Testament and to A itself, where the Christian's sufferings are primarily the sufferings of Christ! And this suffering results from the fact that no supernatural power is bestowed as a *habitus* upon the Christian as a Christian, to lift him above the suffering and make him for ever immune to sufferings in any form. But if his life with and in Christ does not make him immune to suffering in the world (seen purely in bodily/existential terms), then something similar is true of the human reason : A Christian's life with Christ bestows nothing upon him which could spare him from further use of human reason to verify the gospel. It is at this point that his suffering arises in his thinking, namely that he has nothing in his hands or head which would exclude the possibility of "blasphemy" because of his preaching and of opposition to that preaching. His suffering consists in the fact that his preaching must be so human and that *he* has nothing in his hand to distinguish his speech from the rest of human speech—unless God himself reveals to the hearer that here in this human word God's own message is conveyed. Just as God's Word himself "became flesh", so the witness *to* this incarnation of the divine Word must also "become flesh" fully and completely if it is to be really witness *for* men— otherwise it will be addressed to God and not to men.

What is ultimately involved here is shown by an extreme example (which though extreme yet represents the far less extreme but basically just as false attempts), namely the phenomenon of the temptation to place too great emphasis on "speaking in tongues" in early Christianity. Here the Christians are tempted no longer to be ὁμοιοπαθεῖς ... ὑμῖν ἄνθρωποι (14, 15) but to be, not θεοὶ ὁμοιωθέντες ἀνθρώποις who have κατέβησαν πρὸς ἡμᾶς (14, 11), which is the possible non-Christian misunderstanding, but ἄνθρωποι ὁμοιωθέντες θεοῖς who ἀνέβησαν πρὸς θεούς, as if the Lord who is present in the preaching were to pass over the bounds of human knowledge.

This passing over of the human possibilities of knowledge into the *visio beatifica*, this anticipation of the eschatological state (which is also attested on other levels), which also occurs in those less extreme forms of preaching that try, in various ways, to remove the aspect of verification which is proper to them, implies two things :

1) here one is trying and wanting, yet without success, to abolish man's will and his execution of the preaching with all its limitations and problems; one wants something to vanish from the reality of creation and a gap to appear and naked, divine reality to appear somehow in that gap, scarcely hidden by the mere vestiges of the appearance of human reality.

2) Here one is trying and wanting, yet without success, to fly away from the "struggle for faith in the gospel" and the representative sufferings of Christ into the eschatological condition, into the *visio beatifica*—and this on the level of the νοῦς and of φρονεῖν. Here one does not enter into the sufferings of Christ which really ought to result from the character of preaching as witness; here one does not account for the sufferings of Christ on the level of thinking. And thus one does not leave it to God to wipe away the tears, including the tears of one's thoughts and thinking (Rev. 7, 17; 21, 4; Is. 25, 8), but here one has oneself washed away the tears already on earth.

§ 2. The "Intellectual Element"
in Paul's Method of Preaching
with Respect to the Aim :
the "Persuasion "of his Hearers

Introduction

We are concerned here with the question of the relation of faith
and knowledge in Paul's theology. A glance at the Book of Acts and
the Pauline corpus immediately discloses that the idea of "persuasion"
and "being persuaded" played an important part in the early missionary preaching. The frequency of this word, always in the closest
possible relation to the preaching of the gospel, reveals that it was
used as a *terminus technicus* in missionary terminology. Of course we
are not dealing with just this one expression; rather the complex of
ideas connected with "persuasion" attaches to itself a whole cluster
of related motifs. To give but one example,[1] there is the constant
emphasis on the fact that one simply cannot speak convincingly and
well; one reproaches one's opponents for saying much and doing
little. Thus an especially important part of the whole complex of
motifs which goes with the concept of "persuasion" is the continual
argument from one's own conduct, whereas at the same time we
must not overlook the fact that the emphasis on one's inability to
speak seems to have no real basis in the texts at our disposal. When
we also note that "persuasion" is actually used as a t.t. in early
Christian missionary terminology then we are surely justified in
denoting a special study to this motif. For, if "persuading" really
does play such a large part in early Christian preaching as we suppose,
then this is directly relevant to our question of faith and reason,
especially with respect to the methods of Paul's preaching.

We will investigate this as follows : in five separate chapters we
will examine five different contexts in which the idea of "persuasion"
plays some part. Initially we will limit ourselves entirely to classical
Greek literature, without considering any possible relations to the

---

[1] A fuller presentation of the NT data cannot be given here; but cf. already R. Bult-
mann's article on πείθω in *TDNT* VI, 1-11.

New Testament. The first chapter concerns the role and significance of πείθειν in the earliest literature; here we must ask in particular how it is evaluated and whether it has already acquired for itself a fixed and clearly defined place in men's thinking and speaking. In the second chapter we will examine the early tragedians and comedians; here we will find not only that the word πείθειν conveys more and more definite ideas and concepts, but also that it takes on a definite role in the circles of ideas involving life and death. This will be confirmed by an investigation of the early historians (chapter C) and also especially the Attic orators (chapters D and E). Πείθειν is particularly at home here. Here too the important question of the "power" of persuasion arises.[2]

The purpose of this investigation is therefore to find out (1) what meaning πείθειν had by the 1st cent. AD at the advent of Christianity, and (2) why the idea of πείθειν was taken over by the first Christians to describe the process of the preaching of the gospel and assent to it. What was (and is) it which makes πείθειν suited for that purpose? Is not one thereby adopting for a context that should rather be moulded by the operations of the Holy Spirit a "dangerous", because too intellectual, concept? Or, on the other hand, were ideas and concepts already associated with πείθειν in its earlier usage which predestined it for adoption into the language of Christian preaching? And, as a corollary, did a necessary element in Christian preaching perhaps thereby find expression, an element which, if understood aright, indicates to us the proper relation of faith and reason within Paul's theology?

The consequences to be drawn from this investigation, devoted solely to classical literature, for the New Testament and for Paul can only be indicated in section 2.

---

[2] I have not had time to extend my studies much beyond the 4th. cent. BC. Yet I think that the most important elements in the range of meanings attached to the word πείθειν have come to light in this investigation even though it is limited to the period of the 4th-8th cents. BC.

Section 1 : Observations

A) Πείθειν in early Greek epic and lyric poetry [3]

I) The Problem

The meaning, i.e. the evaluation and content, given to πείθειν [4]
by the early Greek epic and lyric poets can largely be expressed in
terms of a striking contrast. This contrast is marked by the use of
the verb in the optative on the one hand and in the indicative on
the other. That is to say that on the one hand little hope is offered
of any success attending one's persuasion [5] and it is rather regarded
as something peripheral and without importance in itself.[6] One can
certainly try to persuade [7] and, unsure of one's powers, one pleads
for the assistance of the gods;[8] but that does not alter the fact that
one remains basically sceptical and opposed to the business of πείθειν.
On the other hand it is striking to observe the frequency of the

---

[3] Texts and tools for Homer, Hesiod, Pindar, Theognis, Bacchylides, Orphic Lit.
s.v. Bibliography.

[4] Cunliffe 319 : 1) to induce or win over to an act or a course of action, to persuade,
win over, prevail upon, urge successfully, to do or refrain from doing sth.; 2) to induce
to regard one with favour, win or bring over, prevail with ...; 3) to induce to believe
in the truth of something, win to a belief or assurance, convince ...

Ebeling 152 πεῖσαι = durch Gründe überreden, persuadere πεπιθεῖν = durch
Bitten bereden, exorare.

When Ebeling wants to translate πεπιθεῖν by "durch Bitten bereden", exorare, he must
be thinking particularly of *Il.* 1, 100; 9, 181. 184. But that is certainly not always the
case. *Il.* 14, 208, where Hera wants to lead Okeanos and Thetis back to a state of marital
harmony, and that through words or arguments (?), for nothing is said here about
asking (cf. too 23, 37 and *Od.* 24, 119), and other examples (cf. also *H. Apoll.* 275, where
nothing is said of asking, but only of arguments) show rather the intensity (that is the
point of the reduplication) of persuasion which can succeed through requests or arguments (cf. also the fut. πεπιθήσω which occurs only in *Il.* 22, 223; it comes from the
reduplicated aor. root and has the same factitive meaning as this root. This is the
trans. form of the intrans. πιθήσω in *Od.* 21, 369).

Autenrieth 252 persuade, win over, talk over.

[5] ... εἰ πεπίθοιεν ... *Il.* 23, 40
    ... οὔτις ... ἀνὴρ ... ἀγγέλλων πείσειε ... *Od.* 14, 123 (potential opt. : opt. after οὐ.
    This form only in Homer)
    ... οὐδέ κεν ὡς ἔτι θυμὸν πείσει᾽ *Il.* 9, 386.
[6] ... ἱλασσάμενοι πεπίθοιμεν *Il.* 1, 100.
    ... ἀρεσσάμενοι πεπίθωμεν *Il.* 9, 112.
[7] ... πειρᾶν ὡς πεπίθοιεν *Il.* 9, 181.
[8] ... πολλὰ μάλ᾽ εὐχομένῳ ἐννοσιγαίῳ ... πεπιθεῖν ... *Il.* 9, 184.

categorical,[9] almost formulaic and adversative,[10] repudiations of any attempts at persuasion, and the many emphatic [11] statements that attempts at persuasion have failed.[12]

This poses the two basically interrelated questions which we must try to answer :

1) What are the reasons for this antipathy and scepticism towards πείθειν, and
2) What are the reasons for the continual failure of πείθειν ?

II) Attempt at a solution

(1) The scepticism arises because πείθειν is from the start in bad odour. For one knows that those who practise it often do so with the intention of deceiving : they talk one into things rather than convincing. One knows that πείθειν qua "convince" is, as it were, continually overshadowed by the sense of "deceive" and is indeed often swallowed up by this meaning. So from the start one feels uneasy and insecure and counters it with the hash formulae referred to above or with what amount to curses.[13]

---

[9] οὐδέ σε πεισέμεν οἴω Il. 5, 252.

οὔτ'ἐμέ ... πεισέμεν οἴω ... Il. 9. 315

(οἴω = I think, namely of that which is assumed to be definite, or of a firm decision)

Μηδείς σ'ἀνθρώπων πεῖσαι ... Thgn. lol

[10] οὐδέ με πείσει(ς) : Il. 1, 132; 6, 360; 9, 345.386; 11, 648; 18, 126; 24, 219.433; Od. 14, 363; Thgn. 839; 1363 = you will not deceive me. In Il. 24, 433 and Od. 14, 363 used parenthetically, otherwise to conclude a sentence.

οὐδέ = neque enim, explanatory, adversative.

[11] In most passages the negative is placed first in emphasis : "but in no way ..." (cf. n. 12).

[12] Il. 12, 173 οὐδὲ ... πεῖθε φρένα ταῦτ'ἀγορεύων

Il. 9, 587 ἀλλ'οὐδ'ὡς τοῦ θυμὸν ἐνὶ στήθεσσιν ἔπειθον

Il. 17, 33 ... τὸν δ'οὐ πεῖθεν

Il. 22, 78.91 οὐδ'Ἕκτορι θυμὸν ἔπειθε/ἐπειθόν

Il. 22, 357 οὐδ'ἄρ'ἔμελλον πείσειν

Od. 1, 43 ἀλλ'οὐ ... πεῖθ' ...

Od. 7, 258 ; 9, 33 ; 23, 337 ἀλλ'ἐμὸν οὔ ποτε θυμὸν ... ἔπειθεν/ἔπειθον

Od. 9, 500 αλλ'οὐ πεῖθον ἐμὸν ... θ' ...

Od. 14, 392 οὐδέ σε πείθω

Od. 14, 337 ἀλλὰ τοῦ οὔ ποτε θυμὸν ... ἔπειθεν

H. Cer. 329 ἀλλ'οὔτις, πεῖσαι δύνατο ...

H. Ven. 7 ; 33 τρισσὰς δ'οὐ δύναται πεπιθεῖν

cf. also Hes. Sc. 450, etc.

[13] Cf. e.g., Od. 14, 156f. ἐχθρὸς ... μοι κεῖνος ὁμῶς 'Αΐδαο πύλῃσι γίγ ...

a)　This deception has already begun when one does not say what one really thinks.[14]

b)　This deception leads logically to the attempt to persuade someone by talking him round. To do this one must by various means paralyse and disarm the vigilance [15] of the *νοῦς* of the person addressed,[16] in order to "bypass" it [17] and so to "steal" [18] the other's conviction—without his realizing it.

---

[14] Cf. e.g., *Il.* 9, 312f.; *Od.* 2, 90-3; so also Thgn. 96-101 : ὃς κ᾽εἴπῃ γλώσσῃ λῷα φρονῇ δ᾽ἕτερα.

[15] An analysis of the only passage in Homer which describes a successful and legitimate *πείθειν* may help to show a) how this *πείθειν* was achieved and b) what the original reasons for the scepticism with which it was viewed were.
In *Od.* 23, 172 Odysseus says of Penelope : ἦ γὰρ τῇ γε σιδήρεον ἐν φρεσὶ ἦτορ. (This section dealing with an attempt at persuasion successfully undertaken ends at 1.230 : πείθεις δή μεν θυμόν, ἀπηνέα περ᾽μάλ᾽ἐοντα). But how can it succeed here ? Odysseus, by way of a *μέγα σῆμα* (188; σῆμα = token by which any one's identity or commission was certified : L-S; das Zeichen, Kennzeichen, Mahl, Merkmal, überh. Alles, woran man etwas erkennt oder unterscheidet—cf. *Il.* 10, 466; 23, 455 etc. : Ps; signum, nota indicium : Bechtel; something adduced as proof, an evidence : Cunliffe), describes in the following passage τὸ λέχος ἀσκητόν (190-201) and then explains : οὕτω τοι τόδε σῆμα πιφαύσκομαι. Then, σήματ᾽ἀναγνούσῃ τά οἱ ἔμπεδα πεφραδ᾽ Ὀδυσσεύς (206), Penelope is convinced (that is already the case in 1.205 : Ὣς φάτο, τῆς δ᾽αὐτοῦ λύτο γούνατα καὶ ...). She apologizes to Odysseus for her original scepticism, for αἰεὶ γάρ μοι θυμὸς ἐνὶ στήθεσσιν φίλοισιν ἐρρίγει μή τίς με βροτῶν ἀπάφοιτο ἔπεσσιν ἐλθών ... (215-7). And, she continues, νῦν δ᾽, ἐπεὶ ἤδη σήματ᾽ἀριφραδέα κατέλεξας εὐνῆς ἡμετέρης, ἣν οὐ βροτὸς ἄλλος ὀπώπει, ἀλλ᾽ ... (225-7). And this is enough evidence for πείθεις δή μεν θυμόν ... (230) : "Now you (finally) persuade my reluctant heart". Conclusions : a) Legitimate *πείθειν* can only succeed if τόδε σῆμα πιφαύσκεσθαι on the part of the speaker coincides with σήματα ἀναγινώσκειν on the part of the person addressed. The evidence cited must thus be basically open and accessible to the latter, so that when he is thus able to test things for himself *πείθειν* is achieved. b) The initial σιδήρεον ... ἦτορ (172) was rooted in the fear (ῥιγεῖν) that others could come with the purpose of ἀπαφίσκειν (= to cheat or beguile with words = ἀπατάω, lead astray, deceive) ἔπεσσιν. Thus one knows exactly what *πείθειν* really means and implies and involves and so is sceptical towards false attempts at *πείθειν*.

[16] Cf. e.g., *Od.* 2, 106 (= 19, 151; 24, 141) : ὡς τρίετες μὲν ἔληθες δόλῳ καὶ ἔπειθεν Ἀχαιούς.

[17] *Il.* 1, 132 : παρελεύσεαι suggests the idea of the bypassing of the *νοῦς* and the corresponding ἀναγινώσκειν (παρέρχεσθαι really means "overtake" and is thus a metaphor from racing—*Od.* 8, 230; cf. also παρεξελθεῖν, *Od.* 5, 104.138. Then it comes to mean fig. "outwit", "delude"; cf. *Od.* 13, 291; 5, 104 : παρ ... Διὸς νόον Thgn. 1285 : δόλωι παρελεύσεαι). So here speed is required in order to convince someone deceitfully (cf. 2 Th 2, 2 : ταχέως = without proper awareness, which must come through the

Proper πείθειν on the other hand is marked by

i) the fact that it takes time [19] and is often difficult [20] because it

---

νοῦς). The understanding of the person to be persuaded is here not sought; rather the persuader leaves him stranded in incomprehension.

[18] *Il.* 1, 132 : here πείθειν is to be achieved through κλέπτειν νόῳ (= keep one's own counsel, feign, think with, secrecy and cunning; cf. πάρφασις ἥ τ'ἔκλεψε νόον ... *Il.* 14, 217; οὐκ ἔστι Διὸς κλέψαι νόον Hes. *Theog.* 613, also Pi. *P.* III 29; *N* VII 23; A. *Ch.* 854; S. *Tr.* 243; etc.; κ'τὴν ἀκρόασιν Aeschin. 3, 99. νόος is here "cleverness", "intelligence", but the word κλέπτειν gives it the overtones of δόλος), which literally means : to commit theft with the assistance of the νοῦς (νόῳ is here instrumental, not local; lit. "by thought", in contrast to force; cf. S. *El.* 56 : λόγωι κλέπτουντες). And, just as κλέπτειν generally means appropriating something for oneself unnoticed, so here the conviction of the other is "stolen"—without his consent—by means of the νοῦς. But in that case persuasion has become "talking into" and thus what was described in *Od.* 23 as ἀναγινώσκειν is here deliberately bypassed.

Od. 2, 106 : πείθειν = λανθάνειν δόλῳ = to escape notice through δόλῳ : keep from knowing and so persuade them. This is basically no different from πείθειν by κλέπτειν νόῳ; it is by circumventing knowledge that persuasion becomes "talking into" and thus deception.

Thgn. 704 : ... πείσας ... ἥτε βρότοις παρέχει λήθην βλάπτουσα νόοιο ... ;

Hes. *Theog.* 613 : ἀλλ'οὐκ ἔστι Διὸς κ λ έ ψ α ι νόον οὔτε π α ρ ε λ θ ε ῖ ν.

[19] 1) μή με κάθιζ' ... *Il.* 6, 360

οὐχ ἕδος ἐστί ... οὐδέ με πείσεις *Il.* 11, 648 (a pregnant phrase for οὐχ ἕδους καιρός ἐστιν = it is no time to sit around—cf. 23, 205—sc. "which would be necessary if you were going to persuade me").

2) Often expressed through the impf. which conveys the ideas of a long time and repeated attempts : *Il.* 4, 104; 6, 51.162; 9, 587; 12, 173; 16, 842; 17, 33; 22, 78.91; *Od.* 1, 43; 2, 106; 7, 258; 9, 33.500; 19, 151; 23, 337; 24, 141; *H. Apoll.* 113; *H. Merc.* 396.

3) Some examples in more detail :

Od. 2, 106 = kept someone convinced = kept someone believing; thus ἔπειθον also appears here as a factitive verb meaning "believe" (2, 103, similarly 19, 148.151; 24, 138.141). So too in 7, 258 : here it is preceded by the lines (255-7) ἐνδυκέως ... πάντα. Not just once did she make her proposal; each time it failed again and she could never talk him round.

Od. 9, 500, frequent repetition (similarly *Il.* 17, 33). Here we must think of the activity of πείθειν as split up into various stages which are effected by Menelaos' words (this is also the case in the positive statements of *Il.* 6, 51; 4, 104; 16, 842). So also *Il.* 12, 17; 6, 162 and *Od.* 1, 43.

Od. 14, 392 : Odysseus, still disguised as a begger, cannot persuade the swineherd Eumaios that his master will soon return : "in truth your (τοι = dat. sympath.) heart is unbelieving in your breast; not even by an oath could I persuade you". S II 259 : "es will mir trotz aller Anstrengungen nicht gelingen, überzeugend auf dich zu wirken". ἄπιστος here means "unbelieving", "mistrustful", "incredulous", "suspicious" (cf. *Od.* 14, 150) and not "disobedient" (according to L-S ἄπιστος in this latter sense is not found before Sophocles).

Il. 6, 51.61 : The readings ἔπειθε in 6,51 and παρέπεισεν in 6, 61 are contested. Bekker,

frequently meets with "stern" resistance;[21] πείθειν is only easy and speedy for the gods [22] or for those who can obtain it from them by asking for it;[23] and

ii) the fact that it submits to the judgment of the νοῦς of the person addressed.

c) Hence i) πείθειν can be identical with ἀπατᾶν [24] and (ἐξ) απαφίσκειν [25] attempts at πείθειν are made by

following few MSS, reads ὅρινε in 51 (cf. 2, 142 and 4, 208). Yet ὅρινε does not fit here. For the prisoner does not appeal to Menelaos' sympathy but promises him a trefty ransom; this neither greatly excites Menelaos nor moves him (cf. the meaning of ὀρίνειν on p. 114, n. 45); rather he is won over in his thinking and is persuaded to grant the prisoner his life. Besides, almost all MSS have ἔπειθε(ν) and only a few ὅρινεν. If then ἔπειθε and παρέπεισεν can stand, we can see here a contrast between the imperfect (expressing the repeated attempts) and the aorist (expressing the single final change of heart). Thus the passage would have to be translated : "thus he spoke and gradually persuaded him, with one word after the other". Or again : "he was beginning to persuade him".

Il. 22, 91 (cf. 5, 358) : here Priam and Hecuba plead with their son not to fight with Achilles outside the walls : ὣς τὼ γε ... ἔπειθον. Here too is a reference to a repeated action. We have the same formula a couple of lines before after Priam alone has first urgently begged him not to do it : 76f. ἦ ὁ ῥ'γέρων ... ἔπειθεν. If one looks more carefully then one sees that here too the action is repeated. Neither his father's words nor his tearing out of his hair can sway Hector.

Il. 16, 842 : "thus he spoke with you and thus with one word after the other he persuaded your foolish heart". A repeated action. Patrokles is gradually won over by Achilles with one word after another. So too 4, 104.

Il. 9, 587 : here too the reference is to a repeated action, for it says above :

πολλὰ δέ μιν λιτάνευε γέρων ἱππηλάτα Οἰνεύς ...

πολλὰ δὲ τόν γε κασίγνηται καὶ πότνια μήτηρ ἐλλίσσονθ' ...

πολλὰ δ'ἑταῖροι ...

[20] σπουδῇ παρ πεπίθοντες, Il. 23, 37; Od. 24, 119.

[21] ἦ γὰρ σοί γε σιδήρεος ἐν φρεσὶ θυμός Il. 22, 357 (σιδήρεος = hard, relentless, as in Il. 24, 205.521; Od. 5, 191; 4, 293; 12, 280; 23, 172); πείθεις δή μευ θυμόν, ἀπηνέα πέρ μάλ'ἐόντα Od. 23, 230; στορεῶς δ'ηναίνετο μύθους H. Cer. 330; αὐτὰρ ὅ γ'ἠρνεῖτο ἑτερῶς ... Il. 23, 42.

[22] H. Merc. 396 ῥηιδίως γὰρ ἔπειθε Διὸς νόος ...

[23] Il. 9, 183f. πολλὰ μάλ'εὐχομένω γαιηόχῳ ἐννοσιγαίῳ ῥηιδίως πεπιθεῖν ...

[24] Dolo quem permoveo, move someone by craft, beguile : Il. 1, 32; 4, 104; 6, 162; 16, 842; Od. 2, 106; 19, 151; 24, 141; H. Ven. 7, 33; Pi. N. V. 28; etc. So also already in Il. 1, 132 where πείθειν takes on the sense of "deceive" from its context (κλέπτειν/νόῳ and παρέρχεσθαι). But Achilles' speech in Il. 9, 308-429 gives a really classic illustration of how πείθειν and ἀπατᾶν are interchangeable. This affects the use of πείθειν in 315, 345 and 386. Taking as his starting-point ἐχθρὸς γάρ μοι κεῖνος (312) Achilles lays particular emphasis in the debate on two closely connected ideas :

— δολόεσσα Καλυψώ,[26] together with διὰ θεάνων [27]
— Κίρκη δολόεσσα [28]
— ἀλῆται who are ἄνδρες κεχρημένοι κομιδῆς and hence seek to ψεύδεσθαι; hence their attempt is identical with ἀπατήλια βάζειν,[29] resulting from their αἶψά κε ... ἔπος παρατεκταίνεσθαι.[30]
  ii) πείθειν is the exact opposite of αἴσιμα παρείπων.[31]

  d) Hence it follows quite naturally that
  i) only the fool lets himself be "talked into" something. Only lack of understanding makes πείθειν in the sense of deception possible.[32]

---

1) Agamemnon's intentions are not honourable : he has *deceived* me once and is trying to do so again;

2) Agamemnon will not talk me round.

Complementary to these is the idea that Achilles wants to speak frankly; he claims for himself uncompromising openness. The argument in that part of the speech that interests us is divided thus :

1) 312-377 : ἐχθρὸς γάρ μοι κεῖνος

2) 378-392 : ἐχθρὰ δέ μοι τοῦ δῶρα.

The structure is thus as follows :

312 theme : ἐχθρὸς γάρ μοι κεῖνος.

313 key-word : ἀπάτη (ὅς χ'ἕτερον μὲν κεύθῃ ἐν φρέσιν, ἄλλο δὲ εἴπῃ) in contrast to Achilles in

314 αὐτὰρ ἐγὼν ἐρέω ὥς μοι δοκεῖ εἶναι ἄριστα (cf. also ἀμφαδόν in 370 : Achilles' "openly" is in contrast to Agamemnon's "deceit")

315 key-word : οὔτ' ... πεισέμεν ...

Pt. 1, 314-343

344 key-word : ἀπάτη (... εἵλετο καί μ'ἀπάτησε)

345 key-word : οὐδέ με πείσει

Pt. 2, 346-374

375f. key-word : ἀπάτη (... μ'ἀπάτησε καὶ ἤλιτεν ... ἔξαπαφοιτ'ἐπεεσσι

386 key-word : οὐδέ ... πεί σει ... (key-word ἀπατᾶν occurs three times in 370-7)

Conclusions : Achilles resists the attempt to talk him round, not so much, indeed, because this attempt is in fact being made, as because he knows only too well the cause of and motive for this sort of persuasion and disapproves of it. Cf. K. Reinhardt, *Die Ilias und ihre Dichter*, ed. by U. Hölscher, 1961, p. 231 : "Überreden an sich wäre noch nichts Anfechtbares, aber dass sie ihn jetzt zu etwas bringen suchen, was zuletzt nur ihren Zwecken dient, ihnen nicht von Herzen geht, das ist es, worüber er nicht wegkommt".

25 Cf., e.g., *Il.* 9, 376.
26 *Od.* 7, 245.250.258; 22, 45.
27 *Od.* 9, 29; cf. also 23, 333-7.
28 *Od.* 9, 32f.
29 *Od.* 14, 124-7.
30 *Od.* 14, 131.
31 *Il.* 6, 51.61f.
32 Cf., e.g., *Il.* 4, 104; 16, 842.

ii) One successfully repulses false πείθειν by intelligence [33] and the cleverness that comes from experience.[34] Deceitful πείθειν comes to grief when pitted against prudence.

iii) If one comes whose persuasion is sincere but who can bring no verifiable evidence then he is not trusted.[35]

Conclusions: the history of the usage of πείθειν is "sick" from birth, so to speak. The term is called in question from the start and suffers from the fact that it represents not only that which it really means, but also a corruption of that. It is certainly fundamentally important for the history of this word that right from the start it possessed this dubious character and thus almost always had a pejorative sense.

(2) The continual failure of πείθειν is due to the fact that although there are many different means of persuasion those do not seem to have been used which could alone lead to conviction. This became clear from our analysis of Od. 23, 230. One does not use verifiable arguments to achieve a successful πείθειν, and therefore one employs other means as substitutes and hopes to persuade by means of these.[36] Even though πείθειν is always [37] basically a matter of speech and

---

[33] Il. 6, 162 : ἀλλὰ τὸν οὔ τι πεῖθ' ἀγαθὰ φρονέοντα, δαίφρονα βελλερο ... ἀγαθὰ φρονέοντα = a good or virtuous man (and not a well-meaning person or one giving good advice—as in Od. 1, 43; cf. Il. 23, 305 : εἰς ἀγαθὰ φρονέων)

δαίφρονα = prudent.

Hesych. δαίφρων · συνετός, πολεμικός, τὰ πολέμια φρονῶν

[34] Il. 9, 345 (εὖ εἰδότος Schol. : καλῶς ἐπισταμένου μου ὅτι ἀπατεών ἐστιν).

[35] 1) This is clearly shown by the train of thought in the speech of Od. 14, 122-132 : "We cannot trust any traveller who brings news of Odysseus : for they think up untrue stories to pass the time. And how can we be sure that you are not such a one ? There are so many untrue travellers' tales in circulation that we cannot trust you either".

2) So also Il. 24, 219-224 (ἄλλος ἐπιχθυνίων = another who is mortal and not the messenger of the gods); Od. 1, 42f.; 14, 378ff.

[36] Od. 7, 254-7 (= 9, 29-33) is a particularly good example of the different means and ways of persuasion.

[37] Also Il. 1, 100 ἱλασσάμενοι πεπίθοιμεν = after having appeased (his wrath) we might persuade him (so also 9, 386; cf. too Ar Ra 1168 : Pl. Lg. ix, 857 A; X An 3, 1, 26). Two things are obviously referred to here :

1) The first refers back and comes about through two actions : i) πατρὶ φίλῳ δόμεναι ἑλικώπιδα κούρην ἀπριάτην ἀνάποινον; ii) ἄγειν θ'ἱερὴν ἑκατόμβην ἐς χρύσην

2) πεπίθοιμεν on the other hand refers to the subsequent attempt to move him by words to avoid further misfortune. Thus ἱλασσάμενοι is epexegetic of the τότε : "then, that is when we ..."; hence "then, perhaps, after having propitiated, we may persuade him".

Those actions that are in the strictest sense atoning must already have occured

words [38] and is achieved, or not achieved, through speaking,[39] yet these words can be given additional force by other things, especially when they themselves do not possess the power to persuade. Yet these "other things" are plainly subordinate to the accompanying words [40]—their job is to reinforce the words. Here we can no longer speak of "persuading with arguments", but only of "talking someone into something"; this comes about by

i) influencing him through "special" words and (or) gestures,[41]

---

before πείθειν can take place. We therefore cannot render it : "we could perhaps through atoning actions placate him". The same applies to 9, 112 : ἀρεσσάμενοι = after we have placated him; cf. on this passage (ἀρεσσάμενοι—[root ἀρεσ-]—πεπίθωμεν) Gal 1, 10 : ἀρέσκειν-πείθειν.

[38] Ὡς φάτο ... (οὐ)πείθειν, ἔπειθε : Il. 4, 104; 6, 51; 12, 173; 17, 33; Od. 1, 43; 2, 103; 9, 500; 19, 148; 24, 138; etc.

ἀγόρευε ... πεισέμεν Il. 5, 252

πεπίθωμεν ... ἔπεσσι ... Il. 9, 112.

[39] Cf. the frequency with which πείθειν coincides with φάσκειν.

[40] A good example is H. Cer. 325-30 : Demeter's father sends μάκαρας θεοὺς αἰὲν ἐόντας πάντας and, these πολλὰ δίδον περικαλλέα δῶρα, τιμάς θ', ἅς κ'ἐθέλοιτο μετ'ἀθανάτοισιν ἐλέσθαι. Yet—ἀλλ'οὔτις πεῖσαι δύνατο φρένας ... Rather στερεῶς δ'ηναίνετο μύθους—and that when it had spoken before of πολλὰ δίδον ... δῶρα! So too Il. 9, 386 = not even so (i.e. despite gifts !) shall A any more persuade ...

[41] 1) fair and attractive words :

ἔπεα πτερόεντα προσηύδα Il. 4, 92.104; 5, 242-252; H. Apoll. 111; Hes. Sc. 445.450;

πεπίθωμεν ... ἐπεσσί τε μειλιχίοισι ... Il. 9, 112f.; Od. 9, 492f.

μελιγάρυες ὕμνοι Pi. P. III 65 (cf. O. X 4; N. III 4)

πείσας ... αἱμύλιοισι λόγοις ... Thgn. 704 (cf. Od. 1, 56; H Herm. 317).

2) passionate words :

λίσσεσθαι Il. 6, 45.51; 9, 574.585; 22, 20f.

λιτανεύειν Il. 9, 581

οὔτε γὰρ εὐχαῖσιν πείθηι, μόνος οὔτε λιταῖσιν Orph. H. 87, 9.

3) oaths :

οἷόν σ'οὐδ'ὀμόσας περ ... οὐδέ σε πείθω Od. 14, 392

4) gestures :

γουνόμαι Il. 9, 583

Ἦ ῥ ὁ γέρων πολιὰς δ'ἄρ'ἀνὰ τρίχας ἔλκετο χερσὶ τίλλων ἐκ ... Il. 22, 77

καί μιν δάκρυ χέουσ'ἔπεα ... Il. 22, 81

Ὡς τώ γε κλαίοντε προσαυδήτην φίλον υἱόν ... ἔπειθον Il. 22, 90f.

ii) influencing him through his emotions, either of anxiety/fear,[42] or of love/friendship/good will,[43] or

iii) influencing him through money and gifts.[44]

Despite this range of possible aids to persuasion, such attempts are almost always doomed to failure. The reason for this is that one all the time realizes what πείθειν really means, if not clearly and consciously, yet vaguely and intuitively. Hence one will have no truck with influencing through substitutes for arguments and refuses to regard one's feelings as conviction.[45]

---

[42] μή τι φόβονδ'ἀγόρευ'ἐπεὶ οὐδέ σε πεισέμεν οἴω Il. 5, 252. Cf. also 1, 33 and Od. 9, 492-500 (together with "fair" words).

[43] Il. 18, 126 μηδέ μ'ἔρυκε μάχης φιλέουσά περ ...

Il. 6, 360 μή με κάθιζ', Ἑλένη, φιλέουσά περ ... (φιλέουσά περ = though you want to show your love for me; i.e. however good your intentions are; K. Reinhardt, op. cit. 263 translates: "Heiss mich nicht sitzen, so lieb du es meinst, du beredest mich doch nicht");

Od. 1, 42f. ἀλλ'οὐ φρένας Αἰγίσθοιο πεῖθ'ἀγαθὰ φρονέων (πεῖθ'ἀγαθὰ φρονέων = Il. 6, 162 = good though his intentions were; so Il. 24, 173; 4, 219: Od. 7, 15; similarly Il. 23. 305).

[44] Il. 9, 112 πεπίθωμεν δώροισίν τ'ἀγανοῖσιν ...

Il. 9, 576 ὑποσχόμενοι μέγα δῶρον

Cf. also Il. 1, 100; 9, 385f.; 24, 433f.; Od. 7, 255f.; 9, 23-33; 23, 337; also relevant are Hes. f. 361 (= f. 87 in Gaisford, Poetae Minores Graeci I): δῶρα θεοὺς πείθει δῶρ'αἰδοίους βασιλῆας. Suides δ 1451 (II 135, 12 Adler): "δῶρα - βασιλῆας". οἱ μὲν Ἡσιόδειον οἴονται τὸν στίχον, εἴρηται δὲ καὶ Ἡλάτωνος ἐν τρίτηι Πολιτείαι.

[45] This can be illustrated from many examples. We cite only some of the most striking:

1) In Il. 9, 574ff. neither λίσσεσθαι nor λιτανεύειν nor γουνόομαι help in πείθειν, but only when his wife κατέλεξεν ἄπαντα ... ὅς ... (594) do we hear of something taking effect; but then it is not πείθειν but τοῦ δ'ὠρίνετο θυμὸς ἀκούοντος κακὰ ἔργα (595).

2) It is interesting how in Od. 14, 361-5 Eumaios ἦ μοι μάλα θυμὸν ὄρινας ταῦτα ἕκαστα λέγων ὅσα δὴ πάθες ἠδ'ὅς'ἀλήθης achieves ὀρίνειν θυμόν through his story of suffering. But at the same time—for ἐγὼ δ'εὖ οἶδα καὶ αὐτός (365)—one is quite aware that ἀλλὰ τά γ'οὐ κατὰ κόσμον (κατὰ κόσμον = aright; here we must supply εἶπες in anticipation of οὐδέ με πείσεις εἰπών) οἴομαι, for the presumption is that this is a case of a beggar's ψεύδεσθαι for the sake of currying favour. Thus, despite the θυμὸν ὄρινας, there is no trace of "persuasion". That is on another level.

3) The phrase οὐδέ με πείσεις of Il. 11, 648 occurs elsewhere but only here does the speaker thereby convict himself of lying. For Patroklos remains so long until it says in 1.804: Ὣς φάτο, τῷ δ'ἄρα θυμὸν ἐνὶ στήθεσσιν stirred in his soul.

4) So also H. Ven. 1-7: the story of the ἔργα πολυχρύσου Ἀφροδίτης could ὦρσε (from ὄρνυμι = arouse passion) but it οὐ δύναται πεπιθεῖν φρένας (so also 33). Θυμὸν ὀρίνειν means: to stir the heart with passionate excitement, so Il. 2, 142; 3, 395; 4, 208; 11, 804; 13, 418.468; 14, 459.487; 17, 123; 19, 272; 24, 568; Od. 8, 178; 17, 47; etc.

III) Summary

It is certainly not without relevance for the further history of this idea that it was from birth an unwanted child and so that its first appearance in the extant literature is accompanied by rejection and active hostility. Πείθειν has, with a few exceptions, really no proper role in this early literature : either it passes over into the realm of the emotions and comes to mean ὀρίνειν, or it is synonymous with ἀπατεῖν, or it is simply doomed to failure. Πείθειν has not yet found its proper function in this early literature. This function it must slowly win for itself by a growing distinctness over against other ideas (ὀρίνειν-ἀπατᾶν). So we cannot learn here the real meaning of πείθειν because proper πείθειν hardly ever occurs. All we can discover from the texts are hints and clues to its real meaning. Such a clue is the idea, gleaned from the continual experience of the opposite, that πείθειν should really be directed at man's *understanding*. That becomes clear

1)   where it is stated that fraudulent persuasion is possible because of the other's lack of understanding; the unspoken presumption is that if he had used his brains such false πείθειν would not have been possible;

2)   where πείθειν is achieved by bypassing the scrutiny of the understanding;

3)   where it is clearly distinguished from ὀρίνειν;

4)   where it is plainly felt that πείθειν *qua* deceitful talking round is not πείθειν *qua* convincing;

5)   where one feels compelled to say explicitly that πείθειν often comes about by one's saying what one does not think.

We will now briefly enlarge upon this consciousness of the real meaning, function and purpose of πείθειν which lurks somewhere here in the background.

IV) Preview

The starting-point of πείθειν, the means it uses and the goal to which it is directed all indicate the sphere in which the nature and character of the πείθειν will one day be found.

Only in *Il.* 11, 792; 15, 403; *Od.* 14, 361; 15, 486 could one take it to mean "touch" ' "move".

1) The starting-point : the source of πείθειν is often not mentioned or may simply be generally characterized as "man" with all his wishes, desires and ambitions. Yet there are some more precise indications of the ideas that men had of the starting-point of πείθειν :

   i) the attempt at πείθειν comes from the νοῦς and is contrasted with λανθάνειν (cf. especially Pi. P. III 28) and stands in a special relation to νοεῖν;[46]

---

[46] νοῦς :

1) In Il. 1, 132 it is precisely the point that πείθειν should not come about through κλέπτειν τῷ νόῳ (n.i. : this κλέπτειν τῷ ... is certainly reminiscent of 2 Th 2, 2 : do not be ταχέως shaken from νοῦς, from dispassionate reasoning, by means of ἀπατᾶν; n. ii : K. Fritz in Classical Philology xxxviii, 1943, pp. 79-93 sees in Homer's use of νόος and νοεῖν "one original and fundamental concept which may be defined as the realization of a situation ... to plan, to have an intention". Yet in respect of this passage it would be more correct to think of νόος as an explicitly intellectual concept : "way of thinking, attitude of mind", without finding any practical aspect here. This first occurs in Horace's usage (Ep. 1, 2. 20 and Ars 142).

2) Od. 7, 258.263 : the original πείθειν comes from νόος ... αὐτῆς.

3) H. Merc. 396 : ῥηιδίως γὰρ ἔπειθε Διὸς νόος αἰγιόχοιο.

4) Pi. P. III 28 : ... κοινᾶνι παρ᾽εὐθυτάτῳ γνώμαν πιθών, πάντα ἴσαντι νόῳ Boeckh and Dissen want to follow the single manuscript Z (Vienna) and restore γνώμᾳ πιθών and compare γνώμᾳ πεπιθὼν πολυβούλῳ in I. IV 72 and P. IV 109. Mommsen comments : "quod nec traditum est nec Graecum nec nisi superflua addit" (163). Most of the MSS have γνώμαν, which is also supported by the τὴν πρόγνωσιν of the Scholia-Commentary; the scholia and glossators treat πιθών (in several cases πεπιθών—perhaps culled from I. IV 72—but πιθών is called for by the metre; a gloss indeed has πείσας) as a transitive form = πείσας. A few MSS have γνώμαν πυθών (for πυθόμενος ?). It must thus be translated : "But Laxias, who dwelt in the Python rich in victims, heard it and persuaded his mind (cf. O. III 41; IV 16; P. IV 84) through his surest guaranty, his own omniscient reason". In this version Pi. emphatically (πάντα ἴσαντι νόῳ) corrects Hesiod (f. 148 = f. 29—Gaisf.—) who says that the information was given through the ravens of Eoie (Schol. 52 a.b). Pi. opposes this : Apollo convinced himself. Hence the active form πιθών is emphasized—and this is through the most "direct" and quickest and best "messenger", his omniscient νοῦς.

νοεῖν :

We can see how far πείθειν was understood in connection with νοεῖν from a proverb which first appears in Hes. Op. 295 but is often quoted down the centuries as a popular saying :

   293 Οὗτος μὲν πανάριστος,
   294 ὃς αὐτὸς πάντα νοήσῃ
   295 ἐσθλὸς δ᾽αὖ κακεῖνος,
   296 ὃς εὖ εἰπόντι πίθηται
   297 ὃς δέ κε μήτ᾽αὐτὸς νοέῃ,
   298 μήτ᾽ἄλλον ἀκούων ἐν θυμῷ βάλληται,
           ὃ δ᾽αὐτ᾽ἀχρήιος ἀνήρ.

"But he too is noble who trusts one who speaks sensibly and listens to him". Parallel

ii) πείθειν comes from a preceding φράξεσθαι;[47]

iii) πείθειν comes from "deep insight";[48]

iv) πείθειν is nevertheless not a purely "human" matter (cf. here the connection between faith in God as Creator and faith in God as the one who in the last analysis stands behind man's intellectual activity [49]).

2)   The means : the sheer fact of the formulaic repudiation of every attempt at πείθειν as well as the resultant failure of all these attempts using the most diverse means may indicate that a conscious idea of πείθειν lies behind this and that the methods used did not match up to the qualities expected from this. A preliminary indication of the meaning and scope of real πείθειν is perhaps to be found in the οὕτω τοι τόδε σῆμα πιφαύσκομαι and corresponding σήματ'ἀναγνούσῃ (Od. 23, 202-6), but also in the successfull πέπιθε φρένας (H. Apoll. 275), achieved through the giving of reasons (257-74). One constantly tries to persuade but does not "get through" or only rouses emotions.

This much we can see, then, that it is realized that bribes, feelings, etc., are not the proper "arguments" by which to "persuade". But there are grounds for hope that the hitherto but vague concept of πείθειν may in the course of time form its own vocabulary to express comprehensively the meaning of πείθειν.

---

to this run 297f. : "but he who himself does not think and also shuts up his heart to another's advice is a worthless and useless man" (adapted from Th. v. Scheffel's translation).

[47] Il. 9, 112 : how far πείθειν here is treated as an "act of mind and thought" can be seen by the connected words shortly before : οὐ γάρ τις νόον ἄλλος ἀμείνονα τοῦδε νοήσει... (104f.). This φράξεσθαι (to think upon, consider, ponder) occurs ἐνὶ φρεσὶ (Il. 9, 423) or μετὰ φρεσίν (Hes. Op. 688), etc. and also θυμῷ (Il. 16, 646).

[48] Pi. I. IV 72; in Homer (Il. 5, 260; Od. 16, 282) πολύβουλος is an attribute of Athene, and in H. hymn. Is. 26 one of Isis. It is remarkable that Pindar uses it of γνώμᾳ, an abstraction, but not surprising if we consider phrases like καθαρᾷ γνώμᾳ O. IV 16, ἀποτρόπῳ γνώμᾳ P. VIII 94, πολύστροφον γνώμαν f. 214. This passage seems to require a trans. sense of πεπιθών. It tells how the boy Melissos, thanks to his unflagging trainer Orseas (here likened to a helmsman), has won a competition : κυβερνατῆρος διακοστρόφου γνώμᾳ πεπιθὼν πολυβούλῳ. Dornseiff (Pindar, übersetzt und erläutert, Leipzig, 1921): "... als er seines steuerwendenden Leiters Einsicht noch folgte, der vielverständigen ...". According to Mommsen all MSS read πεπιθών; only Z has γνώμα, the rest have γνώμᾳ. A possible solution is to read πεπιθώς for πεποιθώς (Hartung) or πίσυνος (Hermann); we should not, however, exclude the possibility that πεπιθών can also have a transitive meaning. For, while πιθήσω is intransitive, πεπιθήσω is transitive.

[49] Cf., e.g., Il. 9, 184.

3) The goal : the attempt at persuasion is not directed at men *simpliciter* without further qualification,[50] but specifically at their φρένες,[51] θυμός,[52] κῆρ [53] or ἦτορ [54]. If it is going to lead to successful πείθειν then certain conditions must be met which are imposed upon it by these discriminatory faculties. To be more exact, we should add that all seems to hinge on the ability of these faculties to carry out their functions. Hence the πείθειν, directed at the φρένες of men, can only be effective and successful if this faculty is also active in σωφρονεῖν,[55] if real σωφροσύνη is present,[56] and if a man is really σοφός.[57] Thus τοὺς ξυνετοὺς δ᾽ ἄν τις πείσειε τάχιστα λέγων εὖ.[58] On

---

[50] *Il.* 1, 100; 5, 252; 9, 112.181; 15, 26; 17, 33; 22, 223.357; 23, 40; *Od.* 2, 106; 14, 123.392; 19, 151; 24, 141;

H. Merc. 396; Pi. *O.* III 16; *N.* V 37; VII 95; *Il.* 1, 132; 6, 360; 9, 315.345; 11, 648; 18, 126; 24, 219.433; *Od.* 14, 363.

[51] *Il.* 4, 104; 12, 173; 16, 842; *Od.* 1, 42f.; *H. Apoll.* 275; *H. Ven.* 7, 33;

Il. 9, 184 μεγάλας φρένας

Il. 6, 162 ἀγαθὰ φρονέοντα

H. Cer. 329 φρένας καὶ νόημα

[52] *Il.* 6, 51; 9, 386.587; 22, 78.91; *Od.* 7, 258; 9, 33; 23, 230.337; *H. Apoll.* 113

Od. 9, 500 μεγαλήτορα θυμόν (so also Hes. *Sc.* 450)

Cf. also *Il.* 6, 51.61 θυμός/φρένες

Il. 22, 357 ἐν φρεσὶ θυμόν

H. Cer. 329f. φρένας οὐδὲ νόημα θυμῷ χωομένης.

[53] *Il.* 23, 37.

[54] Pi. *O.* II 80 : ... ἐπεὶ ζηνὸς ἦτορ λιταῖς ἔπεισε ... τὸ ἦτορ = L-S : "of the reasoning powers" ἐν δέ οἱ ἦ στήθεσσιν ... διάνδιχα μερμήριξεν *Il.* 1, 88; cf. 15, 252; Pi. *O.* II 79. According to L-S the mother's πείθειν is here directed towards τὸ ἦτορ as the "reasoning power" of Zeus. Her πείθειν therefore seeks to influence this power. It is striking here how this direct appeal to the "reasoning power" can achieve its aim also through λιταῖς; that means that "prayers" too can take the form of "persuasion". In contrast cf. Pi. *Pae.* VI 13 ἦτορ, δὲ φίλῳ παῖς ἅτε μητέρι ... πειθομένος = "like a child obeying its beloved mother, so I obeyed my sweet heart"—the element of "reasons" is here simply excluded; similarly in Pi. *P.* IV 200 : obedience (πιθόμενοι; cf. also *P.* I 59) is offered on the basis not of "reasons", but of an external pressure, a command, the Θεοῦ σάμασιν (= thunder and lightning) which make a forceful impression (ἀμπνοὰν ἔστασαν).

[55] i.e. one must distinguish between the mind and the actual process of thinking; one can have a mind and yet at the same time be ἀφρονῶν. And even in the presence of a God (*Il.* 4, 104) there should be no relaxing of this σωφρονεῖν. Pandoras has the real choice of agreeing to the proposal or not, and the fact that a god is trying to persuade him does not excuse his "imprudence".

[56] Pi. *P.* III 63 εἰ δὲ σώφρων ... χείρων ... πίθον ...

[57] Pi. *f.* VI 52 ταῦτα θεοῖς μὲν πιθεῖν σοφοὺς δύνατον ....

[58] Euenus of Paros 1, 5, cited in Ath. 9, 367e. The context is interesting : apparently Euenus's reference to πείθειν-συνετούς is an attempt to go beyond the λόγος ... ὁ παλαιός

the other hand if for any reason ὑφαιρεῖται νόημα in the φρένες then there can be no successful πείθειν.[59]

B) Πείθειν [60] in the major tragedians and comedians [61]

I) Introduction

A good starting-point is a passage in Aeschylus' Agamemnon.

(= the old answer), which one always says in case of irreconcilable ἀντιλέγειν : Σοὶ μὲν ταῦτα δοκοῦντ'ἔστω, ἐμοὶ δὲ τάδε.

[59] B. 9, 16ff.

Cf. also 11, 107,.

[60] For A : Dindorf 280, persuadeo, oratione flecto

For Ar : Sanxay, to persuade, to convince, to consult

For S : Ellendt/Geuthe 616f., permovendo dictis, cum ad credendum, tum ad faciendum

Dindorf 394 (as above).

We do not propose to deal here with attempts at persuasion that succeed through deceitful means and carried out for deceitful purposes; cf., e.g., A Eu 724; Pr 559f., 1063-70; Ch 1064; E Alc 700; Hec 131-33; El 1021 (cf. with that IT 24ff.); Hipp. 1311f.; IT 1049; Med 586f. (πείσαντά με ... ἀλλὰ μὴ σιγῇ φίλων = behind your friends' backs); 944f. 964f. : πείθειν δῶρα καὶ θεοὺς λόγος χρυσὸς δὲ κρείσσων μυρίων λόγων βροτός (cf. Pl. R III 390 E; Ov Ars 3, 653f.; Hor Carm 3, 16); 982; S Ai 148-51 (τοιούσδε λόγους ψιθύρους—cf. Pi P. II 75—πλάσσων ... πείθει). Contrast 156; S OC 1298 (πόλιν δὲ πείσας has in the context a ring of deceit, since οὔτε νικήσας λόγῳ οὔτ'εἰς ἔλεγχον χειρὸς οὐδ'ἐργοῦ μολών). Only in S do we find πείθειν unambiguously distinguished from ἐν δόλῳ λέγειν for the first time, while hitherto the latter was often included in the former and only the immediate context revealed the intended sense.

In contrast S Ph 90ff. distinguishes

i) πρὸς βίον (90.103)

ii) δόλοισιν (91); (τὸ) ψευδῆ λέγειν (100.108); (ἐν) δόλῳ (101f.107); cf. already 54f. : τὴν φ ... σε δεῖ ψυχὴν ὅπως δόλοισιν ἐκκλέψεις λέγων.

iii) πείθειν (102).

Neoptolemos clearly and deliberately distinguishes "conviction" based on facts and "stories of lies".

Similarly in E Hel 815ff. If rescue (σωθῆναι) should come ὠνητὸς ἢ τολμητὸς ἢ λόγων ὑπο or on the other hand 825 εἴ πως ἂν ἀναπείσαιμεν ἱκετεύοντά νιν—(in 828 the uncompounded form πείσανε δὲ echoes this compound; cf. on this phenomenon the material in K-G I 552 and furthermore :

Wackernagel, Vorlesungen über Syntax II 177

Fränkel, Zum Text der Vögel des Aristophanes, in : Studien zur Textgeschichte und Textkritik—Festschrift Jachmann, Köln, 1959, p. 21f.).

But contrast E Tr 982.

[61] Texts and tools for

Aeschylus,

In 1051f. Clytemnestra states as it were a hermeneutic maxim for every proper process of πείθειν : εἴπερ ἐστὶ μὴ χελιδόνος δίκην,[62] ἀγνῶτα [63] φωνὴν βάρβαρον κεκτημένη then the rule applies : if one wants to persuade someone then ἔσω φρενῶν [64] λέγουσα πείθω νιν λόγῳ.[65] It must therefore involve a sort of λόγος which penetrates to the φρένες and there perform its proper task.

Hence we have a natural twofold division of attempts at persuasion, which often become necessary because of "discord" [66] and often then take place within the context of a "discussion":[67]

On the part of the speaker(s)—the reality of πείθειν here : what does true πείθειν mean here—the contribution of πείθειν here—what are the conditions for any πείθειν here—what is required here ?

Aristophanes,
Euripides,
Sophocles and
Menander
s.v. Bibliography.

[62] Hesych. χελιδόνος δίκην : τοὺς βαρβάρους, χελιδόσιν ἀπεικάζουσι διὰ τὴν ἀσύνθετον (= ἀσύνετον) λαλίαν.

Hesych. χελιδόνων μουσεῖον : ὡς βάρβαρα καὶ ἀσύνετα τοιούτων τῶν τραγικῶν with reference to 1.93.

i.e. i) the twittering of the χελιδόνος was a byword among the Greeks for a foreign, i.e. barbarian tongue. Hence comes the identification : ὁ χελιδών = ὁ βάρβαρος : Ar Ra 91; 683:; etc. (cf. also χελιδονίζειν).

ii) βάρβαρος is synonymous with ἀσύνετος and thus here emphasizes the ἀγνῶτα φωνήν : Hesych. βάρβαρα : ἀσύνετα, ἄτακτα.

[63] ἀγνοεῖν (ὕπνος, e.g., produces ἀγνοεῖν—A Eu 134) = not to perceive, to recognize; mostl. c. acc. : to be ignorant of : Hdt 4, 156; S Tr 78; fail to understand.

[64] πείθειν is therefore operative within the person addressed "within his mind", mind as seat of the mental faculties, perception, thought (L-S) : ὥστε σὴν πεῖσαι φρένα E Hipp 1337. This recalls the Homeric phrase τοῦ θυμὸν ἐνὶ στήθεσσιν ἔπειθεν. Cf. also S Ph 1325 γράφου φρενῶν ἔσω and E Med 316f. λέγεις ἀκοῦσαι μαθακ', ἀλλ'ἔσω φρενῶν ὀρρωδία μοι μή τι βουλεύσῃσις κακόν.

[65] "I must speak with him and convince with my argument (dat. instr.) and that within his φρένες".

i) Note the close connection between φωνή (here act.—ἀγνῶτα— = which does not understand and pass.—βάρβαρον— = outlandish, not to be understood) and φρένες.

ii) That does not rule out the possibility that πείθειν in A Ag twice has the meaning "believe" : 1212; 1239. Cf. however συνιέναι in 1243 which interprets πείθειν qua "believe" as "conscious acceptance" in contrast to ἐκ δρόμου πεσὼν τρέχω 1245.

[66] A Pr 202f. στάσις τ' ἐν ἀλλήλοισιν ὡροθύνετο, οἱ μὲν θέλοντες ... οἱ δὲ ... σπεύδοντες E Hec 130 : the context within which πείθειν is practised is the λόγοι κατατεινόμενοι "words of hot contention" (cf. also Pl Prt 329 b; etc.); E Ph 81 ἔρις.

[67] Cf. ,e.g., S OC 801 ἐς τῷ νῦν λόγῳ (πείθειν 797 and 803) = in our present discussion (starting from 728); λόγῳ ... πείθειν cf. OC 1296.

On the part of the person(s) addressed—the reality of πείθειν here :
What does true πείθειν mean here—what part does πείθειν play
here—what is required here—what are the necessary presuppositions
and conditions here which would allow the πείθειν to reach a successful
conclusion ?

II) πείθειν : the speaker

We can describe more exactly the process that is involved for the
speaker in πείθειν as follows :

(1)   The instrument [68]

i)   in general :

a)   πείθειν is essentially accomplished through the φωνή φωνεῖν.[69]
Thus πείθειν is achieved through the articulation of words, arguments,
speech :
b)   πείθειν (ἐν)λόγῳ, λόγοις [70]
     πείθειν (ῥῆσιν) ... λέγων.[71]

ii)   in detail :

Important as εὖ λέγειν is for the process of πείθειν, yet it is no guarantee
of its success.[72] But in any case εὖ λέγειν is not marked by a needless

---

[68] Instrumental ἐν (= by means of) λόγοις πείθειν S *Ph* 1393; cf.
ἐν λιταῖς = by means of prayer S *Ph* 60
ἐν δόλῳ ... ἄγειν S *Ph* 1393
ἐν ὀφθαλμοῖς ... S *Ant* 764 (cf. *Il.* 1, 587 ἐν ὁ ... ἴδωμαι)
ἐν ὄμμασιν S *Tr* 241; etc.
ἐν γλώσσαις S *Ant* 961
ἐν φοναῖς S *Ant* 696; cf. also 1003; 1201.

[69] Cf. A *Ag* 1061; *Pr* 1063.

[70] A *Ag* 1052; S *Ph* 593f.; 612; 1393f.; E *Hec* 294; *IA* 1011.13; 1211f.; *Rh* 663;
Supp 347; 354f.; cf. also E *IA* 97f. ... πάντα προφέρων λόγον ἔπεισε ... and also A *Pr*
1014; *Ch* 781; Ar *Ach* 626; Men *Epit* 510.12. That πείθειν essentially takes place through
λόγοισιν is clear from the fact that when there is a λήγειν τῶν λόγων a successful πείθειν is
quite impossible : S *Ph* 1395.

[71] A *Supp* 615; cf. 273; *Ag* 1322; S *Ai* 156; f. 142, 20; Ar *Lys* 1229; cf. also E. *Alc*
827f.; *Rh* 935-37; *Ion* 840; Men. *Epit.* 510.514.

[72] Cf., e.g., E *Or* 943.946.

"squandering" [73] of "many" (πολλά) or even μυρίος[74] words or arguments, which are often mostly "irrelevant and dragged in by their hair" (παρασύρειν ἔπος),[75] but by "few" words (βραχέα) though "timely" (τὸ εἰπεῖν τὰ καιρία).[76] For only this can avert the danger of ... λόγοι πρὸς αἰθέρα φροῦδοι μάτην ῥιφέντες ...[77]

iii) two basic elements in the meaning of πείθειν :

a) πείθειν means a process in which above all something is made clear. This explains its close connection with διδάσκειν.[78] Concretely that means λέγειν σαφῆ λόγον [79] and calls for a μακρὸν καὶ σοφὸν λόγον,[80] which in individual cases can involve a τοιαῦτ' ... λόγοισιν ἐξηγεῖσθαι.[81] In the case of an argument with one who is trying to persuade by deceitful means [82] the way of proper πείθειν is characterized by, e.g., δηλοῦν/δηλοῦσθαι,[83] the motif of τεκμήριον-σῆμα,[84] the help of δεῖγμα (τῶν ἐμῶν λόγων) [85] and the practice of δεικνύναι.[86]

b) From this making something clear πείθειν can take on the

---

[73] E Med 325 λόγους ἀναλοῖς · οὐ γὰρ ἂν πείσαις ποτέ. Yet cf. "persistence" Men. Epit 54 : ὅλην τὴν ἡμέραν κατέτριψε (sc. δεόμενος). λιπαροῦντι καὶ πείθοντί με ...

[74] E Med 965.

[75] A Pr 1065 (adapted from Ps-transl.); L-S : "to drag a word in, use it out of time and place".

[76] S OC 808 = ἐν καιρῷ λέγειν (809) "in season, timely". Cf. χρὴ λέγειν τὰ καίρια A Th 1, cf. Ch 582; also S Ant 724. Men f. 472, 3 (f. 472 ΥΜΝΙΣ : Stob Fl 37.18 = 3. p 70 1Η—π'χρηστότητος—Plu Mor 33e, 801c; Max Conf 15.580; Isid Pel Ep 5.13, Μενάνδρου ·Υμνις) : τούτῳ λαλήσας ἡμέρας σμικρὸν μέρος → πείθειν (cf. however Epit 54 ὅλην τὴν ἡμέραν).

[77] E Hec 334f. 340.

[78] A Supp 516-23 : ἐγὼ δὲ λαοὺς ξυγκαλῶν ἐγχωρίους πείσω (MSS : πιετω; Wilam. στείχω, Wecklein πατῶ; aber cf. πείθω 523) τὸ κοινὸν ὡς ἂν εὐμενὲς τιθῶ, καὶ σὸν διδάξω πατέρα ποῖα χρὴ λέγειν ... Ar Nu 96-99; E El 580.594 : διδάσκειν and πείθειν are here synonymous.

[79] A Ag 1047; cf. Th 82; σαφής = clear, plain, distinct, of things heard, perceived or known.

[80] E Rh 838.

[81] A Pr 216; ἐξηγεῖσθαι = to interpret, explain.

[82] Besides n. 1, cf. S OC 794f. : τὸ σὸν δ'ἀφῖκται δεῦρ'ὑπόβλητον στόμα πολλὴν ἔχον στόμωσιν.

S OC 802 : γλώσσῃ σὺ δεινός = OT 545 λέγειν σὺ δεινός (opposite : γλῶσσαν ἀργόν S Ph 97).

[83] S OC 783.1513.

[84] Cf., e.g., S OC 1510.1512.

[85] E Supp 354.

[86] E Hipp 1008.

basic sense of "advise", "counsel":[87] τὰ λῶστα βουλεύειν[88], σὺν νῷ χρηστὰ βουλεύειν.[89]

(2) The object

This should above all be πιστά,[90] i.e. persuasion should succeed through what is true and real, and so should have the truth itself [91] as its object and not just something "fashioned out of falsehood to resemble truth" (ἀληθῶς οὐδὲν ἐξηκασμένα).[92] But this has two possible consequences :

i) it is possible that the πείθειν, which often indeed has an ὀρθοῦν as its goal,[93] must be preceded by the condemnation of previous error [94] or the call to ἐκστρέφειν.[95]

ii) So too [96] the counsel of the good statesman is often at the

---

[87] In addition to the two following nn. cf. also E *Hec* 294 where πείθειν is synonymous with παρηγορεῖν (288) = to advise, give counsel; Men f. 575 (= Stob *ecl* III 37, 5 ... Μενάνδρου ... σοιπρέπει) : here πείθειν is synonymous with παραινεῖν = to give advice, teach.

[88] A *Pr* 206; cf. 307 παραινέσαι τὰ λῶστα

Ag 1053 τὰ λῶστα τῶν παρεστώτων λέγει.

[89] E *Or* 909 (here in contrast to ὅταν γὰρ ἡδὺς τοῖς λόγοις φρονῶν κακῶς πείθῃ τὸ πλῆθος ...).

[90] A *Ag* 1213; πιστός = trustworthy, sure; cf. 272.352.

[91] i) This idea underlies the fact that the power of πείθειν is suspended for a certain time because of an earlier ἐψευσάμην (A Ag 1208.1212)

ii) An ἀληθόμαντις (A Ag 1241; opposite : ψευδόμαντις) seeks to "persuade" by ὀρθομαντείᾳ.

iii) S *OC* 1515 f. : πείθεις με πολλά γάρ σε θεσπίζονθ' ὁρῶ κοὐ ψευδόφημα.

S *Ph* 102 : πείσαντ' i.e. Ph should realize that it is to his own advantage that he should come to Troas—instead of the deceitful plea πλεῖς δ'ὡς πρὸς οἶκον (58); hence πείσαντ' = "through persuasion" is here equivalent to "after one had told him the truth".

E *Hec* 1206 τίνα δοκεῖς πείσειν τάδε ; ...

E *Hec* 1207 εἰ βούλοιο τ'αληθῆ λέγειν, ...

(i.e. if he told the truth he could also expect a successful πείθειν).

[92] A *Ag* 1244.

[93] Cf. ,e.g., Men f. 730 (Stob f. 83.12 = 4. p 651 H [ὁποίους τινὰς χρὴ εἶναι τοὺς πατέρας περὶ τὰ τέκνα, καὶ ὅτι φυσική, τις ἀνάγκη ἀμφοτέρους εἰς διάθεσιν ἄγει] Μενάνδρου. ὀρθοῦν here = "to set straight" (L-S); "Krummes, Gebogenes, Schiefes, gerade machen ... gerade richten, lenken ... verbessern" (Ps). The point here is that πείθειν should replace the λυπεῖν that seems necessary for ὀρθοῦν.

[94] Cf., e.g., S *OC* 736.753f.

[95] Cf., e.g., Ar *Nu* 87-90.

[96] Cf. here E *Or* 907ff.

time unpleasant but later proves beneficial. From this point of view
(ὧδ'ἰδόντα) must one judge the statesman. For he is in a similar position
to the physician, whose remedies can also be bitter at the moment.

But radically different is the πείθειν of the "loud-mouth", the
demagogue, who "has doors before his mouth" [97] and, θορύβῳ ...
πίσυνος, yet gains "credibility" (πίθανὸς ἔτ᾽) even if he were to ἀστοὺς
περιβαλεῖν κακῷ τινι. [98] Therefore, ὅταν ἡδὺς τοῖς λόγοις φρονῶν κακῶς
πείθῃ τὸ πλῆθος, τῇ πόλει κακὸν μέγα. [99] This is the reason for Menander's
saying : ἑτέρους λαλοῦντας εὖ βδελύττομαι,[100] and for Euripides'
decided aversion to the demagogues who can certainly speak well
(οἱ καλοὶ λίαν λόγοι [101]) but by this τερπνὰ ... λέγειν destroy cities
and houses, instead of so speaking that ἐξ ὅτου τις εὐκλεὴς γενήσεται.[102]
Sophocles' judgment is this :[103] λόγῳ μὲν ἐσθλά, τοῖσι δ᾽ἔργοισιν κακά.
This therefore distinguishes proper πείθειν, which seeks the real
advantage of the person addressed, from the πείθειν of him who
through ὁ ποικιλόφρων κόπις ἡδυλόγος δημοχαριστής [104] yet "by
means of charm" (ἐπάδουσα [105]) produces κηλεῖν [106]—in short σκληρὰ
μαλθακῶς λέγων.[107] Not only is τὸ λέγειν εὖ [108] if it brings βλαβήν to
the person addressed but in such cases this λέγειν εὖ does not even bring
the speaker any real advantage. Certainly the "fair speaker" is a
man ὅστις ἐκχανῶν λόγοις πρὸς κέρδος ἴδιον ἄλλοτ᾽ἄλλοσε στρέφει·
ὁ δ᾽αὐτίχ᾽ἡδὺς καὶ διδοὺς πολλὴν χάριν ...;[109] but this κέρδος ἴδιον is

---

[97] This is the lit. translation of ἀθυρόγλωσσος in E *Or* 903 (like Thersites in *Il.* 212f.;
cf. εὐθύγλωσσος Pi *P* II 86, ἀθυρόστομος S *Ph* 188 and Thgn 421).

[98] E *Or* 905f.; on πιθανός (act.) cf. Th 3, 36, 6; 4, 21, 3; 6, 35, 2; Ar *Th* 268; *Eq* 629;
Pl *Grg* 458e 7; A *Ag* 485f.; θορύβῳ ... πίσυνος = "trusting in his loud voice" (cf. the
"bluster" of Tynd. 630).

[99] E *Or* 907f.

[100] f. 472, 6.

[101] E *Hipp* 487.

[102] 488f.

[103] S *OC* 782.

[104] E *Hec* 131-33; W. Nestle, *Euripides*, 1901, p. 289 tr. : "Den verschlagenen Schalk
und Schmeichler des Volkes mit dem süssen Geschwätz". Cf. also S *OC* 761f.

[105] A *Ag* 1021; cf. Pl *Lg* 773d; Tht 149d.

[106] E *IA* 1211f.

[107] S *OC* 774.

[108] Men f. 472, 8f. τὸ γὰρ λέγειν εὖ δεινόν ἐστιν εἰ φέροι βλαβήν τινα ·

[109] E *Supp* 412-4.

ultimately an illusion. For, according to E *Med* 580-3,[110] his being σοφὸς λέγειν (= λέγειν δεινός) brings only harm to him who is ἄδικος ὤν (= Jason) : ἐμοὶ γὰρ ... πλείστην ζημίαν ὀφλισκάνει. Hence Medea can decry Jason as an incarnation of wordly wisdom. Ar *Nu* 423 provides a good commentary on this : Strepsiades thinks that he can conceal the wrong he has done by learning the art of persuasion but is forced to confess that this turns out to have a boomerang effect. Thus those who παρ' ὄχλῳ μουσικώτεροι λέγουσιν [111] but are of no real use to them or to themselves are really ἐν σοφοῖς φαῦλοι.[112] All these passages echo the contemporary moral problem posed by the increasing use of sophisticated methods of persuasion.

(3) The person

This shows clearly that proper πείθειν is not only a matter of certain qualities residing in the "words",[113] not only a matter, e.g., of the speaker's being a σαφὴς ἔτυμος ἄγγελος,[114] important and essential though this may be ; rather the power of πείθειν is produced by the whole life [115] of the speaker : τρόπος ἔσθ' ὁ πείθων τοῦ λέγοντος,

---

[110] Already in 576-8 the chorus reproaches Jason : οὐ δίκαια δρᾶν, although he εὖ ... τούδ'ἐκοσμήσας λόγους ;

[111] Or : ὅσοι δημηγόρους ζηλοῦτε τιμάς ... πρὸς χάριν λέγητέτι (E *Hec* 254f.).

[112] E *Hipp* 988f.

[113] E *Hipp* 984-9 ; U. Wilamowitz-Möllendorf, *Hippolytos*, 1891, p. 141, tr. : "Indessen die Sache, die du so beredt verfichtst, ist, wenn man sie genau betrachtet, schlecht. Hingegen mir gebricht es an der Gewandtheit, mich vor dem grossen Haufen zu verteidigen. Vor meinesgleichen und im kleinen Kreise versteh ich's besser. Und das ist natürlich. Denn was gebildeter Geschmack verwirft, hat für das Ohr der Menge vollsten Klang". The phrase here ἐγὼ δ'ἄκομψος (L-S "rude I am in speech") was frequently used in the Athenian courts. (eg. Lys 1, 3 ; 19, 2 ; Is 8, 5 ; 10, 1 ; D 27, 2 ; 55, 7) to secure the jury's sympathy.

[114] A *Th* 82f. ἔτυμος = true = in accordance with the facts. The point here is that this is all so (σαφής + ἔτυμος) despite the ἄναυδος. The same applies (as much or even more) to an αὐδήεις = speaking with a human voice (here με πείθει = I know). S *OC* 1510-17 ; the idea exists that the trustworthiness of the gods (ψεύδοντες οὐδὲν) extends to that of their messengers (οὐ ψευδόφημα), but that the τεκμήριον or σῆμα, i.e. that which establishes a claim or demonstrates it and which is ultimately essential for πείθειν (τῷ δ'ἐκπέπεισαι ... τεκμηρίῳ + πείθεις με) is in the hands of the gods αἱ πολλὰ βρονταὶ ... τὰ πολλά τε στάψαντα, but their messengers have their experience of earlier prophecies that have come true (cf. 606ff. and 1037).

[115] That is the point of E *Hipp* 1007 : καὶ δὴ τὸ σῶφρον τοὐμὸν οὐ πείθει σ'ἴσως (καὶ δὴ as *Med* 386.1107 ; *Hel* 1059, introducing an assumption, here = εἰ δέ) "And, assuming that the appeal to my σωφροσύνη does not convince you of my innocence"—and that should really come about through the proof (introduced by πρῶτα δέ 991) of the im-

οὐ λόγος.[116] So we read that τὸ ἀξίωμα[117] is helpful for πείθειν or that really only the ἀνὴρ δίκαιος can really practise aright the εὖ λέγειν[118] necessary for πείθειν while the final verdict on the σοφὸς λέγειν or the λέγειν δεινός of him who is ἄδικος ὤν : ἔστι δ'οὐκ ἄγαν σοφός = his cleverness proves to be folly.[119]

III) πείθειν : the person addressed

Since πείθειν is basically directed towards ἰδεῖν [120] a prerequisite is "openness" [121] for thinking over a new state of affairs [122] and readiness for real ἀκούειν and not just κλύειν.[123] Also required is ἔχειν νοῦν [124]

---

probability of the act *ex vita*—so δεῖ δή σε δεῖξαι τῷ τρόπῳ διεφθάρην (1008); this is then followed by the proof of the improbability of the act *ex causa*.

[116] Men f. 427.7 : τρόπος here = way of life, habit, character. The same contrast occurs in f. 575, 2f. : ... οὐχ ὁ σὸς λόγος ... ὁ δ'ἴδιος πείθει τρόπος.

[117] = honour, reputation; cf., e.g., E *Hec* 293-95 : τὸ δ'ἀξίωμα ... τὸ σὸν πείσει. λόγος γὰρ ἐκ τ'ἀδοξούντων ἰὼν κἀκ τῶν δοκούντων αὐτὸς οὐ ταὐτὸν σθένει.

[118] S *OC* 806f.

[119] E *Med* 580-83.

[120] Cf., e.g., E *IT* 1048f. : λάθρα δ'ἄνακτος ἢ εἰδότος δράσεις τάδε ; πείσασα μύθοις'οὐ γὰρ ἂν λάθοιμί γε.

[121] ἴσως γὰρ ἂν πείσαις ἐμέ = I am open to conviction; I have an open mind (Ar *Pax* 405); but cf. A *Pr* 335; S *OC* 797; *Ph* 624f.; 1393f.; E *Hipp* 1062; *Med* 185.325.941 (cf. *Alc* 48); *Hipp* 1336; E *Or* 1610 πεῖθ'ἐς 'Αργείους μολὼν—proverbial (*Scholia in Euripidem* collegit recensuit edidit E. Schwartz, vol. I, Berolini 1887) : "persuade the Argives" = to undertake a pointless task (cf. 714f.).

[122] Thus Jebb (The Electra, p. 141) describes the meaning of πείθον in the present as "to allow the reasoning to weigh with thee"; cf. S *El* 1025 and *OC* 520, but especially *El* 1015f. where the following words explain what is meant by πείθειν : προνοίας οὐδὲν ἀνθρώποις ἔφυ κέρδος λαβεῖν ἄμεινον οὐδὲ νοῦ σοφοῦ. Cf. also E *Hel* 1393 and 994 : μαλλόν γε μέντοι τοῖς ἐμοῖς πείθου λόγοις ... "be persuaded by my arguments" and not by the argument of πόθος (1395f.); cf. also E *Andr* 233 and f. 440.

[123] A *Ag* 1064; Paley, FA (*The Tragedies of Aeschylus*, 1855, p. 375) comments : "The Greeks made a distinction between κλύειν and ἀκούειν (*Prom* 456; *Cho* 5), and consequently between mere words, and words which entered the mind of the hearer". A good example of this is also E *Ba* 787 : πείθει μὲν οὐδέν, τῶν ἐμῶν λόγων κλύων. But, on the other hand A *Supp* 623.

[124] The false σὺ ταῦτ'ἔπεισας of Teiresias in E *Ba* 255 was only possible because of the νοῦν οὐκ ἔχον of his respected grandfather. Pentheus is deeply moved since τῷ γήρᾳ φιλεῖ χὠ νοῦς ὁμαρτεῖν (f. 260); cf. the similar reproach in S *OC* 930 : here νοῦν (οὐκ)ἔχειν clearly has the first of the two possible meanings : i) to have sense, be sensible; ii) to have one's mind directed to something (L-S). Cf. too the failure of deceitful πείθειν to make any impression on the νοῦς in S *OC* 810.

or ἔχειν λόγον.[125] For only the σοφός [126] who has the capacity of συνιέναι [127] and is φρονῶν ἃ χρὴ φρονεῖν [128] and so is anything but an ἀσύνετος [129] can δέχεσθαι λόγον.[130] Hence he must not let himself be convinced just by what is before his eyes but by what he himself really knows and has experienced.[131] If after all he cannot be convinced [132] this obstacle can be removed with an additional help, perhaps in the form of an ἑρμηνεύς.[133]

Only when these presuppositions are fulfilled by the speaker and the person addressed is it possible for an essential part of πείθειν to be realized, the voluntary assent of the person addressed which corresponds to the element of "advising" in it.[134] For, since πείθειν

---

[125] E *Alc* 51 1; cf. 48 : οὐ γὰρ οἶδ᾽ἂν εἰ πείσαιμί σε (= ἴσως ου ; cf. *Med* 941 : οὐκ οἶδ᾽ἂν εἰ πείσαιμι, πειρᾶσθαι δὲ χρῆ : cf. K-G I 246 for similar examples). ἔχειν λόγον = "to possess mentally to understand the argument" (so also A *Ag* 582; cf. also ἔχεις τι; do you understand ? Ar *Nu* 733; etc.).

[126] But that implies the μὴ οὐ πείσῃς σοφούς (cf. the context : τὸ σὺν κακὸν κοσμοῦσα) in E *Tr* 982.

[127] A *Ag* 1243; cf. 887; S *El* 1479; etc.

[128] E *Ba* 1124 : Pentheus' πείθειν is unsuccessful because his mother ἐκ βακχίου κατείχετ᾽ (ἐκ denoting the origin of her mental state; cf. Xen *Smp* I 10 ἐκ θεῶν τοῦ κατεχόμενοι) and thus οὐ φρονοῦσ᾽ἃ χρὴ φρονεῖν = her mind not as it should be (cf. 851-53.332; *Med* 1129.1329; etc.).

[129] A *Ag* 1060 : ἀξυνήμων = not comprehending; only here (instead of the more usual ἀσύνετος = void of understanding).

[130] A *Ag* 1060 : (L-S) of mental reception, take, accept; (Ps) mit den Ohren aufnehmen, vernehmen, hören; cf., e.g., S *El* 688; A *Ag* 1653; X *An* 1, 8, 17; thus "to accept, approve" e.g. τὸν λόγον E *Med* 924; Hdt 9, 5; τοὺς λόγους Th 1, 95.

[131] E *El* 594 : his own experience of πόνων in Troy is more persuasive than that which comes from τίς οὖν διδάξει σ᾽ἄλλος ἢ τὰ σ᾽ὄμματα (580).

[132] Cf., e.g., A *Ag* 1245 : τὰ δ᾽ἀλλ᾽ἀκούσας ἐκ δρόμου πεσὼν τρέχω.

[133] E.G. A *Ag* 1060 : εἰ δ᾽ἀξυνήμων οὖσα, μὴ δέχῃ λόγον ἑρμηνέως ἔοικεν ἡ ξένη τόρου δεῖσθαι; ὁ ἑρμηνεύς = interpreter, esp. of foreign tongues; here simply "interpreter, expounder", also 616 and Pi *O* II 85. τορός = clear, distinct, plain; here the ἑρμηνέως ... τοροῦ is the same as the τοροῖσιν ἑρμηνεύσιν in 616.

[134] A *Supp* 940f. ταύτας δ᾽ἑκούσας μὲν κατ᾽εὔνοιαν φρενῶν ἄγοις ἄν, εἴπερ εὐσεβὴς πίθοι λόγος (κατ᾽εὔνοιαν φρενῶν with ἕκουσας i.e. not ἀκούσας βίᾳ φρενῶν—cf. 943 ... μήποτ᾽ἐκδοῦναι βίᾳ ...-).

Ar *Pl* 600 : οὐ γὰρ πείσεις, οὐδ᾽ἢν πείσῃς; i.e. you may convince me by argument, but "a man convinced against his will is of the same opinion still".

S *Ph* 90-103 : πρὸς βίαν ... πείσαντ᾽ ... ; 594 : ἢ λόγῳ πείσαντες...ἢ πρὸς ἰσχύος κράτος... ; 612 : πείσαντες λόγῳ = 1332 ἑκὼν αὐτός (cf. E *Phoen* 476).

1394 : πείθειν ἐν λόγοις should produce the state of ἑκών (1392) = (Ps) freiwillig, aus eignem Willen, auf eignen Antrieb, gern; mit Wissen und Willen; E *Supp* 347-55 : πείσας (355) synonymous with συγχωρεῖσθαι (E *IT* 741f.); E *Ion* 840f. : πιθών σε ... εἰ δὲ σοὶ τόδ᾽ἦν πικρόν ... The problem of the relation of πείθειν and ἀνάγκειν to one another is

is by definition opposed to any idea of force,[135] πείθειν can contain within itself no element of intellectual compulsion in the sense of a desire for power over the understanding and will of the other.[136] Rather πείθειν is like the activity of a midwife : it seeks by advice to help the other to make his own evaluations and so his own decisions.

IV) Provisional statement

If what has been said so far has given the impression that we are correct in our twofold division of the reality of what is meant by πείθειν, and that we have described these elements, if not comprehensively, at least in their essentials; then this impression must be drastically revised. For to describe the reality of what is meant by πείθειν, with "intellectual" and "moral" concepts, assigned to the speaker and to the person addressed, is but to concentrate on the phenomena and thus the forms within which the process of πείθειν appears.

However the comprehensive character of the reality of πείθειν can only become apparent if we can answer the question as to the essence (das Sein) of these forms. What is it that is essentially being expressed in and through these forms ? What ultimately lies behind these "intellectual" and "moral" concepts ? *What* is it that is "convincing"

---

posed in an interesting way in E *Or.* In 28f. we clearly hear Electra's reluctance to accuse God (28 φοίβου δ'ἀδικίαν is emphatic : "but, as regards the—alleged—injustice of Phoebus, what good is it to accuse him of that ?" μὲν = μὴν—*Alc* 146; *Med* 676; cf. De 366; the following δέ—29—is perhaps equivalent to ἀλλὰ—after the negation implied in the question— : "but yet he persuades—cf. *Hec* 133—Or".—cf. De 166). But contrast 286 (ἐπάρας), 599 (ὁ κελεύσας) and 1665 (ἐξηνάγκασα). Men *PK* 248.252 πείθειν-ἐκβιάζειν.

E *Or* 706 : πρὸς βίαν (adv. in a formulaic usage : *Andr* 730.753; *Herc* 550; *Med* 1216; *Suppl* 454f.385; cf. S II 511) in contrast to 705 πεῖσαι τῷ λίαν χρῆσθαι καλῶς.

ἀναπείθειν in particular is used of "persuasion" contrary to one's own opinion (e.g. Ar *Nu* 96.340) and inclination (e.g. Ar *Nu* 868; 1019). The ἀνα—here can either convey the idea of falsehood, and thus "to seduce, to mislead, to corrupt" (e.g. Ar *V* 101) or the element of "back, contrary" (e.g. Ar *V* 116.278.568.586.784.974). The importance of the idea of voluntary agreement, which causes difficulties for both sides and hard and strenuous work, is expressed by the words ἀνά τοι με πείθεις.

[135] In addition to the preceding n. cf. also E *Supp* 346f. εἶμι καὶ νεκροὺς ἐκλύσομαι λόγοισι πείθων · εἰ δὲ μή βίᾳ δορός ...

[136] Thus πείθειν should not be achieved βίᾳ δὲ θυμοῦ = against my inclination (E *Alc* 829; cf. 826 = ἠσθόμην ... ἰδὼν ...; 827 ἀλλ'ἔπειθέ με ...) like βίᾳ φρενῶν (A *Sept* 612) "against his better reason" and βίᾳ καρδίας (A *Supp* 798).

(πειστικός) in the λόγος ?[137] We can only throw out hints here, but it seems plain that this being which lies behind the different forms can best be described by and through a further description of the two "Sitze" in which the power of πείθειν "dwells".

V) πείθειν : "Sitz im Leben"

The nature and the power of πείθειν have their "Sitz im Leben" on the border between life and death, salvation and destruction. By the power of πείθειν either existing life is destroyed—this only in a few cases—or on the other hand life is preserved, either by averting threatening death or by overcoming already present death.

(1) Destruction of existing life

Someone "persuades" another to slay someone (πείθειν—κτείνειν).[138] The power of πείθειν (πάντα προσφέρων λόγον) is especially clear if someone lets himself be persuaded to kill against his own intentions.[139] However the ἀπολλύναι/ἀπόλλυσθαι [140] produced by πείθειν can also simply take the form of someone's being sent into exile.[141] Here too belong the prophecies of death and destruction, given through a prophetess [142] or τῷ τεκμηρίῳ,[143] which are aimed at "persuasion".

(2) Preservation of life

Πείθειν is essentially directed towards an action.[144] Yet the purpose of πείθειν is not the release and application of some wonderful, almost

---

[137] Cf. Men f. 472, 4 πειστικὸν (πίστι ...) λόγος = πειστήριος = persuasive, convincing — captivating; cf. E IT 1053 πειστήριοι λόγοι ; πειστικιότεροι λόγοι Xen. Cyr 1, 6, 10.

[138] A Eu 84; E Med 9; Or 29f.

[139] Cf., e.g., E IA 96 : ... ἐγώ ... εἶπον ... ὡς οὔποτ᾽ἂν τλὰς θυγατέρα κτανεῖν ἐμήν ... μ᾽ἀδελφός ... ἔπεισε τλῆναι δεινά.

[140] Cf., e.g., E Hipp 487.

[141] Cf., e.g., S OC 1298 — 1292 : γῆς ἐκ πατρῴας ἐξελήλαμαι φυγάς.

[142] A Ag 1239 (— θάνοντες 1219; τεύξαται κακῇ τύχῃ 1230; φονώς 1231; μόρος 1246; ἀποκτείνειν 1250). But to what purpose? καὶ τῶν δ᾽ὅμοιον εἴ τι μὴ πείθω. τί γάρ ; τὸ μέλλον ἥξει.

[143] S OC 1509-16 : τὸ τεκμήριον ἐκ πέπεισται τοῦ μόρου πείθεις με.

[144] Basically all πείθειν passages show this. Yet cf. especially S OC 15/16 and Men f. 575, 2f. (connection of πείθειν/ποιεῖν).

magical, power, ὥσθ'ὁμαρτεῖν μοι πέτρας ...,¹⁴⁵ but the removal of
τὸ ζῆν ἄνευ σωτηρίας.¹⁴⁶ That can mean

i) (negatively) avoiding it : by πείθειν another is held back from
dying ¹⁴⁷ or killing,¹⁴⁸ or from a possible κακοῦσθαι ¹⁴⁹ or ἐκ πατρῴας
φυγάς.¹⁵⁰

ii) (positively) restoration : the power of ἐν λόγος succeeding πείθειν
makes possible the ending of the state of τὸ ζῆν ἄνευ σωτηρίας ¹⁵¹
and the restoration of that of σωτηρία.¹⁵² It can also simply mean
that the use of πείθειν enables one to free another from fear,¹⁵³ from
the state of δύσμορος,¹⁵⁴ ὥστε τῶν δέ σ'ἐκλῦσαι πόνων ...¹⁵⁵. But if
such a saving power is ascribed to πείθειν, then it is not surprising
that time and again the Ancients speculated about the power of
persuasion with regard to a death that had already occurred. Can the
power of persuasion bring the dead back to life? Some can recount
such cases,¹⁵⁶ others see here the limit of the power of πείθειν.¹⁵⁷

---

145 E *IA* 1211.

146 S *Ph* 1396.

147 S *OC* 1442 (Polyneices).

148 E *Alc*; *Andr* 39 οὐ κτείνειν (= κωλύειν θανεῖν 14);
    E *Ba* 1121.1124; *Or* 943.946 οὐ κατακτείνειν
    E *Hec* 288.294 οὐ ἀποκτείνειν
    E *Or* 1610; *Alc* 699f. οὐ θνήσκειν
    E *Hec* 338.340 μὴ στερηθῆναι βίου.

149 E *Med* 183.185.

150 E *Hipp* 990.1048; *Med* 904f.

151 S *Ph* 1393-6.

152 Through   πείθειν — σώζειν/σώζεσθαι/σωτηρία S *Ph* 1393-6.100-109;   E *Hel* 828
(cf. 815). 1039.1041; *Or* 705.710.712 (πείθειν = σώζειν σοφίᾳ, μὴ βίᾳ); *IA* 1209.1212
(συσσώζειν); Men *Epit* 510.

153 E *IA* 1011.1013 πείθωμεν ... οἱ λόγοι ... καταπαλαίουσιν φόβους.
    E *Rh* 663f. σύ τοί με πείθεις, σοῖς δὲ πιστεύων λόγοις ... εἰμ'ἐλεύθερος φόβου.

154 S *OC* 736.749.

155 A *Pr* 335.341.

156 Cf., e.g., A *Eu* 724 (Apollo) Μοίρας ἔπεισας ἀφθίτους θεῖναι βροτούς. (ἔπεισας =
οἴνῳ παρηπάτησας—728, but without οἴνῳ—; cf. E *Alc* 11f.: παιδὸς φέρητος ὃν θανεῖν
ἐρρυσάμην, Μοίρας δολώσας; 33 : Μοίρας δολίῳ σφήλαντι τέχνῃ. The story is found in
Hesiod; cf. Schol. E *Alc* 1 and 33). An optimism derived from this has left its mark
on   Ar *Ra* 68 :   κοὐδεὶς γέ μ'ἂν πείσειεν ἀνθρώπων τὸ μὴ οὐκ ἐλθεῖν ἐπ'ἐκεῖνον ... πότερον
εἰς Ἅιδου κατω; cf. also E *Supp* 346f. : εἶμι καὶ νεκροὺς ἀκλύσομαι λόγοισι πείθων ...

157 Cf., e.g., E *Alc* 48 : Apollo tells death, who is about to kill Alc : οὐ γὰρ οὐδ'ἂν εἰ
πείσαιμί σε ... (but contrast A *Eu* 724). S *Ph* 623f. : πείθειν cannot ἐξ Ἅιδου θανὼν πρὸς
φῶς ἀνελθεῖν.

(3) Conclusions

The power of πείθειν is the power which brings or destroys life. Hence it is clear that what is meant by πείθειν is not to be comprehended in terms of purely intellectual concepts. Rather the intellectual power of πείθειν must be closely related to its existential power. We assume that the process of πείθειν basically cannot achieve more "intellectually" than it can existentially.[158] This means that the power of arguments within the context of πείθειν lies in their ability to give life.

VI) πείθειν : "Sitz im Himmel"

Not only οἱ σοφοί ... τὸ θεῖον εἰδότες μάντεις [159] are able to succeed in πείθειν;[160] for the power of πείθειν is for all men essentially a δωρεά of the gods.[161] Therefore in πείθειν and διδάσκειν one must turn to the gods to ask for success.[162] In the same sense the λόγος which one is going to use to "convince" is occasionally qualified by εὐσεβής [163] and the Cyclops warns : ἀλλ'ἐμοὶ πιθοῦ ... τὸ δ'εὐσεβὲς τῆς δυσσεβείας ἀνθελοῦ.[164] Thus the successful outcome is nothing but the result of divine and human cooperation.[165]

---

[158] That is at any rate the argument in S Ph 623f. Since the power of πείθειν is inadequate to recall me, once dead, to life I will not be persuaded now by your arguments. I.e. πείθειν's power to convince intellectually is demonstrated and gauged by its existential power—here by whether it is able to bring the dead back to life.

[159] Cf. too θεσπίζειν directed at πείθειν : in A Ag 1210.1212.

[160] E Rh 65f.

[161] A Pr 341f. αὐχῶ γὰρ αὐχῶ τήνδε δωρεὰν ἐμοὶ δώσειν Δί', ὥστε τῶνδέ σ'ἐκλῦσαι. In 335 πείθειν is described as the means whereby ὥστε ... πόνων can be effected.

[162] A Supp 520 πρὸς ταῦτα (= πείσω, διδάξω) μίμνε καὶ θεοὺς ... λιταῖς παραιτοῦ.

[163] Cf., e.g., A Supp 941.

[164] E Cyc 309.311.

[165] A Supp 615 τοιάνδ'ἔπειθεν ῥῆσιν ... λέγων ἄναξ Πελασγῶν ... 623 δημηγόρους δ'ἤκουσεν εὐκιθὴς στροφὰς δῆμος Πελασγῶν. Ζεὺς δ'ἐπέκρανεν τέλος. F. A. Paley (The Tragedies of Aeschylus, 1855, p. 52) tr. : "it was the people, as I said that heard the eloquent appeal, but it was Zeus who put it into their hearts to ...".

C) *Πείθειν* [166] *in the major historians* [167]

I) The situation that makes *πείθειν* necessary

Generally speaking, the situation in which *πείθειν* occurs or should occur involves some problem. It can be 1) purely a question of information, of understanding some unfamiliar phenomenon. One wonders at something and wants or needs an explanation of it.[168] But 2) the necessity of what is meant by *πείθειν* arises existentially in a situation involving a matter of life or death.[169] Often man is faced only with these alternatives.[170] But often it is a matter of hotly contested [171] and important decisions to be taken in a *συνόδῳ* [172] or *συνεδρίῳ*.[173] In each case the person or the whole people that is in in this position hope by means of a successful process of *πείθειν* to find clarification in their confusion [174] and thus the means of reaching a decision.[175] Finally, *πείθειν* seeks to turn men to deeds and action.[176]

---

[166] Schweighäuser persuadere.

Powell to persuade, convince ... carry one's point.

[167] Texts and tools for Herodotus, Thucydides and Polybius sv. Bibliography. We have not dealt with Xenophon because of lack of time.

Since Schweighäuser's Polybius-Index is incomplete and Mauersberger's Lexicon has not yet reached π, the 49 cases of the use of *πείθειν* in the act. are listed here (as given by Prof. Mauersberger in a personal letter): 1, 43, 5; 1, 54, 6; 2, 2, 6; 2, 22, 3; 2, 52, 1; 2, 56, 11; 3, 41, 7; 3, 98, 11; 4, 29, 3; 4, 36, 6; 4, 53, 1; 4, 64, 2; 4, 82, 7; 5, 1, 9; 5, 50, 11; 5, 54, 5; 5, 54, 11; 5, 60, 1; 5, 63, 3; 7, 2, 1; 8, 35, 6; 9, 5, 1; 9, 24, 7; 9, 27, 11; 10, 11, 5; 12, 25, 4; 12, 26, 1; 13, 7, 6bis; 18, 9, 2; 18, 9, 5; 18, 45, 12; 21, 5, 12; 21, 31, 16; 21, 34, 13; 23, 3, 9; 24, 11, 8; 28, 20, 10; 28, 21, 1; 29, 3, 7; 29, 4, 7; 30, 2, 10; 31, 17, 5; 38, 7, 8; 38, 13, 6; 39, 3, 5; fr 96; 147; 184.

[168] Hdt 2, 150, 2 : ἐπείτε δὲ τοῦ ὀρύγματος τούτου οὐκ ὥρων τὸν χοῦν οὐδαμοῦ ἐόντα, ἐπιμελὲς γὰρ δή μοι ἦν ... εἰρόμην τοὺς ... 3, 12, 2 : θῶμα δὲ μέγα εἶδον πυθόμενος παρὰ τῶν ἐπιχωρίων 9, 53, 4 : ἐθώμαζέ τε ὀρέων τὸ ποιεύμενον ἄτε οὐ παραγενόμενος τῷ προ ...

[169] Hdt 1, 71; 112, 2; 2, 121dl; 3, 119, 3; 4, 83, 2; 5, 24, 1; 26, 2; 104, 2; 9, 120, 4.

[170] Hdt 1, 11, 4; 24, 3.

[171] The context of *πείθειν* is ἡ ἐν αὐτοῖς ἀμφισβήτησις = quarrel, dispute, questioning, argument; cf., e.g., Plb 18, 9, 5.

[172] The place where *πείθειν* takes place is ἡ σύνοδος = gathering, assembly; cf., e.g., Plb 18, 9, 2.

[173] The place where *πείθειν* is practised is τὸ συνέδριον = a gathering for the purpose of discussion; cf., e.g., Plb 18, 45, 10.12.

[174] Hdt 1, 97; 6, 35, 3; Th 1, 58, 2; 111, 1.

[175] Th 3, 42, 2 : the λόγοι are the διδάσκαλοι τῶν πραγμάτων (similarly Pericles' words in 2, 40, 2) and that man is ἀξύνετος εἰ ἄλλῳ τινὶ ἡγεῖται περὶ τοῦ μέλλοντος δυνατὸν εἶναι καὶ ἐμφ ....

[176] In essence this can be shown from every *πείθειν*-passage. But the connection between *πείθειν* and act is most pregnantly expressed in Th 8, 27, 5 : ὡς δὲ ἔπεισε, καὶ

In Th and Plb it is frequently the πρέσβεις who, representing the people, have the task of practising πείθειν.[177] 3) We often find πείθειν also used in the context of this last-mentioned situation, but in a rather specialized sense, when it is a matter of procuring the services of important men or soldiers, and also of ships for war, with or without money.[178]

II) The way by which πείθειν is achieved

Especially striking is the relatively high number of cases of attempts at persuading or convincing that do not succeed.[179] This may have something to do with the fact that these attempts often take the form of an appeal to the emotions.[180]

Let us examine the cases of successful πείθειν.[181] If we leave out of consideration both cases of deception [182] and those where "favourable"

ἔδρασαν ταῦτα. It is not without difficulty that we supply ἔπεισε with a personal object (the other commanders) and ἔδρασαν with a subject (the commanders as a whole). ἔδρασαν is a necessary improvement by Wilamowitz-Möllendorf in Hermes 1, 1936; the MSS read ἔδρασε but this is unsuitable, since, if Phrynichos' purposes could have been carried out by him alone, the assent of his fellow commanders would have been quite unnecessary.

[177] 1, 58, 1; 2, 67, 1.2; 73, 14; 3, 3, 1; 4, 4; 36, 5f.; 71, 2; 72, 1; 86, 3; 100, 1; 4, 17, 1; 22, 1; 58, 1; 87, 2; 5, 4, 5f.; 61, 3; 6, 46, 5; 73, 2; 76, 1; 88, 7-10; 7, 12, 1; 32, 1; 8, 32, 1. Plb 4, 53, 1; 6, 64, 2; 21, 5, 12; 31, 16; 28, 20, 10; 38, 7, 8.

[178] Hdt 1, 163, 3; 2, 152, 5; 4, 151, 3; 6, 5, 2; 9, 33, 3; Th 1, 14, 3; 2, 29, 5; etc.

[179] Hdt 2, 11, 4; 24, 3; 71, 4; 112, 2; 163, 3; 2, 121, dl; 3, 137, 4; 138, 3; 4, 83, 2; 105, 2; 155, 4; 5, 36, 2; 104, 2; 6, 52; 7, 139, 6; 160, 1; 210, 1; 8, 4, 2; 80, 2; 109, 1; 9, 13, 2; 55, 1; 109, 3; 120, 4. Th 1, 35, 4; 65, 1; 3, 21, 1; 31, 1; 75, 4; 59, 3; 4, 4, 12; 71, 2; 87, 2; 5, 4, 6; 6, 50, 1; 54, 11; 7, 73, 26.

[180] Attempt at πείθειν through

ἱκετεύειν	1, 11, 4
λίσσεσθαι	1, 24, 3
δακρύσασα καὶ λαβομένη τῶν γουνάτων τοῦ ἀνδρὸς ἐχρήιζε	1, 112, 2
κελεύειν	1, 163, 3
χρηστήρια φοβερά ...	7, 139, 6
ταῦτα ὑπισχόμενος	8, 4, 2 = ἐδέοντο 8, 120, 4

Yet cf. Hdt 3, 119, 3 κλαίεσκε ἂν καὶ ὀδυρέσκετο and Th 6, 88, 10 δεομένους πείθειν as examples of successful attempts.

[181] Without any further qualification Hdt 1, 154; 4, 98, 4; 6, 5, 2; Th 1, 14, 3; 58, 2; 111, 1; 2, 29, 5f.; 33, 1; etc. Plb 5, 54, 5; 7, 2, 1; 9, 5, 1; 21, 34, 13.

[182] Through bribery: Hdt 3, 152, 5; 4, 151, 3; etc. Th 1, 31, 1; 2, 96, 2; 4, 80, 13; 5, 16, 18; etc. Plb 3, 41, 7; 5, 60, 1; through deceit: Hdt 3, 72, 4; 155, 4; 4, 154, 2; Th 6, 46, 22; 8, 47, 1; Plb 5, 50, 11.

A special case is provided by the necessity of πείθειν ἀπάτῃ in the face of the περινοίος of the Athenians (= "the excess of an active mind, which not only sees all that is really to be seen in a subject, but fancies something more ... Thus the περινοία of the Athenians

conditions [183] are mentioned, then it emerges that in general the problematic πείθειν-situations are resolved when two elements are present :

(1) The speaker : the element of the clarification of an otherwise strange state of affairs—through giving sensible reasons.[184]
Thus the attempts at

i) are made by such as have knowledge [185] or at least claim to [186] and who can moreover speak "convincingly";[187]

ii) use rational [188] arguments.[189] Thus πείθειν declines to follow

consisted in an oversuspiciousness of the motives of public men, in a disbelief of human virtue"—so Th. Arnold, *The History of the Peloponnesian War*, vol. I, 1830, p. 486) in Th 3, 43. Here it was very difficult to get good counsels accepted because they were excessively inclined to suspect selfish motives in the speakers and reject the proposals out of hand.

[183] Th 5, 78, 2 καὶ ἐπειδὴ ἡ μάχη ἐγεγένητο, πολλῷ μᾶλλον ἐδύνατο πείθειν τοὺς πόλλους ἐς τὴν ὁμολογίαν as fear is very often a decisive factor and an important prerequisite; cf. ,e.g., Th 3, 75, 5; 101, 2, 8; 8, 44, 2; etc.

[184] Th sets great store by giving the reasons which should lead to πείθειν as exactly as possible, either before (e.g. 3, 81, 1; 7, 86, 4; 8, 27, 5) or after (e.g. 3, 75, 2; 8, 12, 1; 93, 2) or before and after (e.g. 5, 46, 2), introducing them with λέγων (6, 60, 3; 8, 12, 1), λέγοντες (2, 80, 1; 8, 93, 2), φάσκων (2, 85, 5) and νομίζων (1, 93, 3).
Example from Hdt : 3, 12 is a good example. Hdt is describing the difference in the hardness of the skulls of fallen Persians and Egyptians. The people there inform (ἔλεγον Impf.) him that the reason for the hardness of the Egyptians' skulls is that from childhood they go around with shaved heads and the bones would be hardened by the sun ... καὶ ἐμέ γε εὐπετέως ἔπειθον "and they easily convinced me". ἔπειθον plainly comes about here by the giving of what are for the questioner thoroughly sensible reasons. αἴτιον appears in all four times in this short section. Finally he says : ταῦτα μέν νυν τοιαῦτα. I.e. the giving of αἴτιον δὲ τούτου is the direct cause of the πείθειν. Similarly too in 5, 24. Example from Th : 7, 86, 5 καὶ ὁ μὲν τοιαύτη ἢ ὅτι ἐγγύτατα τούτων αἰτίᾳ ἐτεθνήκει (= πείσαντες ... ἀπέκτειναν αὐτόν [4]).

[185] Cf., e.g. Th 3, 102, 3 : Δημοσθένης ... προαισθόμενος τοῦ στρατοῦ ... 8, 12, 1 : γνοὺς δὲ ὁ 'Α' ... πείθει; Plb 5, 1, 8f. : συλλογισάμενος ... πείσ.

[186] Cf. Th 6, 33, 1 : πείθων γε ἐμαυτόν (a common rhetorical phrase : cf., e.g., And 1, 70; D 5, 3; 23, 19) σαφέστερόν τι ἑτέρου εἰδὼς λέγειν.

[187] Cf. Th 4, 21, 3 : ... κλεών ... ὢν τῷ πλήθει πιθανώτατος ... καὶ ἔπεισεν αὐτοὺς ... πιθανώτατος τοῖς πολλοῖς Th 3, 36, 6; 4, 21; 6, 65. Cf. Th 3, 42, 3 : the speaker who fails to convince does so because he ἀξύνετός ἐστίν. I.e. the presupposition for πείθειν is the speaker's being συνετός.

[188] Cf., e.g. Th 6, 76, 2. where Hermocrates characterizes the other side's attempt to persuade by saying : οὐ γὰρ δὴ εὔλογον τὰς ... εὔλογος = admitting of a rational explanation which may convince the hearer (cf. in the same speech the εὔλογος/ἄλογος antithesis in 79, 2 and on the lips of Euphemos in 84, 2-85, 1).

[189] Th 6, 86, 2; 2, 81 : λόγῳ πείθειν
    Th 5, 61, 3 : πείσαντες ἐν τῶν λόγων ...
    Th 3, 66 : λόγοις πείσειν ....

the way of κατὰ πλήσσειν τοῖς λόγοις and follows that of προσκαλεῖσθαι in the sense of "inviting discussion" and "verifying";[190] πείθειν thus comes about through "proof",[191] μετ'ἀποδείξεως πείθειν,[192] necessarily preceded by διδάσκειν,[193] as well as συνιστάνειν,[194] διατίθεσθαι,[195] ὑποδεικνύναι,[196] "reflection",[197] "counsel, reason,[198] in short διαλέγεσθαι;[199]

---

[190] Plb 12, 26d, 1. καταπλήσσειν τοῖς λόγοις (= strike with amazement, astound ... of orators Arist *Rh* 1408a, 25—L-S; in Erstaunen, Verwunderung setzen—Ps) may certainly ἀνάγκακε δ'αὐτῶ προσέχειν but only διὰ τὴν ἐπί φασιν τῆς ἀληθινολογίας. In contrast true πείθειν attempts, as it were, to "summon" the other "as a witness" (προσκαλεῖσθαι has this meaning as well as "summon", "call to oneself"); he himself should test whether the ἀποδείξεις adduced are sound or not.

[191] The ideal towards which all who attempt to πείθειν must strive is proof, i.e. achieving the limits of ἀκριβές and not "proving something not quite rigorously" (ἐντὸς τοῦ ἀκριβοῦς πείσαντά τινα). A. W. Gomme al. *A Historical Commentary on Thucydides* Vol IV, 1970, p. 165, tr.: "... (to persuade his judges or public opinion) even short of the exact limits".

[192] Cf., e.g., Plb 12, 26d, 1; 9, 27, 11 : ὁδὲ Μάρκος δοὺς πίστεις ὑπὲρ ἀσφαλείας ἔπεισεν.

[193] Πείθειν is preceded by διδάσκειν (= explanation περὶ τῶν πεπραγμένων): Th 3, 71, 2; 5, 27, 3. Apparently διδάσκειν should prepare the ground for πείθειν. For διδάσκειν and 5, 30, 1 διδάσκαλον γίγνεσθαι mean "counsels well supported by reasons" (cf. also 2, 93, 1; 4, 83, 3; 7, 18, 1; 8, 45, 2; Plb 5, 63, 3; etc.).

[194] Cf., e.g., Plb 28, 20 (21, 1 = συνιστάναι = hinstellen, darlegen, darthun, erweisen—Ps; exhibit, give proof of, prove, establish L-S).

[195] Cf., e.g., Plb 13, 7, 6 ... διετίθετο λόγους ... ὑποδεικνύων ... πείθειν ... διατίθεσθαι = seine Rede ordnen, in Ordnung darlegen, daher überhaupt eine Rede vortragen, halten (Ps). Also simply, as in e.g., 30, 2, 10 (διατιθέμενος → ἔπεισε), διατίθεσθαι propose, explain, expound.

[196] Cf., e.g., Plb 13, 7, 6; 4, 64, 2 : ... διετίθετο λόγους ... ὑποδεικνύων ... πείθειν ... ; ὑποδεικνύναι = beweisen, darthun (Ps); show, indicate, teach (L-S).

[197] Πείθειν comes about through ἐδίδοσαν σφίσι λόγον = to deliberate Hdt 1, 97, 3.

[198] 1) Πείθειν comes about through συμβουλεύειν; cf. 7, 173, 4, where gradually (Impf. ἐπείθοντο) conviction (cf. τὸ πεῖθον) came about through συμβουλεύειν (here three times in quick succession)—so also in 5, 36, 2; 4, 83, 2; to Hdt' mind it was ἀρρωδίη. 2) Πείθειν comes about through (πολλάκις) παρηγορεῖσθαι = to counsel, to advise, to reason: 5, 104; 9, 55, 1 (where ἐπειρῶντο πείθοντες in 53, 4 is picked up by παρηγορέοντο τὸν ...) and is identical with ἐνάγειν = to urge, to persuade: 5, 104; cf. also 3, 1; 4, 79, 145; 5, 49, 90.

[199] Cf., e.g., Th 8, 93, 2 ... διελέγοντό τε καὶ ἔπειθον ...

Plb 3, 98, 11; 18, 9, 2.4f : διαλεχθεὶς ἔπεισε ...

4, 29, 3 : ... ... διελέγετο περὶ ... ἔπεισε ...

4, 64, 2 : ... διελέγοντο κατὰ τὰς ἐντολάς καὶ ... ἔπειθον ...

28, 20, 10 : ... διαλεχθεὶς καὶ πείσας ...

iii) are directed above all at man's reason [200] since they seek his voluntary assent;[201] often a μεταγινώσκειν [202] must be asked of him if the ἀναγνωσθέντες [203] is to be possible.

(2) The person addressed : The element of readiness [204] to scrutinize for oneself such explanations as are given [205]—often by means of reminding [206] and remembering.[207] One is not convinced by "incre-

---

[200] Cf. Th 8, 93, 2 : ἐλθόντες ... τινὲς ... πρὸς αὐτοὺς ... καὶ ἔπειθον οὓς ἴδοιεν ἀνθρώπους ἐπιεικεῖς αὐτούς ... ; Th 4, 17, 3 : λάβετε δὲ αὐτοὺς (= τοὺς λόγους) ... μηδ' ὡς ἀξύνετοι διδασκόμενοι. I.e. the Athenians should put out of their minds the idea (which has apparently occured to them) that the envoys wanted to teach them as if they were fools.

[201] 1) A good example is Th 5, 18, 5 : ἢν δὲ Ἀθηναῖοι πείθωσι τὰς πόλεις βουλομένας ταύτας ἐξέστω ξυμμάχους ποιεῖσθαι αὐτοῖς Ἀθηναίους. I.e. πείθειν is meant to convince the other in such a way that he is under no compulsion. Cf. also, e.g. Th 4, 67, 3 ; 78, 2 ; 7, 43, 1.
2) Cf. on the contrast "persuade—force" :
Th 2, 81, 2 εἰ μὴ λόγῳ πείθοιεν ἔργῳ πειρῶντο τοῦ τείχους ...
3, 66, 2 μήτε νεωτερίσαι ἔργῳ λόγοις τε πείθειν ...
4, 38, 4 πείθων-κολάζων
87, 2 οὐ πείθω-πειράσομαι/βιάζεσθαι
Hdt 3, 138, 3 ... ἔπειθον, βίην δὲ ἀδύνατοι ἦσαν.

[202] Th 4, 92, 2.

[203] Hdt 4, 154, 2.

[204] Cf. Th 8, 32, 1 : καὶ αὐτὸν μὲν πείθουσιν ὡς δ' οἵ τε Κορίνθιοι καὶ οἱ ἄλλοι ξύμμαχοι ἀπρόθυμοι ἦσαν .... Apparently the πρόθυμος here is the presupposition for the πείθειν. So also in 6, 88, 8 (πάσῃ προθυμίᾳ) and 4, 17, 3 : λάβετε δὲ αὐτοὺς (= τοὺς λόγους) μὴ πολεμιώς (= in a hostile spirit; so also 3, 59, 1 ; 6, 53, 3).

[205] We find a good example of the hearer's own controling contribution to the whole event of πείθειν in Hdt 2, 150, 2. Hdt asks the inhabitants how the excavated masses of earth in the Nile delta had been transported : οἱ δὲ ἔφρασάν μοι ἵνα ἐξεφορήθη, καὶ εὐπετέως ἔπειθον (aor. ἔφρασαν). Why?—γὰρ λόγῳ καὶ ἐν Νίνῳ τῇ πόλει, γενόμενον ἕτερον τοιοῦτον. I.e. simply that the hearer himself could verify the correctness of the answer given.
Th 3, 36, 5 : καὶ ἔπεισαν ῥᾷον, διότι καὶ ἐκείνοις εὔδηλον ἦν (εὔδηλον εἶναι with part. like 2, 64, 6). A similar sequence of thought appears in Th 6, 33, 1 ... καὶ γιγνώσκω ὅτι οἱ τὰ μὴ πιστὰ δοκοῦντα εἶναι ἢ λέγοντες ἢ ἀπαγγέλλοντες οὐ μόνον οὐ πείθουσιν, ἀλλὰ καὶ ἄφρονες δοκοῦσιν εἶναι.

[206] Cf., e.g., Th 6, 87, 1 : ... καὶ ἔτι ἐν κεφαλαίοις ὑπομνήσαντες ἀξιώσομεν πείθειν.

[207] Πείθειν constantly recurs in the modus of "calling to remembrance" : Th 4, 17, 3 ὑπόμνησιν ... πρὸς εἰδότας forms together the predicate to τοὺς λόγους ἡγησάμενοι "regard our speech only as a reminder of the right way to decide for the benefit of men who know it well (and have perhaps now only lost sight of it)". Cf. also Th 1, 72, 1 where ὑπόμνησιν ποιήσασθαι τοῖς ... πρεσβυτέροις ὧν ᾔδεσαν—and that for the purpose ὅπως μὴ ῥᾳδίως περὶ μεγάλων πραγμάτων τοῖς ξυν ..., πειθόμ. (73, 1). Th 4, 92, 7 : 1) μνησθέντας ἡμᾶς and 2) πιστεύσαντες δὲ τῷ θεῷ together bring it about that τοιαῦτα ὁ Πάγ. τ. παρ. ἔπει (4, 93, 1).

dible" stories even if the narrator swears to their truth.[208] The individual destination of the process of πείθειν evidenced here [209] is echoed by the usage which occurs for the first time in Hdt of the rendering of the reflexive middle by the active with "oneself" as object.[210] The essentially dialogic [211] character of every case of real πείθειν, which often requires considerable time,[212] is indicated not only when either different rival groups (all of whom one must give a hearing if one is to decide aright [213] try to persuade [214] or when

[208] Hdt 4, 105, 2.

[209] Cf., e.g., Th 8, 93, 2 : ἐλθόντες ... τίνες ... πρὸς αὐτοὺς ἀνὴρ ἀνδρὶ διελέγοντό τε καὶ ἔπειθον ; 4, 91 : προσκαλῶν ἑκάστους κατὰ λόχους ... ἔπειθε ...

Plb 4, 64, 2 : the king's reaction to the envoys' attempt at persuasion is 1) he listens to it carefully or till its end (διακούειν) and 2) he promises βουλεύεσθαι περὶ τῶν παρακαλουμένων

[210] Hdt 1, 97, 3 : ταῦτα ... λέγοντες πείθουσι ἑωυτοὺς βασιλεύεσθαι (cf. S II 198 δ : πείθουσι is a hist. pres., replacing the past tense, without being affected by the nature of the action). This is preceded by συνελέχθησαν οἱ Μῆδοι ἐς τὠυτὸ καὶ ἐδίδοσαν σφίσι λόγον, λέγοντες περὶ τῶν κατηκόντων. In the following passage the chief arguments are then briefly mentioned which finally led them to conviction. Cf. also Th 8, 37, 3 ; 4, 22 ; Plb 9, 24, 7 ; 12, 25e, 4.

[211] In addition to n. 25 cf. Th 5, 35, 7 : πολλάκις δὲ καὶ πολλῶν λόγων γενομένων ... ἔπεισαν τοὺς ....

5, 27, 55 : καὶ ... τοὺς λόγους εἶναι ... πείσαντας. (cf. 3, 80, 1).

[212] What is new in Hdt is that πείθειν does not always have to have a sense of a completed action—"persuade", "convince"—, but can also have an inceptive or durative one—"exhort", "talk over with a person" (hitherto the pres. indic. of πείθειν was only used in the former sense; pace B-T 558 n., where it seems to be assumed that both senses are already possible in Homer). Some examples : Hdt 1, 123, 2 ; 2, 152, 5 (πείθει-ἔπεισε) ; 3, 145, 2 (λοιδορεών-κακίζων-λέγων are durative participles which go with ἀνέπειθε) ; 4, 154, 2 ; 5, 63, 1 (κατήμενοι ἀνέπειθον) ; 104, 2 (which tells of a certain Onesilos who often urged Gorgos—πολλάκις ... παρηγορέετο—to rebel against the Great King. When he heard of the Ionians' revolt—τότε δὲ ... πάγχυ ἐπικείμενος ἐν ἦγε—he tried even more to make him rebel ;—ὡς δὲ οὐκ ἔπειθε τὸν Γ.—. But when his repeated attempts at persuasion were of no avail ...further on : ἦρχε ..., he continued his dominion over Salamis καὶ ἀνέπειθε πάντας Κυπρίους συναπίστασθαι and urged all the Cypriots, tried to persuade them—one after the other—to revolt with him ; τοὺς μὲν δὴ ἄλλους ἀνέπεισε he persuaded most of them. His success is expressed by the aor.) ; 6, 23, 2 ; cf. also 7, 173, 4 (ὡς ... συνεβούλευον ... "when they—the Greeks—took counsel—impf. of duration—they were gradually persuaded"—ἐπείθοντο. But Hdt comments : "But to my mind fear was the argument which—gradually—persuaded them"). Th expresses basically the same idea when he says : νομίζω δὲ δύο τὰ ἐναντιώτατα εὐβουλίᾳ εἶναι, τάχος τε καὶ ὀργήν ὧν τὸ μὲν μετὰ ἀνοίας φιλεῖ γίγνεσθαι (3, 42, 1). Cf. also 5, 35, 7 : πολλάκις δὲ καὶ πολλῶν λόγων γενομένων ... ἔπεισαν τοὺς and in 3, 66 νεωτερίσαι ... πείσειν ...

[213] Th 6, 76, 1 ... δείσαντες ... ἐπρεσβευσάμεθα ... τοὺς μέλλοντας ἀπ'αὐτῶν λόγους, πρίν τι καὶ ἡμῶν ἀκοῦσαι, μὴ ὑμᾶς πείσωσιν.

[214] Th 4, 58, 1 ξυνελθόντες ἐς Γέλαν ... ἐς λόγους κατέστησαν ἀλλήλοις ... καὶ ἄλλαι

speakers tackle the recriminations [215] and arguments of their hearers [216] and must arrive at a συμφώνους γενέσθαι περὶ τῶν ἀντιλεγομένων,[217] but also when possible counterarguments which might impede the process of πείθειν [218] are faced in advance in the course of one's own argument or speech.[219]

πείθειν in the Attic orators [220]

D) *Legal Speeches* [221]

In the context of legal speeches that which is meant by πείθειν [222]

τε πολλαὶ γνῶμαι ἐλέγοντο επ'ἀμφότερα ... 3, 36, 6 καταστάσης δ'εὐθὺς ἐκκλησίας ἄλλαι τε γνῶμαι ἀφ'ἑκάστων ...

[215] Cf., e.g., Plb 18, 9, 2.

[216] Th 5, 76, 3 : καὶ γενομένης πολλῆς ἀντιλογίας ... οἱ ἄνδρες ... ἔπεισαν. The attempt at πείθειν produces ἀντιλέγειν : Plb 9, 24, 7 and in Plb 39, 3, 5 διδάσκειν καὶ πείθειν occur ὑπὲρ τῶν ἀμφισβητουμένων.

Th 8, 6, 2 : The attempt at πείθειν takes place amidst πολλὴ ἅμιλλα of the two sides : οἱ μὲν ... οἱ δὲ ....

[217] Plb 18, 9, 5. The result of πείθειν in Th 5, 76, 3 and 8, 6, 2 is : προσεδέξαντο ... τὰ τῶν ....

[218] Th 3, 102, 3; Plb 5, 54, 11.

[219] Cf., e.g., Th 2, 44, 2, where Pericles, in his speech which begins at paragraph 35, takes up the two arguments which impede πείθειν, namely the ὑπομνήματα, and the λύπη. Much as men are aware that they are ἐν πολὺ τρόποις ξυμφοραῖς τραφέντες, and convincingly as one can also show that the present λύπη is εὐπρεπεστάτη, yet convincing them is χαλεπόν.

[220] 1) For ancient sources and for texts and tools for the Attic Orators s.v. Bibliography.

2) Important more recent literature : F. Blass, Die attische Beredsamkeit, 1887-1898; R. C. Jebb, The Attic Orators from Antiphon to Isaeus, 1893; J. F. Dobson, The Greek Orators, 1919; The Cambridge Ancient History, vol. vii; G. Kennedy, The Art of Persuasion in Greece, 1963.

3) The works of the following orators are referred to : Antipho (ca 480-411 BC); Lysias (ca 459-380 BC); Andocides (ca 440-390 BC); Isocrates (436-338 BC); Isaeus (ca 420-350 BC); Aeschines (ca 397-322 BC); Lycurgus (ca 390-325 BC); Hyperides (389-322 BC); Demosthenes (384-322 BC); Dinarchus (ca 360-290 BC); nothing by Demades has been preserved (the speech ὑπὲρ τῆς δωδεκαετίας is not by him).

[221] Under this head come

1) all speeches of Antipho
2) all speeches of Lys, except 2 and 33
3) And 1
4) Isoc 16-19
5) all speeches of Is
6) all speeches of Hyp
7) D 27-59.

is used in the attempts of accusers [223] and accused [224] to persuade the
ἄνδρες δικασταί in the δικαστηρίῳ so that above all ἡ ἀλήθεια ...
γίγνεται φανερά [225] and so λαβεῖν δίκην.[226] Thus πείθειν has its "Sitz
im Leben" in the sphere of the workings of the νόμος and is a valuable
asset in the proceedings in the court. πείθειν here has nothing to do
with dilettante intellectual games but has a judicial character : its
task is no less than to show forth truth as truth and not as falsehood,
and falsehood as falsehood and not as truth (... χρή ... ἢ τἀληθῆ
πιστὰ ἢ τὰ μὴ ἀληθῆ ἄπιστα ποεῖν ...[227]. The seriousness of this judicial
character is further increased by the fact that πείθειν thus stands in
the closest possible relation either to σώζειν/σώζεσθαι/σωτηρία or
to ἀπολλύσθαι.[228] It should help to bring about the former and prevent
the latter. Hence the large number or attempts at πείθειν by bribing
either the accusers or the witnesses is not surprising.[229] But that
need not trouble us any longer here.

Aeschin and Din ("Against Demosthenes") come under political speeches (cf. chapter
E). There are no πείθειν-passages in Lycurg.

[222] In the orators πείθειν is chiefly a t.t. of the courts and hence is most frequently
used in this context. Apart from that πείθειν often appears in an indirect association
with the judicial processes (e.g. Antipho 6, 23.34.35; And 1, 17.19.120f.; 2, 7; Isoc 17,
29.39; 18, 12; Lys 9, 7; 13, 18; 30, 11; 32, 2; D 29, 58; 30, 2; 33, 7; 36, 15; 37, 11.13.
27; etc.), while the remaining occurrences conform to the patterns of earlier usage (cf.,
e.g., Antipho 1, 22; 5, 21; And 4, 17; Isoc 16, 20.21; 18, 60). Here too, as in earlier
works, we can characterize πείθειν more exactly with respect to its opposites (the opposites
of πείθειν are βιάζεσθαι : Lys 1, 32.33; λόγῳ πείσας - κατὰ κράτος εἷλεν : Isoc 16, 21;
λόγῳ πεῖσαι - βίᾳ κρατεῖσθαι : Lys 2, 19; πείθειν with its own form of action is favourably
contrasted in Lys 18, 2 : οὐ βουλόμενος ἀλλ' ἄκων ἠναγκάσθη ποιῆσαι ... πείσαντες ὑμᾶς.

[223] Cf., e.g., Antipho 2, 2, 11; 4, 1, 4; 2, 7; 5, 16, 94f.; 6, 47; Lys 12, 7; 24, 12.14.
18.22; 25, 1.26; And 1, 72; Isoc 16, 9; 19, 15; Is 1, 26.48; 3, 77; D 29, 27; 34, 46;—
κατήγοροι, τῇ κατηγορίᾳ χρῆσθαι, διωκεῖν ... διώκων, ἐπεξέρχεσθαι ;

[224] Cf., e.g., Antipho 1, 23; 2, 2, 11; 6, 14; Lys 14, 20; And 1, 29; etc.—διοκομένος :
φεύγων, φεύγοντες, ἀπολογεῖσθαι, ἀπολογία.

[225] D 36, 17.

[226] Cf., e.g., D 35, 47; δίκην (δίκας) δοῦναι καὶ λαβεῖν (δέχεσθαι) = seine Streitig-
keiten, Rechtshändel führen und entscheiden lassen (Ps).

[227] Antipho 6, 29.

[228] This is true of all orators; cf., e.g., Antipho 1, 8.25; 2, 1.3; 5, 2; etc.

[229] Antipho 5, 50 (through the offer of ἐλευθερία). 56 κατα-ψεύδεσθαί μου; Lys 7, 18.
21; 12, 7 (ἔπεισαν would also be correct here; but here we have the impf. : giving advice
was not hard for them); 20, 10; 26, 7; 30, 34; 31, 32; And 1, 65.120f.; Isoc 17, 12.23.
34f.; D 30, 23; cf. also Hyp 1, 14, 18 (μήτε πεῖσαι ἔστιν μήτε χρήμασιν διαφθείραι); Lys
2, 29 (successful πείθειν through κέρδος καὶ δέος) ; 19, 22 (... ἔπειθε δεόμενος καὶ
ἐγγυώμενος ...—impf. because not everywhere successful); Is 8, 37 (ἔπειθε ... παράγων
ἄνδρα πρεσβύτερον θεραπείαις καὶ κολακείαις ...).

But if πείθειν is in the service of truth itself and its verification
and if it thus belongs to the sphere of the working of the law and its
application to men, then it can be said that ἐμοὶ περὶ πλείστου ἐστὶν
ὑμᾶς πεῖσαι.[230] For ὅπου μὴ πείθων ... ὑμᾶς αυτὸς ζημιώσομαι ...[231].
How can this πείθειν come about? That is to ask after the proper
form of πείθειν if all else is but the assertions and denials (ἀρνεῖσθαι) [232]
that are incidental to "telling the truth". But if πείθειν gets its real
character from its position in the service of truth and the law, then
the proper form of πείθειν is for the most part discernible against the
background of man's capacities.

On the part of the speakers an essential prerequisite is that they
should know how to speak.[233] A more precise description of such an
ability is the subject of continual discussion, but this does not in the
last analysis affect the fundamental point: one must have the gift of
speaking; one must know how to convince with "arguments".[234]
One owes that to the truth. For without this "convincing by arguments" one is of no use to the truth or to the law—or to oneself. But
what guarantee is there that the gift of speaking will be used really
to reveal the truth rather than to suppress it? [235] What assurance has
one that πείθειν will be found among those λέγοντες τἀληθῆ and not
among those ἐξαπατῶντες τῷ λόγῳ? [236]

On the part of the persons addressed an essential prerequisite is that
they practise προσέχειν τὸν νοῦν [237] and that they are εὖ φρονοῦντες

---

230 And 1, 29.

231 *Ibid.*

232 Cf., e.g., And 1, 30: δῆλον γὰρ ὅτι τοῖς μὲν ἡμαρτηκόσι τὰ τοιαῦτα ἁμαρτήματα οὐκ
ἔστιν ἀπολογία ὡς οὐκ ἐποίησαν.

233 Cf., e.g., Isoc 18, 21; 19, 15; etc.; Lys 25, 1f.; etc.

234 And not with prayers and supplications as does occasionally happen (e.g. And
1, 17.19), but which is not regarded as appropriate to the situation (cf., e.g., And 1,
30: ἐμοὶ δὲ ὁ ἔλεγχος ἥδιστος ἐν οἷς ὑμῶν οὐδὲν με δεῖ δεόμενον, οὐδὲ παραιτούμενον
σωθῆναι ἐπὶ τῇ τοιαυτῃ αἰτίᾳ ...).

235 Cf., e.g., D 37, 12 καὶ οὐδὲν ἦν ἁπλοῦν οὐδ'ὑγιὲς τούτων 41, 15 ἀλλὰ δῆλον ὅτι
τούτῳ ... οὐκ ἐλυσιτέλει, φανερῶς ὑπ'αὐτῶν ἐξελεγχόμενω ...

236 Also amidst διαβάλλειν (cf., e.g., D 29, 27), or ψεύδεσθαι or καταψεύδεσθαι or among
ψευδῆ λέγοντες (cf. D 29, 57; etc.).

237 Ps.: den Geist, die Aufmerksamkeit auf eine Person oder Sache wenden ...;
L-S: to turn one's mind, attention to ... to be intent on ...; often simply just προσέχειν;
cf., e.g., Antipho 3, 4, 1; 4, 1, 5; 5, 31; 6, 14, 12; Lycurg 10.75.108; Din 1, 83; Isoc 17,
24; etc.

and εὖ νοοῦντες [238] and are opposed [239] to all ἄνοια [240] and συμφορὰ τῶν φρενῶν.[241] But what conditions must be fulfilled if a πιστεύειν τοῖς λόγοις [242] is to be attained in them?

It is within this structure that we have delineated that πείθειν qua "bringing the truth to light" occurs. On the connection of "speaking the truth" and "convincing with arguments" we need only say this much, that though one knows well that σώζεσθαι/ἀπολλύσθαι in court ought only be achieved through "speaking the truth", yet one is at the same time conscious that the truth, which should have led to σωτηρία, often brought ἀπολλύσθαι instead—and *vice versa*. And this just because the speaker was not able to present the truth *in a convincing fashion*.[243] This experience led in the course of time to the development of two quite distinct methods of argument which were clearly brought into the sphere of the concept of πείθειν. Both should serve to bridge the gap between mere "speaking the truth" on the one hand and "convincing by the truth" on the other.[244]

The one, more a defensive argument, is the constantly emphasized incapacity of a man really to practise this "convincing with arguments",[245]

---

[238] Cf., e.g., Is 2, 14f.; etc.

φρονέω = Ps.: (b) denken ... ὁ φρονῶν = φρόνιμος ... Gewöhnlich steht dann εὖ dabei, klug seyn ... = σωφρονεῖν ... bei Sinnen seyn ...

νοέω im Part. act., verständig, einsichtsvoll, bedachtsam, überlegend, mit Überlegung; L-S: νοῶν καὶ φρονῶν sane and in his right mind ...

[239] Cf. And 2, 7 (admittedly not a court setting but still relevant to an investigation of the elements in the meaning of πείθειν).

[240] Ps.: Unverstand, Unsinn, Unvernunft; Unüberlegtheit, Gedankenlosigkeit, Unbesonnenheit.

[241] Ps.: Krankheit der Sinne, des Verstandes.

[242] Here synonymous with "being convinced by arguments" (cf. Is 1, 50).

[243] Cf., e.g., Antipho 5, 3: πολλοὶ μὲν γὰρ ἤδη τῶν οὐ δυναμένων λέγειν, ἄπιστοι γενόμενοι τοῖς ἀληθέσιν, αὐτοῖς τούτοις ἀπώλοντο, οὐ δυνάμενοι δηλῶσαι αὐτά ...

[244] This gap is well marked out, e.g., in And 1, 72: ... ὅπου μὴ πείθων μὲν ... πείσας δὲ ... ἀλλὰ γὰρ τἀληθῆ εἰρήσεται.

[245] There is plenty of evidence of this. Here we only give some examples:

Antipho 1, 1 Νέος μὲν καὶ ἄπειρος ... ἔγωγε ἔτι ... (ἄπειρος Ps.: unerfahren, unkundig, der in od. von etwas noch keine Erfahrung hat, mit etwas noch nicht zu thun gehabt hat, der mit etwas nicht umzugehen, sich in etwas nicht zu finden weiss, ungeübt, ungeschickt ... unbewandert seyn in etwas, unbekannt seyn mit etwas ...);

Antipho 5, 1: with regard to ἡ δύναμις τοῦ λέγειν ... ἐνδεής εἰμι ...

5, 2: ἡ τοῦ λέγειν ἀδυνασία (= ἡ ἀδυναμία, ἀδυνατία ... τοῦ λέγειν -) βλάπτει με...

5, 5: ... ἐάν τι τῇ γλώσσῃ ἁμάρτω ... then through ἀπειρίᾳ, whereas ἔαν τι ὀρθῶς εἴπω, ... then through ἀληθείᾳ, not δεινότητι ...

Lys 17, 1: ἐγὼ δὲ τοσούτου δέω ... ἱκανὸς εἶναι λέγειν ... 19, 1: in a case of ἀνάγκη which he contrasts with his opponent's[246] display of (too) much confidence in the power of his own speaking.[247]

The other, more a polemical argument, really consists in two different methods whose purpose is to come, despite the above mentioned incapacity, as near as possible to the ideal of "convincing by the truth"—and that means in situations of ἀνάγκη.[248] The spirit that is revealed in such attempts at εὖ λέγειν and πείθειν can be alluded to with the words ... οὕτως ὅπως ἂν δύνωμαι[249] and is diametrically opposed to πιστεύειν τῷ λέγειν.[250]

The one possibility is the practice of recollection which binds speaker and hearer together in a common knowledge.[251] This can, of course, only apply in those cases and events which are and were generally known or should be known.[252] Here the power to convince should be gained by reminding the hearers

1) of the public nature of the event in question and the activity of the accused;[253]

2) of the accused's conduct in his previous career;[254] and

---

one must try to εὖ λέγειν, εἰ καὶ μὴ δεινὸς πρὸς ταῦτα πέφυκα, βοηθεῖν ... οὕτως ὅπως ἂν δύνωμαι ...

Hyp 1, 20 : ἰδιώτῃ δὲ καὶ οὐκ εἰωθότι λέγειν ...

[246] Antipho 3, 2, 2 ; 5, 3 : οἱ λέγειν δυνάμενοι ... Through their gifts of speaking these are able, not only πιστοὶ γενόμενοι τῷ ψεύδεσθαι, but also to use ἡ δόξα τῶν πραχθέντων (as opposed to ἡ ἀλήθεια) to their own advantage. Hyp 1, 19 : ἐπειδὴ δὲ ὁ κατήγορος οὐκ ἀπείρως ἔχων τοῦ λέγειν, εἰωθὼς δὲ πολλάκις ἀγωνίζεσθαι .... But one can also accuse them and say (Lys 25, 2) : ... ἀδυνάτους αὐτοὺς ἡγοῦμαι λέγειν ...

[247] Often attested; cf., e.g., D 35, 42 : ... ἐπεὶ δ'οὖν δεινός ἐστι καὶ πιστεύει τῷ λέγειν ...

[248] For, according to Antipho 5, 2, it is true that ἡ τοῦ λέγειν δυνασία is necessary if one σωθῆναι μετὰ τῆς ἀληθείας εἰπόντα τὰ γενόμενα ...

[249] Lys 19, 1.

[250] Cf. n. 247.

[251] Legal oratory really lived by the idea of 1) μιμνήσκειν (Ps : erinnern, mahnen) and μιμνήσκεσθαι (Ps : sich erinnern, eingedenk seyn, gedenken), 2) ἀναμιμνήσκειν (Ps : Jemanden an etwas erinnern, Pass. : sich erinnern ; L-S : remind one of a thing ... recall to memory, make mention of ...), 3) ὑπομιμνήσκειν (Ps : Einen woran gedenken machen, Einen erinnern, etwas ins Gedächtnis rufen; Pass. : eingedenk seyn, sich woran erinnern ...).

[252] Cf. Aeschin 1, 44 : the rule is ἀναμνῆσαι ... μόνον προσήκει τοὺς ἀκού ...

[253] Cf., e.g., Antipho 6, 19 : τὰ πραχθέντα φανερῶς ἅπαντα πραχθῆναι καὶ ἐναντίον μαρτύρων πολλῶν ; 6, 45 ; the opposite in Antipho 1, 28 : the ἐπιβουλεύοντες do not act μαρτύρων ἐναντίον, ἀλλ'ὡς μάλιστα δύναται λαθραιότατα καὶ ὡς ἀνθρώπων ... cf. D 41, 14 too.

[254] The rule given here is (Antipho 6, 46) οἱ ... ἄνθρωποι τοῖς ἔργοις τοὺς λόγους ἐξελέγχουσιν—or also (Hyp 1, 14) ὁ παρεληλυθὼς χρόνος μάρτυς ἐστὶν ἑκάστῳ τοῦ τρόπου ἀκρι-

3) of their knowledge and insight which comes from 1) and 2) and which they in fact already have.[255]

Such "reminding" serves to give true πείθειν its form. For true πείθειν can only come through the kind of thinking implicit in all reminding and never apart from it.

The other possibility is to formulate valid proofs for events which were not obvious to all and could not be shown to be obvious through a reminder.[256] Then everything depends on one's making the best of one's own knowledge.[257] For this purpose one can make use of

1) δεικνύναι [258]
2) ἐπιδεικνύναι [259]
3) ἀποδεινύναι [260]

βέστατος. Hence Antipho 2, 2, 12 : ἐμὲ δὲ ἔκ γε τῶν προειργασμένων γνώσεσθε οὔτε ... This is followed by a list. And 1, 67 : τῶν δὲ γενομένων ἕνεκα εἰκότως [ἂν] ἀνὴρ ἄριστος δοκοίην εἶναι ... ; Lys 19, 19 : γνώσεσθε δὲ ὅτι ἀληθῆ λέγω ἐξ αὐτῶν ὧν ἐκεῖνος ἔπραττε ... 23, 14 : ἐξ ὧν ἔπραξε ... cf. also 16, 1f.; 21, 1; Aeschin 1, 122 : ... καὶ πεπιστευκότος τῷ βίῳ ......; Hyp 1, 14 : ... ὑμᾶς δ᾽οἶμαι δεῖν οὐκἐκ τῶν τοῦ κατηγόρου διαβολῶν περὶ ἐμοῦ δικάζειν, ἀλλ᾽ἐξ ἅπαντος τοῦ βίου ὃν βεβίωκα ἐξετάσαντας.

255 Cf., e.g., Antipho 6, 14 : πολλοὶ, τῶν περιεστώτων τούτων τὰ μὲν πράγματα ταῦτα πάντα ἀκριβῶς ἐπίστανται ...; And 1, 30 : ... με δεῖ ... ὑμᾶς ἀναμιμνήσκοντα τὰ γεγενή-μενα ... ; Lys 7, 18 : οἳ οὐ μόνον ἀλλήλων ταῦτ᾽ἴσασιν ἃ πᾶσιν ὁρᾶν ἔξεστιν, ἀλλὰ καὶ περὶ ... ἐκείνων πυνθάνονται ...

I.e. Deceitful πείθειν is impossible if the hearers are informed and know about it. This can also be expressed by one's saying (Lys 24, 14) : ὑμεῖς δὲ ·ὃ τῶν εὖ φρονούντων ἔργον ἐστί· μᾶλλον πιστεύετε τοῖς ὑμετέροις αὐτῶν ὀφθαλμοῖς ἢ τοῖς τούτου λόγοις. Aeschin 1, 93 : τὸ πρᾶγμα θεωρεῖτε μὴ ἐκ τοῦ παρόντος, ἀλλ᾽ἐκ τοῦ παρεληλυθότος χρόνου ...; D 40, 11 ὡς καὶ ὑμῶν οἱ πολλοὶ ἴσασι. 45, 33 : ἴστε γὰρ πάντες ...; Is 1, 26 : ... πᾶσι δήπου φανερὸν ὑμῖν ἐστιν ὅτι .... Hyp 1, 4 : ... ῥάδιον [·οἶμαι] εἶναι ἅπασιν ἰδεῖν.

256 Cf. Aeschin 1, 44. The rule is σαφεῖς ... προσήκει τὰς ἀποδείξεις ποιεῖσθαι ... ἡ ἀπόδειξις; Ps : Nachweisung, Darlegung, bes. Darlegung der Gründe; dah. theils voll-ständige und genauere Auseinandersetzung, Beweisführung ... theils der geführte Beweis selbst ... die Demonstration ... und die daraus sich ergebende Conclusion.

257 Cf., e.g., Antipho 2, 1, 3 : ἂν δυνώμεθα σαφέστατα ἐξ ὧν γιγνώσκομεν πειρασόμεθα, ὑμῖν δηλοῦν ὡς ... D 49, 5 : θαυμάσῃ δὲ μηδεὶς ὑμῶν εἰ ἀκριβῶς ἴσμεν ...

258 Ps : zeigen, d.h. i) sichtbar machen, zum Vorschein bringen ... ii) zeigen, wo und wie etwas ist, aufzeigen, vorzeigen, usw ... Einem etwas zeigen, d.h. ihn darüber belehren, es ihm begreiflich machen ... Daher von Anklägern = ἐνδεικνύναι ... Dah. überh. nachweisen, beweisen ... dah. δέδεικται es ist erwiesen ...

259 Ps : zeigen, nachweisen ... beweisen dass ... Mit d. Acc. d. Part ... nachweisen, dass ...; Med/Pass : Zeigen, nachweisen ...; L-S : show, point out ... prove that; cf., e.g., Antipho 1, 3; 5, 19.61; 4, 2, 7; Isoc 16, 37.7.11.25; 17, 54.3.3; 18, 54.31.41.56; etc.

260 Ps : vorzeigen, aufzeigen, nachweisen ... eine Behauptung erweisen; L-S : point out, display, make known ... show by argument, prove ...

4) ἐνδεικνύναι [261]

5) διδάσκειν [262]

6) δηλοῦν [263]

7) διηγεῖσθαι [264]

8) ἐλέγχειν [265]

9 ἀπελέγχειν [266]

10) ἐξελέγχειν [267]

11) ὁ ἔλεγχος [268]

12) ἀποφαίνειν [269]

13) ἐξετάζειν [270]

14) the argument that something is εἰκός, happens εἰκότως, κατὰ τὸ εἰκός, ἐκ τοῦ εἰκότος, ἀπὸ τῶν εἰκότων, ἔστι οὐκ ἀπεικός [271]

---

[261] Ps : anzeigen, bemerklich machen ... nachweisen ... Med : sich oder etwas von sich zeigen, darauf hinweisen ... beweisen, deutlich machen ...

[262] Ps : Klar und verständig auseinandersetzen, darstellen, ... beweisen, darthun ...; Pass; unterrichtet, in Kenntnis gesetzt werden ...; L-S : explain ... show by argument, prove ...; e.g. Antipho 2, 2, 9; 4, 2, 8, where ὑμᾶς ... πείθοντες ... (7) should result from διὰ τὸ ... ὀρθῶς ὑμᾶς διδαχθῆναι (8); 2, 2, 9-11 : διδάξω is followed by ὑμᾶς πείθων (11); And 1, 72 : ... ἐγὼ ὑμᾶς διδάξω ... ὅπου μὴ πείθων ...; Lys 9, 7 : ἔπειθον αὐτοὺς ... διδάσκοντες ὡς οὐκ ἐπιεικὲς εἴη ...; D 35, 43 : ... διδάξαι ὑμᾶς ... πεισάτω ὑμᾶς ... οὔτε διδάξαι οὔτε πεῖσαι; Is 1, 48 : ... καὶ πειρῶνται πείθειν ὑμᾶς ... οὐχ ὡς δίκαιόν ἐστι τὸ πρᾶγμα διδάσκουσιν ὑμᾶς.

[263] Ps : offenbaren, offenbar od. sichtbar machen, deutlich oder bekannt machen, erklären, darstellen, darthun, beweisen, zeigen ...

[264] Ps : auseinander setzen, erzählen, vortragen, erklären; L-S : set out in detail, describe ...; cf., e.g., Antipho 1, 13.18.31; 6, 8: etc.

[265] Ps : überweisen, überführen ... widerlegen ...; Med/Pass : überführt, widerlegt werden ... Überh. beweisen, erweisen ...; L-S : cross-examine, question; test, bring to the proof ... prove ... bring convincing proof ...; cf., e.g., Antipho 2, 4, 10; 3, 5.; etc

[266] Ps : überführen, von Grund aus widerlegen, verstärktes ἐλέγχω. L-S : strengthd. for ἐλέγχω, convict, expose, refute ... procure a conviction ... vindicate; cf., e.g., Antipho 5, 19.36; etc.

[267] Ps : verstärktes ἐλέγχω überweisen, überführen, (durch richtige Darstellung der Sache) widerlegen ... Mit d. Acc. d. Sache : an den Tag bringen, erweisen ...; cf., e.g., Antipho 2, 2, 2; 1, 10; 1, 9,; etc.

[268] Ps : 1) Beweis ... Bes. Beweis od. Aufzählung der Beweise, um einen zu überführen ... zuwiderlegen ...; cf., e.g., Antipho 1, 7.12; etc.

[269] Ps : aufzeigen, aufdecken, vorzeigen, ans Licht bringen, sichtbar machen, kundthun, sowohl durch die That, als durch die Rede; dah. a) Verborgenes od. Geheimes ans Licht bringen; entdecken, enthüllen; beweisen, darthun, darlegen ...; cf., e.g., Antipho 6, 48.27f.; etc.

[270] Ps : ausprüfen, ausforschen ... Dah. untersuchen ... erforschen ... prüfen ...

[271] Ps : es ist natürlich, wahrscheinlich, es lässt sich erwarten; es ist billig, schicklich; L-S : like truth, i.e. likely, probable, reasonable; cf., e.g., Antipho 2, 2, 3; 6, 31; etc.

15) the bringing of τὸ τεκμήριον [272] and τὸ σημεῖον [273]

16) presenting witnesses,[274] who should be πιστοί, in order to βεβαιοῦν.

It is by using these two possibilities, reminding and demonstrating, that what is meant by πείθειν, as opposed to mere "speaking the truth", comes about. In that the truth is thus shown to be truth and falsehood to be falsehood, i.e. it is shown on the one hand ὅτι δὲ καὶ ταῦτ'ἀληθῆ λέγω [275] and on the other ὅτι δὲ μὴ δοκῶ διαβάλλειν αὐτόν,[276] the judge is "convinced by arguments" to which he can "give credence" [277] and one's opponent, καίπερ δεινὸς ὤν,[278] is confuted (ἐλέγχειν). For both are inseparable parts of the situation in court.[279]

E. *Other speeches (political, exhortatory, epideictic, on education)*

I) Introduction

πείθειν [280] is inseparably connected with the idea, and the continual

---

[272] Ps : Umstand, aus welchem sich etw. entnehmen od. schliessen lässt ... Beweismittel, Beweisgrund, Beleg, überzeugender Beweis; Erkennungszeichen, Criterium, Indicium ... im Gegensatz gegen μάρτυρες und μαρτυρίαι, thatsächliche Beweise, überzeugende Gründe ... Daher die Formel τεκμήριον δὲ τούτου τόδε ..., der Beweis dafür ist, wenn eine aufgestellte Behauptung begründet werden soll; gewöhnlich ganz kurz τεκμήριον δέ, wonach dann die Aufzählung der Gründe folgt ...; cf., e.g., Antipho 5, 61; etc.

[273] Das Zeichen, woran man etw. erkennt 1) allg. das Kennzeichen, Abzeichen, Wahrzeichen, a) das sichtbare ... b) das für den Verstand erkennbare, dahmit Rücksicht auf den darauf gegründeten Schluss, der Beleg, das Zeugnis, die Gewähr der Beweis ... 2) bes. a) ein von der Gottheit gesandtes Zeichen, wodurch sie ihren Willen kund giebt ...; cf., e.g., Antipho 2, 3, 8; etc.

[274] παρέχεσθαι τοὺς μάρτυρας ... τούτων ; καλεῖν τοὺς μάρτυρας ... τούτων.

[275] D 40, 15, 44; or : ὅτι τοίνυν ἀληθῆ καὶ ταῦτα λέγω (D 40, 35); ὡς δὲ καὶ ταῦτ'ἀληθῆ λέγω (D 40, 18.52); ὡς δ'ἀληθῆ λέγω (D 40, 7); καὶ ὡς ἀληθῆ λέγω ταῦτα (Is 2, 16).

[276] D 40, 33; 48, 55.

[277] Cf., e.g., Is 3, 77, 79 : ... οὐ πιστεύσετε, ἐὰν μὴ ἀποφαίνῃ, ὑμῖν, ὅπερ ... πρῶτον ... ἔπειτα ... εἶτα ... ἔτι δὲ πρὸς τούτοις ἐπιδειξάτω ὅτῳ ... For otherwise none is so ἀλόγιστος, ὅστις ἂν πιστεύσαι τούτοις τοῖς λόγοις Hyp 1, 5.

[278] D 41, 12.

[279] Cf., e.g., And 1, 30 : πείθειν not by i) δέεσθαι, ii) παραιτεῖσθαι but by i) ἐλέγχειν, ii) ἀναμιμνήσκειν. So also 1, 69.

[280] Cf. also 1) συμπείθειν = join in seeking to win : D 18, 147;

2) And 3, 37 ... τὰ μὲν πείσαντες ...
τὰ δὲ λαθόντες ...
τὰ δὲ πριάμενοι ...
τὰ δὲ βιασάμενοι ...(cf. 38)

claim, that through it the truth expresses itself, or at least should
do so.[281] How then can we define the relation between what is meant
by πείθειν on the one hand and "truth expressing itself" on the other ?
Do both mean more or less the same or does the process of πείθειν
refer to some independent extra ? And how far can this "independent
extra" be defined ?

If a look at the intended result of πείθειν allows us to make inferences
as to its nature and character, then we can say this much, that πείθειν
is always directed towards an action [282] corresponding to the truth
that is expressing itself. We can therefore surmise, as the inference
we mentioned, that the δύναμις peculiar to πείθειν should, as their
starting-point and source, correspond both to the "self-expression"
and to the "action" in the πείθειν-event, and should be composed of
two basically different forms of "argument" :

1) πίστεις αἱ ὑπὸ τοῦ λόγου πεπορισμέναι
2) πίστεις αἱ ἐκ τοῦ βίου γεγενημέναι.[283]

Here it is important to note in advance that to prevent oneself
being convinced by false reasons and motives [284] demands no less
intellectual effort than allowing oneself to be persuaded by good
arguments. The same is true with respect to the πίστεις αἱ ἐκ τοῦ
βίου : to decline to be persuaded on grounds of διαβάλλειν [285] etc., is
just as much an activity of the scrutinizing reason as being "convinced" by a good character. The criteria for the rejection of πείθειν
also apply, vice versa, to correct πείθειν.

Isoc NC 22   ... πεῖσαι ... βιάσασθαι ... ἐκπρίασθαι ... προσαγαγέσθαι ...

Epist. III, 2 ... πείθειν-οἳ ἄγωντες ἠναγκασμένοι (cf. I, 4 : πείθειν by ἐκφοβεῖν); Isoc
4, 162 : here πείθειν and κωλύειν are opposites : κωλύειν seeks to hinder what πείθειν seeks
to achieve. 5, 15f. : πείθειν-βιάζεσθαι (so also D 17, 23);

Isoc 14, 9 : πείθειν-ἀναγκάζειν (so also D 23, 167).

3) πείθειν is often synonymous with προαγεῖν, cf., e.g., Isoc 4, 17f.

[281] Cf. D 36, 17 ἡ ἀλήθεια γενομένη φανερά; Isoc 4, 15.17; 15, 177; D 19, 18 :
παρελθὼν δ'ἐγὼ πάντα τἀληθῆ πρὸς τὴν βουλὴν ἀπήγγειλα ... καὶ συνεβούλευον ... καὶ
ἔπεισα ταῦτα τὴν βουλήν. We pass over deceitful attempts at πείθειν like, e.g., Aeschin 2,
61 : πείθειν through ἐδέοντο and ὑπογενειάζειν and false promises.

[282] διαπράξασθαι = διαλλάσσειν Isoc 4, 16f.

[283] Cf. on this distinction Isoc 15, 278.

[284] Cf., e.g., the rejection of πείθειν in Isoc 6, 9f. in the context of ἐνθυμεῖσθαι.

[285] Cf., e.g., Isoc 5, 73-75, where Philip is slandered (διαβάλλομεν) ὑπὸ τῶν σοὶ φθο-
νούντων, in order that thereby πολλοὺς πείθουσιν. So also Lys 12, 58 : διαβάλλων ὅτι ... καὶ
ἄλλα λέγων οἷς ᾤετο πείσειν ...

II) Situations involving πείθειν

Situations in which πείθειν is particularly at home are

1) discussions in the βουλῇ ἐπὶ τοῦ βήματος, or ἐν ἐκκλησίᾳ on problems relating to inter-state relations [286] (here one often finds that all are "not of one mind",[287])

2) πείθειν as the task of envoys,[288] and

3) the public trials in which the ἄνδρες δικασταί must be persuaded [289]—with all its evil concomitants.[290]

III) The process of πείθειν I : πίστεις αἱ ὑπὸ τοῦ λόγου πεπορισμέναι

1i) Just to speak the pure truth is not enough if one wants to achieve something thereby.

ὁ ... ἐπίδειξιν ποιούμενος [291] is not reproached, as one might expect, with *not* telling the truth but with telling *nothing more* than the truth,[292] and also with not wanting to achieve anything further.[293] On the contrary, the πείθων has as his goal the διαπράττειν of those addressed.[294] Hence it follows that the πείθειν-event is not primarily

---

[286] D 5, 5; 6, 35; 8, 49.53; 10, 26, 56; etc.

[287] i) And 2, 1 οἱ παρίοντες μὴ τὴν αὐτὴν γνώμην ἔχοντες πάντες ἐφαίνοντο
ii) Isoc 4, 19 ἀμφισβητεῖσθαι.

[288] πείθειν is often the task of πρέσβεις of a state :
πρέσβεις And 3, 41; D 12, 6; 18, 179.214; etc.
πρεσβεύειν, ἡμᾶς And 3, 35
πρέσβεις αὐτοκράτορες And 3, 39
Here the activity of the πρέσβεις, namely to πρεσβεύειν, is identical with "to negotiate" (e.g. And 3, 34; etc.).
πρεσβεύειν εἰρήνην = to negotiate peace : And 3, 23; Isoc 4, 177; D 19, 134; etc.; πρεσβεύειν ὑπὲρ τουτωνὶ τὰ βέλτιστα D 19, 184; πρεσβεύειν πολλὰ καὶ δεινά ibid.; εἰρήνης δὲ περὶ πρεσβεύοντας ... And 1, 34.
Pass. : τὰ αὐτῷ πεπρεσβευμένα his negotiations ib. 20; πολλὰ καὶ δεινὰ πεπρεσβεῦσθαι ib. 240.

[289] D 20-26; 21, 30; etc.

[290] D 21, 85f.; etc.

[291] Isoc 4, 17.

[292] Isoc 4, 15 : ἀληθῆ μὲν λέγουσιν ...

[293] The same contrast also occurs in Isoc 6, 15 : Οὐδὲ πώποτε δὲ λόγους ἀγαπήσας, ἀλλ' ἀεὶ νομίζων τοὺς περὶ τοῦτο διατρίβοντας ἀργοτέρους εἶναι πρὸς τὰς πράξεις ...

[294] πείθειν's function between ἀκούειν and ἀσκεῖν is well expressed in Isoc 8, 36 : Ἠβουλόμην δ'ἂν ὥσπερ πρόχειρόν ἐστιν ἐπαινέσαι τὴν ἀρετὴν οὕτω ῥᾴδιον εἶναι πεῖσαι τοὺς ἀκούοντας ἀσκεῖν αὐτήν. Similarly too in D 15, 1 : ἐγὼ δ'οὐδεπώποθ' ἡγησάμην χαλεπὸν τὸ διδάξαι τὰ βέλτισθ' ὑμᾶς ... ἀλλὰ τὸ πεῖσαι πράττειν ταῦτα.

interested in the fact *that* the truth can be told, but in the way that it can be told [295] in order to stir men to action. So the business of πείθειν does not simply coincide with "telling the truth". Rather between the latter and "convictions" lies the whole realm of λόγος, of εὖ λέγειν as the area of the manner of the telling of the truth. Between "telling the truth" and "conviction" lies a συμβουλεύειν which is to be based on the truth and which seeks the interests of the hearers.[296]

lii) If one wants to achieve anything by "telling the truth" one must also make use of the power of λόγος, of εὖ λέγειν.

If a διαπράττεσθαι is therefore to follow "telling the truth" then one must, generally speaking, πολὺν ἀναλίσκειν λόγον and that essentially means in each case [297] seeking out the δύναμις [298] peculiar to the λόγος. As far as possible (καθ᾽ ὅσον ὁ λόγος δύναται) this must be brought into action. One must therefore take the trouble to make the fullest use of the power inherent in the proper arguments to stir men to action and that power is not simply that of "telling the truth"; it means first

a) ἐκείνους τοὺς λόγους [299] ζητεῖν, οἵ τινες τῷ πόλη τούτῳ πείσουσιν [300]

b) ἐντεῦθεν ποιοῦντα τὴν ἀρχὴν ὅθεν ἂν μάλιστα συστῆσαι ταῦτα δυνηθεῖεν.[301]

---

[295] In, e.g., Isoc 4, 15 (cf. 17) that takes the form of argument : ἀληθῆ μὲν λέγουσιν, οὐ μὴν ἐντεύθεν ποιοῦνται τὴν ἀρχὴν ὅθεν ἄν ...

[296] Cf., e.g., D 19, 18.

[297] Whether it is that men ῥᾴδιον ... πραγοῦσιν—perhaps because of their own εὐπειστία (Aeschin 1, 57) or that they δυσπείστως ἔχουσιν cf. Isoc 14, 18; δύσπειστος ον = hard to persuade, opinionated. The reason here is that παρειλήφασι ... ψευδῆ λόγον ... Or another reason : D 13, 13 τὰ ὦτα ... ὑμῶν ... διέφθαρται γάρ.

[298] Cf. Isoc 4, 129 : καθ᾽ ὅσον ὁ λόγος δύναται. The same idea also occurs in Isoc 6, 15 : after Isoc has expressed his general scepticism towards overmuch wordiness he continues : νῦν οὐδὲν ἂν περὶ πλείονος ποιησαίμην ἢ δυνηθῆναι περὶ τῶν προκειμένων ὡς βούλομαι διελθεῖν. ἐν γὰρ τῷ παρόντι διὰ τούτων ἐλπίζω μεγίστων ἀγαθῶν αἴτιος ἂν γενέσθαι τῇ πόλει.

[299] It is οἱ λόγοι, the arguments, which bring about πείθειν (to διαλλάσσειν) but not just telling the naked truth.

[300] "He who wants not only to give a pretty speech but also to achieve something must seek the arguments which will convince".

[301] Isoc 4, 15; cf. § 19 : ...ἐντευθεν ἄρχεσθαι ...

I.e. the truth must be declared with the help of arguments (i) and in a particular way (ii) as seems best fitted to lead to actions conforming to this truth.

This δύναμις of argument "breaks out" (as distinct from arising or originating from the truth as its source or from putting itself at the service of what is truly beneficial) in confrontation, in objections to a particular *interpretation* of the truth, rather than in Truth itself. Thus the business of πείθειν can be likened to a contest.[302] This disagreement is marked by θαυμάζειν,[303] ἀντιλέγειν,[304] ἐνστῆναι,[305] ἐναντιουμένοι,[306] θορυβεῖν.[307]

Thus πείθειν means the process of the realization and effective employment of the δύναμις inherent in the arguments. Hence πείθειν has to do above all with "arguments", with the art of arguing (oratory).[308] and not just with stating or reciting the "truth". And if the qualification καθ' ὅσον ὁ λόγος δύναται automatically restricts the power of the λόγος to influence the hearer then the same can be even more baldly stated : εἰρήσεται γὰρ τἀληθὲς εἰ καὶ μωρὸς ὁ λόγος ἐστίν.[309]

These conclusions force us to ask what this "power" of persuasion is. Isoc 15, 253 ff. provides as it were a phenomenology of the power of πείθειν from which, according to the trend of these paragraphs, he infers the true nature of πείθειν from its observable powerful effects. I.e. it speaks of the power of πείθειν first in the sense of its effects and then of its true nature. The first point concerns us particularly here.

The two main points to notice in the effects of the power of πείθειν described here are that this δύναμις is at once too great and too intimate for its effects to be confined

---

[302] And 4, 2 : the undertaking of πείθειν can also be likened to a contest : ὁ μὲν οὖν ἀγὼν ὁ παρὼν οὐ στεφανηφόρος, ἀλλ' ... οἱ δ'ἀνταγωνιζόμενοι περὶ τῶν ἄθλων τούτων ...

[303] E.g., Isoc 7, 71 ; etc.

[304] And 3, 36 : ἀναγκαίως οὖν ἔχει καὶ πρὸς ταῦτ'ἀντειπεῖν 3, 40 : the ἀντιλέγοντες should παρίοντες ... αὐτοὶ διδασκόντων ὑμᾶς ...; D 5, 5; 16, 11 : λόγος παρὰ τῶν ἀντιλεγόντων ...

[305] Isoc 5, 39.

[306] E.g., D 18, 175; etc.

[307] E.g., D 13, 14; etc.

[308] E.g., Isoc 15, 232f.; D 12, 17; 20, 105.125.148.

[309] Isoc 15, 177; cf. also D 16, 3.

a) to the narrower context of the ἀμφισβητεῖσθαι among men alone, and

b) to the broader context of the ἀμφισβητεῖσθαι between individuals.

I.e. the sphere of πείθειν's power and effects is here really regarded as universal. That means that, as regards (a), that the starting-point is the statement based on observation that it is only the power [310] to πείθειν ἀλλήλους καὶ δηλοῦν πρὸς ἡμᾶς αὐτούς ...[311] which makes man man and distinguishes him from beasts.[312] For σχεδὸν ἅπαντα τὰ δι' ἡμῶν μεμηχανημένα λόγος ἡμῶν ἐστιν ὁ συγκατασκευάσας. This is further developed, first with regard to the whole cultural scene : this power is the reason why

aa) πόλεις ᾠκίσαμεν
bb) νόμους ἐθέμεθα
cc) τέχνας εὕρομεν

Secondly, with regard to the whole area of reason : by this power of πείθειν καὶ δηλοῦν

aa) τοὺς κακοὺς ἐξελέγχομεν
  τοὺς ἀγαθοὺς ἐγκωμιάζομεν
bb) τοὺς ἀνοήτους παιδεύομεν
  τοὺς φρονίμους δοκιμάζομεν [313]
cc) περὶ τῶν ἀμφιβητησίμων ἀγωνιζόμεθα καὶ
  π ε ρ ὶ   τ ῶ ν   ἀ γ ν ο ο υ μ έ ν ω ν   σ κ ο π ο ύ μ ε θ α
  ταῖς γὰρ πίστεσιν, αἷς τοὺς ἄλλους λέγοντες πείθομεν
  ταῖς αὐταῖς ταύταις βουλευόμενοι χρώμεθα ...[314]

---

[310] Cf. § 157.

[311] § 254.

[312] In Lys 2, 19 civilization is marked by two processes :
  i) νόμῳ μὲν ὁρίσαι τὸ δίκαιον
  ii) λόγῳ δὲ πεῖσαι
Both are practised (ἔργῳ) in order to assist (ὑπηρετεῖν),
i.e. i) ὑπὸ νόμου μὲν βασιλευομένους
  ii) ὑπὸ λόγου δὲ διδασκομένους
(cf. in D 20, 63 : ... πεῖσαι ... ἢ θεῖναι νόμον ...)

[313] § 255.

[314] § 256.

As regards (b): this last point (cc) already briefly shows what we mean by our thesis that the effects of πείθειν are at the same time too intimate to be confined to ἀμφισβητεῖσθαι between individuals. The power of πείθειν is also at work within an individual: καὶ ῥητορικοὺς μὲν καλοῦμεν τοὺς ἐν τῷ πλήθει λέγειν δυναμένους, εὐβούλους δὲ νομίζομεν οἵτινες ἂν αὐτοὶ πρὸς αὐτοὺς ἄριστα ... διαλεχθῶσιν.[315] But if it is possible to regard the power of πείθειν as active within [316] an individual then this must affect our concept of what the nature of πείθειν is. We will deal with that later. Let it suffice here to say that the nature of this power cannot lie in its external manifestations nor in the innermost διαλέγεσθαι within one individual, but must transcend both.

Up till now we have tried to give, descriptively or phenomenologically, a more or less comprehensive cross-section disclosing in general the workings of the power of persuasion; now we must take another cross-section to show in particular its effects within the situation of ἀμφισβητεῖσθαι among men. We wish to analyse these effects with reference to the manner of their working and to their function.

What forms are taken by this "seeking to move one's hearers to action by arguments which in themselves possess limited power?" What concrete form does this power take on? Although the different forms listed below may be very diverse, yet they are bound together by two elements constitutive for the sphere of πείθειν's operations:

a) the element of βουλεύειν/βουλεύεσθαι, συμβουλεύειν, συμβουλεύεσθαι,[317] ἐπιβουλεύειν/ἐπιβουλεύεσθαι [318]—often more precisely qualified by ἀσφαλῶς [319]—and their concomitant σκέπτειν/σκέπτεσθαι. This is one of the fundamental categories within which πείθειν slowly develops.[320]

---

315 *Ibid.*

316 In this context cf. also the ἐμαυτὸν πείθω-passages, e.g. Aeschin 1, 45.

317 E.g. Isoc 15, 233 : σύμβουλεύειν = πείθειν

D 17, 21 : συμβουλεύειν = πείθειν

D 19, 18 : συνεβούλευον (imperf. of continuation) — ἔπεισα (aor. of result)

D 26, 19 : συμβουλεῦσαι καὶ πεῖσαι ....

318 πείθειν through ἐπιβουλεύειν D 19, 304.

319 And 3, 34 : βουλεύσασθαι μὲν οὖν ἀσφαλῶς χρὴ κατὰ δύναμιν ... .

320 Cf., e.g., And 3, 31 : ... πείθοντες ... 24 : βουλεύεσθαι ... Also the 40 days ἐν αἷς ὑμῖν ἔξεστιν βουλεύεσθαι ... And 3, 33.40. βουλεύεσθαι is the time for "discussion" (this meaning is possible in many βουλεύειν-passages), in which one weighs up the pros and cons.

b) The element of "bringing something to light" or "into the open", "revealing".[321]

Negatively that means that λανθάνειν and [ἐξ]απατᾶν are the exact opposite of πείθειν.

Positively it means that πείθειν has the character of being ἐκ τοῦ φανεροῦ.[322] This is really a definition of it. This is the second fundamental category which is proper to every form of the realizing of the power of persuasion.

These two constitutive elements in the process of πείθειν work through the different functions of the human intellect, especially in the forms of

    aa) διδάσκειν [323]
    bb) διαλέγεσθαι [324]

---

[321] Cf. D 19, 17.19, where in a really ideal way πείθειν is practised in an "open" setting :

    17 : καὶ παντὶ πολλοὶ συνίσασιν.

    18 : ἐγὼ πάντα τἀληθῆ πρὸς τὴν βουλὴν ἀπήγγειλα ...

    19 : καὶ πρὸς Διὸς καὶ θεῶν πειρᾶσθε συνδιαμνημονεύειν ἂν ἀληθῆ λέγω.

Contrast the behaviour of his opponent :

    19 : εἶπε δὲ τοιούτους λόγους καὶ τηλικαῦτα καὶ τοσαῦτ'ἔχοντας τἀγαθά, ὥσθ ἅπαντας ὑμᾶς λαβὼν ᾤχετο ...

[322] Cf. And 3, 33; Th 3, 43.

[323] πείθειν

i) directly implies a prior διδάσκειν : e.g. Isoc 4, 15 (cf. 17.19); D 14, 2; D 15, 1 and 23, 157 are instructive for the mutual relation of the two. 23, 157 : while πείθειν tries to influence A's way of behaviour, i.e. to move him to a particular action, διδάσκειν gives the reason for this recommended way of behaviour.

15, 1 : the difference between διδάσκειν and πείθειν is that between theoretical understanding and practical execution. What is meant by πείθειν is the attempt to move someone to do something which he already understands—i.e. apart from πείθειν (= ἅπαντες ὑπάρχειν ἐγνωκότες μοῖ δοκεῖτε).

ii) πείθειν is more or less synonymous with διδάσκειν : cf., e.g., And 3, 41; Isoc 6, 12f. At any rate διδάσκειν is a component of βουλεύεσθαι and contributes to discussion (cf., e.g., And 3, 40) and thus should lead to πείθειν.

[324] Cf., e.g., Isoc 6, 16. The relation of διαλέγεσθαι on the one hand and πείθειν/ συμβουλεύειν on the other can be well illustrated from Isoc 15, 67-72. The following expressions belong to one sense-context :

    § 67 συμβουλεύων ὡς δεῖ ...

    70 διαλεγόμενος ...

    71 ἐπιτιμῶ ... διαλεχθεὶς δὲ περὶ τούτων, παραινῶ τῷ ...

    72 ἐπιχειρῶ δὲ καὶ τοῦτο πείθειν αὐτόν, ὡς χρὴ δεινὸν νομίζειν ...

πείθειν and συμβουλεύειν are directed towards action, while διαλέγεσθαι means more a

cc) ὑποτίθημι [τῷ λόγῳ] [325]
dd) ἐπι-ἀπο-δεικνύναι [326]
ee) ἐνθυμεῖσθαι [327]
ff) παραινεῖν [328]

Of all these forms mentioned here three things are true :

a) Although the ideal goal of σημεῖον οὖν τοῦτο, ὅτι ...[329] should be attained by means of these activities in the realm of understanding, yet these activities are not simply identical with what is meant by πείθειν but are simply aids to it. All these forms of activity can do no more in their particular situations than to bring about the limited δύναμις of argument in the sense of καθ' ὅσον ὁ λόγος δύναται.

b) Often they take the form of reminding.[330] For by use of these forms knowledge is set free and recollections arise of what one has seen oneself or heard from others [331] and thus contribute to the event of πείθειν. Hence the maxim: χρὴ γάρ ... τεκμηρίοις χρῆσθαι τοῖς πρότερον γενομένοις, περὶ τῶν μελλόντων ἔσεσθαι; hence, too, it is only εἰκός that ὑμᾶς πρῶτον ἐκεῖνα σκέψασθαι τὰ τότε γενόμενα.[332] And he who learns from the past is a σώφρων.[333]

c) These activities not only forward proper persuasion, but

---

theoretical discussion (so too Isoc 15, 176f.; D 58, 45). The forms presuppose the latter; the latter is often directed towards individuals (cf. in this connection the distinction between διαλέγεσθαι = private conversation and δημηγορεῖν = public speaking in D 19, 304). And while πείθειν is basically open (often expressed by verbs like πειρᾶσθαι, ἐπιχειρεῖν) and is only completed appropriately by the person addressed, a question can be discussed and it can then be said that it was διαλεχθείς whereas with regard to πείθειν it can be said nevertheless οὐκ ... ἔπειθεν ... (cf. Aeschin 1, 57).

[325] And 3, 10.

[326] Cf, And 2, 3 : σαφεῖς τε καὶ βεβαίους τὰς ἀποδείξεις ...

[327] Cf. Isoc 6, 10 : πείθειν and the preceding call to ἐνθυμεῖσθαι go together (= lay to heart, to ponder, to consider; think much or deeply—and thus "to infer, conclude"). Cf., e.g., Antipho 6, 20; 5, 6; etc.

[328] Isoc 12, 54 where there is an attempt to reach πείθειν by means of παραινεῖν 15, 84f. : παραινεῖν/πείθειν.

[329] Cf., e.g., And 2, 4.

[330] E.g. And 3, 24f. : διδάσκειν based on ἀναμιμνήσκειν.

[331] Isoc 5, 42 : whether it be that αὐτοὶ τυγχάνουσιν εἰδότες or else ἑτέρων ἀκηκόασιν, ὅτι...

[332] And 3, 2.

[333] And 3, 32 : τὰ γὰρ παραδείγματα τὰ γεγενημένα τῶν ἁμαρτημάτων ἱκανὰ τοῖς σώφροσι τῶν ἀνθρώπων ὥστε μηκέτι ἁμαρτάνειν.

negatively, they are also weapons against false πείθειν, without any
basis in understanding or aiming at deceitful ends.[334]

2i)   This λόγος, or εὖ λέγειν should not derive its proper δύναμις
out of its visible manifestations.

But if the power of arguments is not just the power of "telling
the truth", in what does the δύναμις proper to λόγος ultimately
consist ? What law does it follow ?

The real δύναμις of arguments and so of πείθειν does not lie, often
as it seems to, in καλοὺς ... καὶ μακροὺς λόγους,[335] πηγὰς λόγων,[336]
λόγους εὐπροσώπους,[337] εὐφημία ... τῶν λόγων,[338] περιττολογίας,[339]
ὑπερηφανία,[340] τοὺς ματαίους τῶν λόγων.[341] For only the mass τῶν
ἀνοήτων [342] "hang wondering on" (περίστατος [343]) such λόγους (and
only the ἄνθρωποι ἄπειροι λόγων [344] allow themselves to submit to the
ἀπορράπτειν τὸ στόμα ὀλοσχοίνῳ ἀβρόχῳ [345]) and succumb to such
κολακεύειν [346] whenever someone comes to them and ἐνέπλησε τὰ
ὦτα λόγων.[347] Of what use is that (ὠφελεῖν) except to be deceived
(ἐξαπατᾶσθαι;[348] παρακρούεσθαι [349]) ?

2iia)   The δύναμις of εὖ λέγειν comes from that which it serves,
the truth.

---

[334] Cf., e.g., D 15, 35 : 2 arguments are used to counter πείθειν based on lack of
understanding :

    i) καίτοι ... ἅπαντες ἴσασι ...

    ii) οἶμαι δ'ὑμῶν μνημονεύειν ἐνίους, ...

    cf. D 19, 204 : ... οὐ ... δυνήσεται πεῖσαι τοὺς αὐτοὺς ἑορακότας ὑμᾶς καὶ εὖ εἰδότας ...

[335] D 19, 11.

[336] Aeschin 2, 21.

[337] D 18, 149.

[338] Aeschin 3, 168.

[339] Isoc 12, 88; 15, 269.

[340] Aeschin 2, 21.

[341] Isoc 15, 269.

[342] *Ibid.*

[343] *Ibid.* and 6, 95.

[344] D 18, 149f.

[345] Aeschin 2, 21 : (proverbial) ἀπορρ ... ἀβρόχῳ = "sew up or stop his mouth with
unburnt rushes" (i.e. easily).

[346] Cf. And 4, 10f.

[347] D 13, 13.

[348] E.g. Aeschin 3, 168.

[349] E.g. D 6, 35.

But if the power of persuasion does not lie, despite all appearances to the contrary, in externals which, though dazzling, yet are ultimately pointless, nor in more or less deliberate manipulation, suited only to the moment and only serving it, what is it which makes the λόγος practised for the purpose of πείθειν ... τοὺς ἀκούοντας, the εὖ λέγειν,[350] a decisive force moving men in their whole existence, past and present, in distinction to the whole mass of ineffectual rhetorical pyrotechnics? We saw in § 1ii the tremendous effects of this power of πείθειν. Hence it would be best to return to the main passage cited there, Isoc 15, 253ff., and to ask what is there ὁ δύναμις of πείθειν και δηλοῦν what makes it so effective.

The answer can only be that this δύναμις of the εὖ λέγειν necessary to πείθειν τοὺς ἀκούοντας does not simply lie in the εὖ λέγειν itself but in the λέγειν ὡς δεῖ qualifying and limiting this "speaking well". This δύναμις of the λόγος necessary for πείθειν does not simply lie in the λόγος itself, but in the categories of ἀληθὴς καὶ νόμιμος καὶ δίκαιος qualifying this λόγος. In short, the δύναμις of the εὖ λέγειν lies in the λέγειν ὡς δεῖ. And ὡς δεῖ is only the λόγος ἀληθὴς καὶ νόμιμος καὶ δίκαιος.[351] It is by subordinating the εὖ λέγειν to the control of the λέγειν ὡς δεῖ and the λόγος to the λόγος ἀληθὴς καὶ νόμιμος καὶ δίκαιος that their δύναμις is realized. If the nature of πείθειν's power is thus internalized, i.e. sited in its orientation towards the truth and not in its conformity to certain external manifestations, then, despite the apparent contradiction, it follows that

aa)   πείθειν's power can generally be effective within the individual without it's being apparent,[352] and

bb)   in cases of doubt preference will be given, not to εὖ λέγειν, but to what precedes and should form the basis of all εὖ λέγειν, εὐγνω-μοσύνη.[353]

---

[350] Isoc 15, 275.

[351] § 255.

[352] Isoc 15, 256.

[353] The pasage is in Aeschin 3, 170. The starting-point (168) is the statement that one should not look for εὐφημία αὐτοῦ τῶν λόγων in a δημοτικός but for his φύσις (= character) and the ἀλήθεια. In the following, those qualities are listed which should be found both in a δημοτικῷ ἀνδρί and in a σώφρονι. The third of the 5 qualities is that of being σώφρων and μέτριον in contrast to ἀσέλγεια; the fourth quality is (τέταρτον) εὐγνώμονα καὶ δυνατὸν εἰπεῖν. καλὸν γὰρ τὴν μὲν διάνοιαν προαιρεῖσθαι τὰ βέλτιστα, τὴν δὲ παιδείαν τὴν τοῦ ῥήτορος, καὶ τὸν λόγον πείθειν τοὺς ἀκούοντας. εἰ δὲ μή, τὴν γ'εὐγνω-μοσύνην ἀεὶ προτακτέον τοῦ λόγου.

The implications of this definition using not "intellectual" but legal and religious categories, binding ones, will only become plain when we remember that humanity as such is defined by the categories of πείθειν καὶ δηλοῦν.[354] So if Isoc says in § 257 that this power of πείθειν καὶ δηλοῦν qua λέγειν ὡς δεῖ (= λόγος ἀληθὴς καὶ νόμιμος καὶ δίκαιος) is used particularly by οἱ πλεῖστον νοῦν ἔχοντες then it is clear

aa) how much "intellectual" activity and religious-legal thinking go together, i.e. this νοῦν ἔχειν is also subordinated to the category of ἀληθὴς καὶ νόμιμος ... without ceasing to be νοῦν ἔχειν;

bb) how little we can speak of νοῦν ἔχειν as a purely intellectual activity, and

cc) how little this area of the religious and legal can be separated from that of the νοῦς.

2iib)   The δύναμις of εὖ λέγειν comes from that which it serves, the true interests of the hearers. πείθειν and ἀρέσκειν are therefore distinct.

In that the πείθων seeks to move men to διαπράττειν by the "exposition of the truth", he has their true interests (τὸ συμφέρον) in view. He must therefore subordinate his gifts of speech and persuasion to the real interests of the community and put them at its disposal. Some examples :

aa)   It can mean that the speaker must first refer to an earlier offence and warn : δεῖ ... γάρ ... τὸν βουλόμενόν τι ποιῆσαι τὴν πόλιν ἡμῶν ἀγαθὸν τὰ ὦτα πρῶτον ὑμῶν ἰάσασθαι ......[355]

bb)   ἡγοῦμαι ... δεῖν ... τοὺς προὔργον τι ποιεῖν βουλομένους καὶ τῶν λόγων τοὺς ματαίους καὶ τῶν πραξέων τὰς μηδὲν πρὸς τὸν βίον φερούσας ἀναιρεῖν ἐξ ἁπασῶν τῶν διατριβῶν ......[356]

cc) D 14, 1ff. : here D sceptically refers to the mass of those speakers who can certainly speak well (τῷ λόγῳ δύναιτο—§ 1—, λέγειν δεινοί—§ 2—), but οὔ μὴν συμφέροντά γ' ... (§ 1), or, as he says in § 2 : οὐδὲν ἂν τὰ ὑμέτερ'εὖ οἶδ'ὅτι βέλτιον σχοίη.

Such interests are served, speaking quite generally, when one

---

[354] Isoc 15, 254.

[355] D 13, 13.

[356] Isoc 15, 269.

practises the forms of πείθειν mentioned earlier on, here quite specifically, when the πείθειν is preceded by a διδάσκειν based on a knowledge of the facts. Through this alone πᾶς ὁ παρὼν φόβος λελύσεται.

If our findings so far are correct, namely that the power of persuasion is proportionate on the one hand to the measure of its conformity to λέγειν ὡς δεῖ in the sense of the λόγος ἀληθὴς καὶ νόμιμος καὶ δίκαιος and on the other hand to its being directed towards the interests of those addressed, then it must follow that ἀρέσκειν cannot mean the same as πείθειν. In fact this is a commonplace of orators, an insight acquired through continual adverse and painful experience, that "speaking to please" [357] men with fair words may not be substituted for the use of arguments relevant to them. For one knows only too well how difficult it is on the one hand ἢ παραινῶν ἢ διδάσκων ἢ χρήσιμόν τι λέγων and on the other hand, at the same time, ἀρέσκειν. This is often impossible for οἳ ... φθονοῦσι μὲν τοῖς εὖ φρονοῦσιν ἁπλοῦς δ᾽ἡγοῦνται τοὺς νοῦν οὐκ ἐχόντας.[358] This refers to the "bad" orators who avoid the ἀπόκρισις ἀληθὴς καὶ συμφέρουσα, in short who does κεκαλυμμένως ... λέγειν,[359] and only think of ὅπως ἀρέσκοντας ὑμῖν λόγους ἐροῦσιν, without any interest in the interests of the state.[360] As a result ὅσῳ γὰρ ἄν τις ἐπιεικέστερον αὐτὸν ἐπιδείξῃ δῆλον ὅτι τοσούτῳ χεῖρον ἀγωνιεῖται παρ᾽αὐτοῖς.[361] For it is simply unavoidable that, if I speak κεκαλυμμένως ... μηδένα μήτ᾽ἀδικήσω μήτ᾽ἐνοχλήσω μήτε λυπήσω ...[362]. For telling the truth is often "unpopular" : οἶμαι δὲ τοὺς ἀηδῶς ἀκούοντας τῶν λόγων τούτων τοῖς μὲν εἰρημένοις οὐδὲν ἀντερεῖν ὡς οὐκ ἀλήθεσιν οὖσιν ...[363]. On the other hand, aiming at ἀρέσκειν need not rule out that προαιρεῖσθαι ... τῶν τε πράξεων τὰς ὠφελιμωτάτας καὶ βελτίστας καὶ τῶν λόγων τοὺς ἀληθεστάτους καὶ δικαιοτάτους ......[364]

---

[357] It is this that is held against Alk. : τὰ ἥδιστα τῷ πλήθει παραλιπὼν τὰ βέλτιστα συμβουλεύει Or also : And 4, 16f. κολακεύων — πείθειν.

Cf. Isoc 8, 39 : ... προαιρεῖσθαι τῶν λόγων μὴ τοὺς ἡδίστους ἀλλὰ τοὺς ὠφελιμωτάτους. And that implies first (πρῶτον) λόγος ὁ τολμῶν τοῖς ἁμαρτανομένοις ἐπιπλήττειν (cf. also 41, 1-3; 4-9 — I C 14, 23f.).

[358] Isoc 2, 46.
[359] 8, 62.
[360] 8, 5.
[361] 15, 154.
[362] 15, 153.
[363] 12, 62.
[364] 15, 132-4.

2iic)   The δύναμις of εὖ λέγειν comes from that which it serves,
the true interests of the speaker.

What benefit does he who persuades derive from his actions?

aa)   In a bad sense he enriches himself at the others' expense, both
financially [365] and in terms of popularity.[366]

bb)   In a good sense ἐπιθυμεῖν τῆς πλεονεξίας, μὴ τῆς ὑπὸ τῶν
ἀνοήτων νομιζομένης, ἀλλὰ τῆς ὡς ἀληθῶς τὴν δύναμιν ταύτην
ἐχούσες.[367]

For οὐκ ὀρθῶς ἔγνωκεν who thinks that those who in this life are
ἀποστεροῦντας or παραλογιζομένους or κακόν τι ποιοῦντας also πλεο-
νεκτεῖν thereby. Rather χρὴ δὲ καὶ νῦν πλέον ἔχειν ἡγεῖσθαι καὶ
πλεονεκτήσειν νομίζειν παρὰ μὲν τῶν θεῶν ...[368] τοὺς εὐσεβεστάτους
καὶ τοὺς περὶ τὴν θεραπείαν τὴν ἐκείνων ἐπιμελεστάτους ὄντας ...[369]

IV) The process of πείθειν II : πίστεις αἱ ἐκ τοῦ βίου γεγενημέναι
The δύναμις of the εὖ λέγειν necessary for πείθειν is proportional to
the δύναμις of the εὖ ἀναστρέφειν.

If πείθειν is directed towards action it is not surprising that it also
arises, or at least should arise, from action. The speaker's own past
and present life and behaviour is an important "argument" in the
process of πείθειν aimed at action. Alongside the δύναμις of "persuading
through arguments" stands here that of "persuading through one's
life". The truth with which true πείθειν is concerned should be expanded
not only in arguments but also in one's life. How important is this
idea for the orators?

We must start from two observations that we have already made,
namely that it is difficult to start from theoretical knowledge and
arrive at practical actions, and that the δύναμις of persuading with
arguments can often help only to a certain extent. Why is that? The main
reason is that the tension between theoretical knowledge and understanding on the one hand and a living in conformity to it on the other
is recognized as unresolved within the speaker himself. As we have

---

[365] ὁ μισθὸς (D 8, 53; 18, 149; etc.).

[366] αἱ χάριτες (D 8, 53) αὐτοὶ μὲν τοῦ δοκεῖν δύνασθαι λέγειν δόξαν ἐκφέροντα D 14, 1; etc.

[367] Isoc 15, 275; cf. the discussion as to what is truly advantageous in Isoc 3, 2;
8, 28-35.

[368] Cf. Isoc 8, 34.

[369] Isoc 15, 282.

already noted, striking gifts of oratory can deceive many about the existence of this tension. That is particularly relevant in the courtroom. Therefore it is there absolutely essential that the accused should ὑποσχεῖν ... περὶ τοῦ βίου λόγον ...[370] and that the judges ἐκ τῶν ἐπιτηδευμάτων κρινοῦσιν ...[371] For everyone knows [372] that ἀρέσκειν (τοῖς κρινοῦσιν) resulting from a good life, which is nothing else than ἡ τῆς εὐνοίας δύναμις,[373] exercises a strong influence (ἔχειν ῥόπην) εἰς τὸ πείθειν. Therefore, we read, ... Ἀλκιβιάδου τὸν βίον ἀναμνῆσαι βούλομαι ... ;[374] hence too the general appeal, θεωρεῖτ' αὐτοῦ μὴ τὸν λόγον, ἀλλὰ τὸν βίον, καὶ σκοπεῖτε μὴ τίς φήσιν εἶναι, ἀλλὰ τίς ἐστίν...,[375] or simply θεωρήσατ' αὐτόν, μὴ ὁποτέρου τοῦ λόγου, ἀλλ' ὁποτέρου τοῦ βίου ἐστίν ...[376] For only such a test can show up whether οἱ μὲν λόγοι καλοί, τὰ δ' ἔργα φαῦλα...[377] or someone is δεινὸς λέγειν, κακὸς βιῶναι...[378] Once one comes to this conclusion then one begins to doubt the δύναμις of persuasion with arguments. Hence And 4, 10 ff. is a good example of how a reminder of the past deeds of Alkibiades lessens his power to convince with words.[379] Here close attention is paid to

1) his handling of public affairs [380] and
2) his handling of private affairs :[381] ... οἱ ... ἀπὸ τῶν ἰδίων αὐτὸν θεῶνται.[382]

In each case whole lists of vices are explicitly cited.[383] The same is true in Aeschin 3, 174.[384] This tour round a speaker's life in order to

---

370 And 4, 37.

371 And 4, 33.

372 Cf. Isoc 15, 279.

373 ἡ τῆς εὐνοίας δύναμις = the power of good will. Cf. Arist. Rhet II, 1 : ἠθικὴ πίστις has three elements : φρόνησις, ἀρετή, εὔνοια.

374 And 4, 10.

375 Aeschin 3, 176.

376 Aeschin 3, 168.

377 Aeschin 3, 174.

378 Ibid.

379 And 4, 11.39.

380 §§ 410-12.

381 §§ 413ff.

382 And 4, 13.

383 μοιχεία, ἁρπαγὴ γυναικῶν ἀλλοτρίων, βιαιότης, πλεονεξία, ὑπερηφανία.

384 One should scrutinize the life and not the rhetorical gifts of those who allow themselves to persuade other men (176). Hence οὕτω γὰρ κέχρηται καὶ τῷ ἑαυτοῦ σώματι καὶ παιδοποιιᾴ, ὥστ' ἐμὲ μὴ βούλεσθαι λέγειν ἃ τούτῳ πέπρακται.

gauge his power to convince with words is only possible because everyone οἶδε ... τὰς πίστεις μεῖζον δυναμένας τὰς ἐκ τοῦ βίου γεγενημέ-
νας ἢ τὰς ὑπὸ τοῦ λόγου πεπορισμένας ...[385] If that is so then the rule
follows that καὶ μὴν οὐδ'ὁ πείθειν τινὰς βουλόμενος ἀμελήσει τῆς
ἀρετῆς ...[386] That means in concrete terms : ... ὅσῳ ἄν τις ἐρρω-
μενεστέρως ἐπιθυμῇ πείθειν τοὺς ἀκούοντας, τοσούτῳ μᾶλλον ἀσκήσει
καλὸς κἀγαθὸς εἶναι καὶ παρὰ τοῖς πολίταις εὐδοκιμεῖν ...[387] I.e. an
argument is "truer" and more convincing, not when one tries to make
it "truer",[388] but when it is delivered by men in whom this argument
has already worked convincingly : τίς γὰρ οὐκ οἶδε καὶ τοὺς λόγους
ἀληθεστέρους δοκοῦντας εἶναι τοὺς ὑπὸ τῶν εὖ διακειμένων λεγομένους
ἢ τοὺς ὑπὸ τῶν διαβεβλημένων...[389] From here it is only a short step
to give full priority to one's "life" rather than to one's λόγος. Thus
τὴν ἐπίδειξιν ποιεῖσθαι [390] is contrasted with τὸ διὰ τούτων τῶν λόγων
ζητεῖν πείθειν ὡς ... and Demosthenes proclaims τὰ δ'ἔργ'ἡμῶν ὅπως
ἄξια τῶν προγόνων ἔσται σκοπεῖν, μὴ τοὺς ἐπὶ τοῦ βήματος λόγους ....[391]

Therefore both the speaker's intellectual activity in the service of
the truth and of what is really advantageous and his daily life and
conduct together contribute to the δύναμις of πείθειν. It is thus the
truth itself which uses those intellectual and existential arguments to
unfold itself to men and to move them from detached διακρυβοῦσθαι to
committed διαπράττειν.

V) The goal of πείθειν

Since it is the declared purpose of every attempt at πείθειν to move
the hearer to a certain action, we must briefly examine more closely
the state of mind of a man as he makes a decision. What happens
in a man in the moment just before he embarks on an action ? How

---

[385] Isoc 15, 278; cf. Arist. Rhet. 1356a.

[386] Isoc 15, 278. The passage continues : ἀλλὰ τούτῳ μάλιστα προσέξει τὸν νοῦν ὅπως
δόξαν ὡς ἐπιεικεστάτην λήψεταί παρὰ τοῖς συμπολιτευμένοις.

[387] Ibid.

[388] Cf. D 10, 55 : (οἱ) ... ἄλλους λόγους ὡς οἷόν τ'ἀληθεστάτους λέγουσιν.

[389] Ibid.

[390] Isoc 10, 9. Isoc goes on to make it still clearer what he means by this : τοὺς γὰρ
ἀμφισβητοῦντας τοῦ φρονεῖν καὶ φάσκοντα εἶναι σοφιστὰς οὐκ ἐν τοῖς ἠμελημένοις ὑπὸ τῶν
ἄλλων ἀλλ'ἐν οἷς ἅπαντες εἰσιν ἀνταγωνισταί, προσήκει διαφέρειν καὶ κρείττους εἶναι τῶν
ἰδιωτῶν ...

[391] D 14, 41.

can we describe his mental disposition at this point of time after all the functions of the human intellect and of the arguments ἐκ βίου described earlier have come into play and have done their work? Into what mental state has the whole process of πείθειν finally brought the man?

Three features are essential:

1) The goal of the whole πείθειν-process is first a deepened understanding of a thing or a situation (Isoc, e.g., tries πείθειν ... ἡγούμενος ... τὴν διάνοιαν τὴν ἐκείνον μάλιστ᾽ ὠφελήσειν ...[392]), so much deepened that the hearers themselves really understand it for themselves.[393] But since this can only come about through the functions of "bringing to light" described above, what is meant by πείθειν is diametrically opposed to all, even partial, λανθάνειν, (ἐξ)ἀπατᾶν, παρακρούσεσθαι. The πείθειν is therefore shown to be a deceitful one if it "tries to move the hearer from his own viewpoint" in order to attain the speaker's goal.[394] The πείθειν is shown to be a deceitful one if it aims at "stopping the mouth", at φενακίζειν [395] and not at ἀποκρίνεσθαι,[396] and φθέγγεσθαι.[397]

2) Thus it is the goal of the πείθειν-process to banish from man's decision—making every element of conscious or unconscious compulsion, yes, even the compulsion of neutrality and of the love of keeping one's distance.

3) The goal of πείθειν is, finally, to place the man himself in the position of making his free decision [398] and not to take this away

---

[392] Isoc 15, 69.72.

[393] Aeschin 1, 93 : the goal of πείθειν in the hearer is mainly his own understanding : πρῶτον μὲν μηδὲν ὑμῖν ἔστω πιστότερον ὧν αὐτοὶ σύνιστε καὶ ... That this is a basic rule is indicated by the preceding τὸν αὐτὸν τοίνυν τρόπον συνίημι and also later on by the words τῇ ἀληθείᾳ.

D 19, 204 : hence it is not possible by deceitful means πεῖσαι, τοὺς αὐτοὺς ἑορακότας ὑμᾶς καὶ εὖ εἰδότας.

[394] Aeschin 2, 63 : by deceitful πείθειν → τὴν ἐκκλησίαν φέρων

D 19, 19 : εἶπε δὲ τοιούτους λόγους καὶ τηλικαῦτα καὶ τοσαῦτ᾽ἔχοντας τἀγαθά, ὥσθ᾽-ἅπαντας ὑμᾶς λαβὼν ᾤχετο.

[395] Cf. And 3, 33; cf. also λέγων ὑμᾶς ἐφενάκιζε D 22, 70; 24, 177; etc.—Cf. D 22, 35 : ... λόγοι πρὸς τὸ φενακίζειν ὑμᾶς ...

[396] Cf. D 18, 214.

[397] Cf. D 18, 199.

[398] Cf., e.g., And 3, 34 ... ἀποδώσομεν ὑμῖν περὶ αὐτῶν σκέψασθαι ... 3, 41 : ... καὶ ταῦτ᾽ἐφ᾽ὑμῖν πάντ᾽ἐστίν ... τούτων ὅ τι ἂν βούλησθε ἔλεσθε ... τούτων δ᾽ἐστὶ τὸ τέλος παρ᾽ὑμῖν.

from him nor even to spare him it. The whole process of πείθειν
should pave the way for αἱρεῖσθαι.[399] What one decides about in detail
is very diverse. But with regard to that which in general is intended
in πείθειν we can say that this αἱρεῖσθαι finds its wider context in the
overcoming of dissension.

Hence it comes about that πείθειν can simply have the meaning
"give assent to, assent" [400] and can thus be synonymous with μοι
(ὑμῖν) τοῦτο δοκεῖ [401]. So πείθειν is directed towards ὁμολογεῖν/ὁμολο-
γεῖσθαι [402] and is ultimately in the service of διαλλάσσειν,[403] i.e. of
peace-making and salvation.

Excursus I

Isoc 5, 24-29 contains a hermeneutic note by Isocrates on the right
use of aids. Here statements are made in the form of an introduction [404]
(cf. § 30 : ʿΑ μὲν οὖν ἐβουλόμην σοι προειρῆσθαι, ταῦτ'ἐστίν) on the
manner

---

[399] Cf., e.g., Aeschin 2, 20; 3, 42; D 8, 49; 10, 26; the opposite is "without my
assent" : cf. Aesschin 3, 41.

[400] The opposite is μηδενὶ τοῦτο δοκεῖ e.g. D 8, 50.

[401] Cf., e.g., Isoc 4, 19 : ἀμφισβητεῖσθαι → πείθειν → ὁμολογεῖσθαι
Isoc 6, 35 : ὁμολογῶ ... πείσειεν.

[402] Cf., e.g., Lys 12, 58 (60)→53; πείθειν is inseparably tied up with ἀποτρέπειν.
Isoc 4, 130 declares that he does not want to slander the Spartans but to put an end
(παύειν) to their characteristic mentality (129); he states that there is no other means of
averting (ἀποτρέπειν) mistakes and persuading them to strive towards different actions
than by a strong condemnation of their present behaviour (similarly Isoc 7, 77) : ἢν μή
τις ἐρρωμένως ἐπιτιμήσῃ τοῖς παροῦσιν. He emphasizes that his accusations are not aimed
at harming them but at putting things right (νουθετεῖν) in order to help them (ἐπ'ὠφελείᾳ):
χρὴ δὲ κατηγορεῖν μὲν ἡγεῖσθαι τοὺς ἐπὶ βλάβῃ τοιαῦτα λεγόντας, νουθετεῖν δὲ τοὺς
ἐπ'ὠφελείᾳ λοιδοροῦντας. I.e. here we have a general rule for the process of διαλλαγή.
With the help of μιμνήσκειν the two complementary elements in διαλλαγή are brought
about.

   i) ἀποτρέπειν τῶν ἁμαρτημάτων
   ii) πείθειν

Both, however, can only take place when they have been preceded by νουθετεῖν.
For in Isoc 4, 16 διαλλάσσειν is given as the goal of πείθειν (cf. § 15 : διδάσκουσιν ὡς χρὴ
διαλυσαμένους τὰς πρὸς ἡμᾶς αὐτοὺς ἔχθρας and § 129 : προειπὼν ὡς περὶ διαλλαγῶν ποιή-
σομαι τοὺς λόγους.

[403] Cf., e.g., D 19, 95.

[404] One might speculate about such an "introduction" worked out by Paul, even
if only in his mind : what ideas did he have as to the necessary manner of his speech
and the mental disposition of his audience ?

1) of his own style and
2) the necessary state of mind of his hearers;

if one attended to these (μετὰ γὰρ τούτων σκοπούμενος [405]) a successful πείθειν could be attained—even in a matter of [406] ἀναγιγνωσκομένους
λόγους [407] and not of λεγομένους λόγους.[408] On the other hand, failure
to observe these aids (ἀλλὰ τῶν μὲν προειρημένων ἁπάντων ἔρημος
γένηται καὶ γυμνός ...[409]) leads to the consequence that the λόγος
φαῦλος εἶναι δοκεῖ τοῖς ἀκούουσιν..[410]

The starting-point and occasion for this warning is the general
truth that ὅσον διαφέρουσι τῶν λόγων εἰς τὸ πείθειν οἱ λεγόμενοι τῶν
ἀναγιγνωσκομένων ...[411] And, it is added, ταῦτ᾽οὐκ ἀλόγως ἐγνώ-
κασιν ...[412] For if

1) the λογος read aloud lacks
   i) ἡ δόξα ἡ τοῦ λέγοντος
   ii) ἡ φωνή
   iii) αἱ μεταβολαὶ αἳ ἐν ταῖς ῥητορείαις γιγνομέναι
   iv) οἱ καιροί
   v) ἡ σπουδὴ ἡ περὶ τὴν πρᾶξιν

2) the λόγος read aloud is
   i) ἀπίθανος
   ii) καὶ μηδὲν ἦθος ἐνσημαινόμενος (ἀλλ᾽ὥσπερ ἀριθμῶν)

This then has as its consequence : Καὶ μηδὲν ἡ τὸ συναγωνιζόμενον
καὶ συμπεῖθον.[413]

But a speech read aloud can attain to πείθειν

---

[405] § 29.

[406] § 25.

[407] λόγοι ἀναγινωσκομένοι (speeches to be read aloud) are written πρὸς ἐπίδειξιν (4. 17;
5, 17) πρὸς ἐργολαβίαν.

[408] Speeches delivered by the speaker *ex tempore* (§ 25, cf. 29).

[409] § 26.

[410] § 27.

[411] § 25.

[412] § 26.

[413] "There is nothing to assist the speaker in his task or to help in persuading his
audience".

i)   when on the part of the readers

a)   δυσχερής [414]
b)   ἡ δυσχερεία [415]
c)   φθονερῶς δέχεσθαι [416]
d)   simply φθόνος [417] are put aside;

ii)   when they are not

a)   τοὺς τῶν κακῶν ἐπιθυμοῦντας [418]
b)   τοὺς οὐδενὶ λογισμῷ χρωμένους
c)   τοὺς ... οἳ τοσοῦτον ἀφέστασι τοῦ νοῦν ἔχειν ...

even if one's opponents, pretending to φάσκοντες ἀκριβῶς εἰδέναι, but in fact just φλυαροῦντες, try to talk them round by "raising an uproar"; [419]

iii)   when they practise

a)   ἡσυχάζουσαν ἔχων τὴν διάνοιαν
b)   ἀναλαμβάνω δ'ἕκαστον αὐτῶν εἰς τὴν διάνοιαν ἐξετάζῃς μετὰ λογισμοῦ καὶ φιλοσοφίας [420]
c)   εὐνοικῶς δέχεσθαι [421]
d)   προσέχειν τὸν νοῦν-ἀκούειν-πρόθυμος [422]

iv)   even if on the part of the speaker οὐδὲ ταῖς περὶ τὴν λέξιν εὐρυθμίαις καὶ ποικιλίαις κεκοσμήκαμεν αὐτόν ... [423] and that with the

---

[414] § 24; cf. § 117.

[415] § 29.

[416] Cf., e.g., D 19, 103.

[417] Cf., e.g., D 21, 29.

[418] Isoc 5, 75f.

[419] Isoc 5, 75 : εἰς ταραχὰς καθιστάναι. ταραχή here = disorder, disturbance of the mind : Isoc 2, 6; 2, 12.230; D 18, 218; etc.

[420] § 29.

[421] D 19, 103.

[422] D 18, 147.

[423] § 27 εὐρυθμίαι = general flow of the discourse
            ποικίλαι = rhetorical figure.

In this connection the description of the speaker in contrast to the poet in Evag 9-11

purpose ποιεῖν τοὺς λόγους ἡδίους ... ἅμα καὶ πιστοτέρους.⁴²⁴ That is all no longer possible because of Isocrates' age. But ἀπόχρη μοι τοσοῦτον αὐτὰς τὰς πράξεις ἁπλῶς δυνηθῶ διελθεῖν.⁴²⁵ This has also the additional advantage that ἡγοῦμαι δὲ καὶ σοὶ προσήκειν ἁπάντων τῶν ἄλλων (=εὐρυθμίαι καὶ ποικίλαι) ἀμελήσαντι ταύταις μόναις (= ταῖς πράξεσιν) προσέχειν τὸν νοῦν ......⁴²⁶

If one takes these thoughts to heart then ἄμεινον ἂν βουλεύσαιο περὶ αὐτῶν (= λόγων ἀναγιγνωσκομένων).

Excursus II

Among those practising πείθειν a special group is that of the πρέσβεις. A passage in D 18, 179 shows how much πείθειν is the task of envoys :

οὐκ εἶπον μὲν ταῦτ',
οὐκ ἔγραψα δέ,
οὐδ'ἔγραψα μέν,
οὐκ ἐπρέσβευσα δέ,
οὐδ'ἐπρέσβευσα μέν,
οὐκ ἔπεισα δὲ Θηβαίους ...... ⁴²⁷

---

is instructive; ποιῆται use πολλοὺς κόσμους and employ μὴ μόνον τοῖς τεταγμένοις ὀνόμασιν, ἀλλὰ τὰ μὲν ξένοις, τὰ δὲ καινοῖς, τὰ δὲ μεταφοραῖς, καὶ μηδὲν παραλιπεῖν, ἀλλὰ πᾶσι τοῖς εἴδεσι διαποικίλαι τὴν ποίησιν ...

... Moreover they work μετὰ μέτρων καὶ ῥυθμῶν .... And these have χάριν ὥστ'ἂν καὶ τῇ λέξει καὶ τοῖς ἐνθυμήμασιν ἔχῃ κακῶς ὅμως αὐταῖς ταῖς εὐρυθμίαις καὶ ταῖς συμμετρίαις ψυχαγωγοῦσι τοὺς ἀκούοντας ... The orator is contrasted with this : τοῖς δὲ περὶ τοὺς λόγους οὐδὲν ἔξεστιν τῶν τοιούτων, ἀλλ'ἀποτόμως καὶ τῶν ὀνομάτων τοῖς πολιτικοῖς μόνον καὶ τῶν εὐθυμημάτων τοῖς περὶ αὐτὰς τὰς πράξεις ἀναγκαῖον ἐστὶ χρῆσθαι.

⁴²⁴ § 27 : ἡδίους with regard to the effect on the hearing, πιστοτέρους with regard to the effect on the hearer's thinking.

⁴²⁵ ἁπλῶς (simple manner) denotes here a style of speaking which dispenses with adornments (κοσμεῖν). This is no reason why it should not nevertheless persuade. On the contrary the ἁπλότης of the style, so the argument runs, allows one to concentrate on essentials.

Similarly παρρησία is a rhetorical term.

⁴²⁶ § 28.

⁴²⁷ 18, 179 οὐκ εἶπον μέν ...—the famous (the only one in D and in the Attic orators as a whole) example of κλίμαξ (gradatio), translated by Quintilian 9, 3, 55 as follows : "non enim dixi quidem sed non scripsi, nec scripsi quidem sed non obii legationem, nec obii quidem sed non persuasi Thebanis" (quidem for μέν and sed for δέ). The climax is developed in stages with two main ideas, of which the second is also the first of the following stage; by means of it the different stages of an action are artfully disclosed

Note too how in the following passage the envoy's complete dedication to his task and to those men who have put their confidence in him and for whom he is responsible is expressed : καὶ ἔδωκ'ἐμαυτὸν ὑμῖν ἁπλῶς ... In D 19, 4f. there is a list of the qualities which one should expect in all envoys : εἰ σκέψαισθε παρ'ὑμῖν αὐτοῖς ... καὶ λογίσαισθε τίνων προσήκει τῇ πόλει λόγον παρὰ πρεσβευτοῦ λαβεῖν. πρῶτον μὲν τοίνυν ὧν ἀπήγγειλε, δεύτερον δ'ὧν ἔπεισε ...

ἐφ'ἅπασι δὲ τούτοις, εἰ ἀδωροδοκήτως ἢ μὴ πάντα ταῦτα πέπρασκαι.

I.e. the πρεσβεύτης is responsible

1) for his report (ἀπαγγέλλειν) on his return from his mission;
2) for the advice which he gives and for persuading the people in accordance with his reports; for τὸ βουλεύεσθαι (= αἱ συμβουλίαι = πείθειν) follows ἐκ τῶν ἀπαγγελίων and is the interpretation of these and that in respect of the actions which aim at the true benefit of the hearers;
3) for following their instructions;
4) for judging the favourable times and opportunities to use or for omitting to do so;
5) in general, for his integrity or lack of it during his mission.

Section 2 : Application of these observations with regard to Acts

A. This section offers no comprehensive examination of the theme of πείθειν in the New Testament, not even in Acts. Nor have we time to interpret the preceding observations in terms of the New Testament in every detail. That would be an undertaking in itself which lies outside the scope of our study.

All we want to do here is, having ascertained the outlines of the general character of πείθειν in classical Greek, to ask now where exactly πείθειν and thus the idea of "persuading" fit into Paul's preaching—according to A. Thus we are asking to some extent about the "Sitz in der Verkündigung" of πείθειν.

For only thus can we infer or confirm anew the significance of the

---

and here in particular it is shown that the speaker, either by merely giving advice or by making a proposal (γράψαι), could have stayed where he was, whereas, in constrat to the ways of earlier statesmen (§ 219), he alone did everything and took the whole responsibility upon himself.

human reason for Christian preaching, as it is expressed in the practice of πείθειν.

B. We recall the four passages (13, 46; 18, 6; 19, 9; 28, 28) which are outwardly characterized by Paul's ostentatious turning away from the Jews (ἀφιστάναι/ἀφορίζειν 19, 9) and towards the Gentiles (εἰς τὰ ἔθνη στρέφεσθαι/πορεύεσθαι 13, 46; 18, 6; τοῖς ἔθνεσιν ἀποστέλλειν 28, 28). These passages describe the judgment which has "come upon you, as it is said in the prophets: Behold, you scoffers, and wonder and perish; for I do a deed in your days, a deed which you will never believe, if one declares it to you" (13, 40f., RSV adapted). Thus is fulfilled the "work" of the apostle for which he has been "set apart", for which he has been "called forth" and which he has "completed", the work of God himself.

The preaching in these four passages is thus not just the announcement of the future judgment but its realization, in the loss τῆς αἰωνίου ζωῆς (13, 46), i.e. τοῦτο τὸ σωτήριον τοῦ θεοῦ (28, 28).

But what are the distinctive features of this situation in relation to our question?

I) The judgment upon the Jews is realized because through the preaching they come to *blaspheme* Christ and not just in some way to show their hatred and emnity against the apostle. The dominant idea in blasphemy is that of violation of the present power, majesty and glory of God. That also explains why 26, 8 and 11 are so close to one another: the Jews' opposition to the "good news" must take the form of blasphemy since it pierces to the very heart of that preaching, the proclamation of the Messiah:

13, 45 : ... καὶ ἀντέλεγον τοῖς ὑπὸ Παύλου λαλουμένοις βλασφημοῦντες ...

18, 6 : ἀντιτασσομένων δὲ αὐτῶν καὶ βλασφημούντων

19, 9 : ὡς δέ τινες ἐσκληρύνοντο καὶ ἠπείθουν κακολογοῦντες τὴν ὁδὸν ἐνώπιον τοῦ πλήθους (cf. Mk 9, 39; I C 1, 23).

28, 25 : ἀσύμφωνοι ... is not so clear as the other passages, yet this idea of rejection is doubtless replaced by the long quotation from Is 9, 6f.

Neither the threat to kill Paul, nor stoning, nor other forms of enmity against him and his message could move Paul to describe the Jews as standing under judgment. But if the "name" that is above all names and that stands for the presence of glory, power and salvation is blasphemed and reviled then there only remains alienation and thus loss of eternal life.

II) Now it is interesting to note how all these situations in which judgment is executed because of blasphemy are characterized by vigorous intellectual efforts on the part of the preacher. In fact, the only examples of L using πείθειν in the active to describe Paul's preaching occur in the context of such judgments. In addition, we must also pay attention to the other predominantly "rational" concepts :

Situation 1 : 13, 43ff.
v. 43 : ... οἵτινες προσλαλοῦντες αὐτοῖς ἔπειθον αὐτοὺς ...

Situation 2 : 18, 4ff.
v. 4 : διελέγετο δὲ ἐν τῇ συναγωγῇ ... ἔπειθέν τε ᾽Ιουδαίους καὶ ῞Ελληνας
v. 5 : ... συνείχετο τῷ λόγῳ ὁ Παῦλος, διαμαρτυρόμενος ...

Situation 3 : 19, 8ff.
v. 8 : ... διαλεγόμενος καὶ πείθων περὶ ...

Situation 4 : 28, 23ff.
v. 23 : ... ἐξετίθετο διαμαρτυρόμενος ... πείθων ...
v. 24 : καὶ οἱ μὲν ἐπείθοντο ... (cf. 17, 4)

It must be added that the practice of πείθειν obviously seeks to bring about the free decision of the other (cf., e.g., 13, 46 : οὐκ ἀξίους κρίνετε ἑαυτοὺς ...) and is thus diametrically opposed to anything like the ἠνάγκαζον βλασφημεῖν in 26, 11. Further, we want to point out that we can see more or less the same situation as confronts us here with regard to the *negative* result of Paul's preaching in its *positive* consequences in I C 14, 24f. There we find that the result of preaching τῷ νοΐ μου (v. 19) is not βλασφημεῖν but προσκυνεῖν τῷ θεῷ (v. 25) whereby the presence of God and thus the encounter with him are *recognized* and explicitly confessed : ὄντως ὁ θεὸς ἐν ὑμῖν ἐστιν.

Even if the word πείθειν is not used here—and in the case of I C that would be only too understandable—yet the same idea obviously is here : the words describing what leads up to the προσκυνεῖν are ἐλέγχεσθαι, ἀνακρίνεσθαι, φανερὰ γίνεται, that is, all words which we found continually in our previous investigation of πείθειν, to be intellectual in tone and to belong particularly to contexts involving judgment.

To the same context belong the charges against Paul (A 18, 13; 19, 26) and the passage in II C 5, 10f. in which Paul speaks of all his preaching of the gospel as essentially πείθειν, and this in the closest possible connection with the idea of the βῆμα.

C) Conclusions

I) The function and significance which L attaches to human reason in Paul's preaching can be gathered in this § 2 from the role which "persuasion" plays in his preaching.

II) This preaching can always only have the character of testimony; yet, at the same time, in view of *what* is testified to here, it is more than a mere (neutral, informal) reference to Jesus. For the risen Lord himself is present in the testimony of his witness, but he has to be identified—and this is the first function assigned to the human reason—so that his presence becomes one that is recognized and so encounter with him becomes reality; because that is so, therefore preaching always brings not just information but also a situation of decision and thus judgment. And it is here that πείθειν has its "Sitz in der Verkündigung" and human reason has its second function in the preaching of the gospel: the preaching is meant, by the use of πείθειν, to help the hearers to make their own decision—for or against Christ—in this encounter.

The φρονεῖν that lies behind the μαρτύριον and thus also the πείθειν is therefore not only the place where, and the means by which, the apostle Paul suffers and bears vicariously the suffering of Christ as blasphemy, but also the place where, and the means by which, the preacher executes judgment, either as salvation or as loss of it. So, significantly, worship (I C 14) and blasphemy (A) take place, not because of a preaching which left the hearers in ignorance and incomprehension, but because of a preaching which sought to explain things as far as possible to its hearers. And the practice of "persuasion" seems in such a context to be something like an "intellectual ultimatum" after which there can only be προσκύνησις or βλασφημία, i.e., acceptance or rejection. Thus the practice of "persuasion" to some extent sums up all the efforts which have been characteristic of the previous preaching, beginning from the "argumentation" from one's sources.

CONCLUSIONS :
THE REASONS FOR AND THE SIGNIFICANCE AND FUNCTION
OF THE HUMAN REASON IN PREACHING

§ 1

1. The use of human reason indicated by words like διαλέγεσθαι, διανοίγειν, or παρατίθεσθαι in the apostolic preaching has as its first important function the identification of the Lord who is present in the testimony of his witness and thus to make possible an encounter with him.

2. The presence of the risen Lord in the testimony of his witness is a presence shaped by suffering, which the witness must bear representatively for Christ. He takes this suffering upon himself primarily in carrying out the preaching itself and thus accounts for it above all on the level of human φρονεῖν.

§ 2

1. We first surveyed the meaning of πείθειν in classical Greek.

2. The use of the human reason indicated by the word πείθειν in the apostolic preaching has as its second important function the identification of the hearer, confronted with the testimony and what he recognizes to be the presence of Christ, as being what he is in his encounter with Christ (coram Deo).

Thus L sees Paul's use of human reason within his preaching as more than a refinement whose use could be left to his own judgment; rather the employment of human reason here is an effort which is demanded by the nature of that which the preaching serves—the identification of Christ and of the hearer.

CHAPTER TWO

1 AND 2 THESSALONIANS

INTRODUCTION

We have seen in connection with our exegesis of Acts that the function and significance of human reason in Paul's preaching became clear when one grasped aright the relation between τὸ εὐαγγέλιον and ὁ λόγος, between διαλέγεσθαι and καταγγέλλειν.

In what follows we will continue with the crystallization of the "intellectual element" within Paul's preaching methods. But in doing so we will quite deliberately adopt the findings of our investigation of Acts as a working hypothesis for the following study and will ask whether the "intellectual element" in 1/2 Th does not also lie hidden in the mutual relationship of τὸ εὐαγγέλιον and ὁ λόγος (and related words). To do this we must first show that this relation really plays a role in Paul's reminiscences of his preaching in Thessalonica and thus in his thought.

In fact it plays an important role :

1) with regard to the subject of his preaching :

τὸ εὐαγγέλιον ἡμῶν	I 1,5	=	ὁ λόγος	I 1,5
τὸ εὐαγγέλιον ἡμῶν	II 2,14	=	αἱ παραδόσεις	II 2,15
τὸ εὐαγγέλιον τοῦ Θεοῦ	I 2,2	=	ἡ παράκλησις ἡμῶν	I 2,3
τὸ εὐαγγέλιον τοῦ Χριστοῦ	I 3,2	=	στηρίξαι, παρακαλέσαι	I 3,2
ὁ λόγος Θεοῦ	I 2,13	=	ὁ λόγος ἀνθρώπων	I 2,13

2) with regard to the activity of the preacher :

κηρύσσειν	I 2,9	=	παρακαλεῖν, παραμυθεῖσθαι	I 2,12

3) with regard to the Thessalonians :

ἐπιστεύθη	II 1,10	=	ἐδιδάχθητε	II 2,15
στήκετε ἐν κυρίῳ	I 3,8	=	στήκετε, κρατεῖτε τὰς παραδόσεις	II 2,15

4) with regard to the goal of all this activity :

εἰς τὸ σωθῆναι I 2,16 ; II 2,10	=	εἰς τὸ μὴ ... σαλευθῆναι ὑμᾶς ἀπὸ τοῦ νοὸς	II 2,2
		εἰς τὸ μηδένα σαίνεσθαι	I 3,3

The following items therefore go together :

1) The *gospel*, God's word, was *preached* and *believed* leading to *salvation*.
2) The *traditions*, men's word, were *taught* and *learnt* leading to *understanding*.

Thus it is clear that the twofold nature of the statements that we found in A 17, 2-4, relating to Paul's preaching and his hearers' reaction, is also preserved in 1/2 Th :

1) On the one hand ὁ λόγος ἀνθρώπων = διαλέγεσθαι, διανοίγειν, etc.
   on the other　　ὁ λόγος τοῦ Θεοῦ = καταγγέλλειν τὸν Χριστόν
2) On the one hand ἐδιδάχθητε　　　= ἀνακρίνειν, πείθεσθαι
   on the other ἐπιστεύθη　　　　= προσκληροῦσθαι [1]

This must be more closely examined in what follows.

---

[1] A connection between A 17, 1ff. and 1/2 Th is also visible in the following points :

i)　σαλεύειν is used only once in A in a figurative sense (apart from A 2, 15, but here it is a quotation of Ps 16), namely of the σαλεύειν of the Thessalonian Jews in Beroea. In 2 Th 2, 2 σαλευθῆναι is the result of opponents' activity in the church

ii)　A 17, 11 : ἐδέξαντο τὸν λόγον μετὰ πάσης προθυμίας ...
　　1 Th 1, 6 : δεξάμενοι τὸν λόγον μετὰ χαρᾶς πνεύματος ἁγίου ...

iii)　Lu 1 (303) remarks on ἀνακρίνειν : "... a noteworthy instance of the right of private judgement". Can we not compare with this the striking frequency of "knowing" etc. (εἰδότες I 1, 4; αὐτοὶ γὰρ οἴδατε 2, 1; καθὼς οἴδατε 2, 2; μνημονεύετε γάρ 2, 9; κάθαπερ οἴδατε 2, 11; αὐτοὶ γὰρ οἴδατε 3, 3; ... καὶ οἴδατε 3, 4; οἴδατε γάρ 4, 2 etc.) ? Cf. here Baur (481), who prefers to see "diese fortgehende Recapitulation" as proof of the unauthenticity of 1 Th.

§ 3. *1* Thessalonians

Section 1 : 1 Th 1, 5

A) The Problem

For our investigation in the Pauline Corpus this verse is of central importance. For on the one hand we find relatively few passages in Paul's letters in which Paul summarizes his previous missionary activity. On the other hand a point of departure is and has been found here for the understanding of Paul's theology which turns out to be, and has turned out to be, influential even for the problematic relation of "faith" and "human reason". In view of these two facts it is very important to understand this passage aright.

I) The *point of departure* simply consists of the fact that the usual [1]

[1] Let us obtain a general view : despite all differences in their explanation of details in I 1, 5, most commentators, with few exceptions (Bor 58; Do 70f.; vH 157; Wo 25), are agreed that τὸ εὐαγγέλιον ... δυνάμει here has "spezifische" (A-R 14) parallels, i.e. "wesentlich wie" (Zö 11), "ganz so wie hier" (Ko 95), in I C 2, 4f.; 4, 19f. (A-R 14; Bi 6; El 8; Hen 51; Ko 95; Mas 85; Mi 3, 9; Mo 16; Ne 17; Pl 1, 10; Schmi 18; Wet 96; Zö 11) and also indeed in Col 2, 23; I J 3, 18 (Ol 406; Zö 11) : "τὸ εὐαγγέλιον ... δυνάμει ist augenscheinlich der Stelle 1 Cor 2, 4 nachgebildet" (Baur 481f.—this is, incidentally, a further proof in his eyes of the unauthenticity of 1 Th). In other words "Paulus hätte auch hier (wie 1 Kor 2, 4) schreiben können : 'Mein Wort und meine Botschaft standen nicht auf überredenden Worten der Weisheit, sondern auf dem Erweis von Geist und Kraft' " (Schü 38). These parallels are then the key to the (parallel) interpretation of I 1, 5 : accordingly the two entities λόγος and δύναμις are here understood as a "Gegensatz" (Ko 93; Schmi 18; Schm 15; Zö 11), "(strong) contrast" (Ea 41; Gl 3; Lin 33; Mo 27f.) and "antithesis" (Ol 406; cf. also Ga 55; Lü 25; Schü 38), occasionally also being explained by means of the supposedly identical contrasting pair of λόγος and ἔργον (Ko 93 with examples; Ol 406). And this "contrast" is no less than one between that which is "negative" and that which is "positive" : "The influence in which the Gospel came to the Thessalonians is ... stated first negatively ... and then positively ..." (Mi 3, 9). "Paulus liebt es, die positive Aussage durch die vorangestellte negative zu heben" (Do 70). Accordingly the λόγος here is but "leer, eitel ... unreel ..." (A-R 23) and the reference is to "a mere word" (e.g. Sa 92), a "blosses Wort" (e.g. Schm 15; Ew 39; Ko 93) ,a "merely ... eloquent instruction" (Mas 85). The idea here is that this λόγος itself is merely something like an empty container which, apart from its being a container, "gar keinen Grund hat" (Ko 93), and thus is a "bedeutungsloses (Wort)" (Ko 93), "ohne (eigene) Kraft und (eigenen) Gehalt" (A-R 23), and is thus "kraft- und erfolglos zugleich" (A-R 23). Such "leere Gerede" (Ko 93), such "empty

interpretation of what Paul means here—appealing to passages like
I C 2, 4; 4, 20—tries to understand it in terms of a contrast between
"word" and "power". Accordingly λόγος here refers to the "empty
and dead eloquence of men",[2] in contrast to which the δύναμις may
change this λόγος, "dem sie einwohnt(e)",[3] to "mighty eloquence".[4]
This transsubstantiation of the word, this transformation through the
δύναμις, "welche nur dem göttlichen Worte eignet"[5] makes any
"Argumentieren"[6] not only unnecessary (for this "mighty eloquence"
is "weit erhaben über blosse worte"[7] and so ultimately has no more
need of them), but even harmful, for it is a betrayal of the Christian
"straightforward narration of that which God has declared and

---

rhetoric" (Mor 1, 57) can only produce "a mere empty sound" (Barn 15), which can do
no more than "to entertain or amuse" (Barn 15).

In contrast to δύναμις, πνεῦμα ἅγιον and πληροφορία, which describe "three kind of
Divine influence" (Dr 19) the λόγος has the miserable fate of being "weiter nichts ...
als ein Wort" (Ko 93). But this "contrast" does not simply exist unchanged but it is
understood as "mediated" in that in the event of the Gospel the δύναμις enters into the
empty vessel of the λόγος and this "das Wort, dem sie einwohnt(e), gewaltig und wirkungsvoll macht(e)" (vH 157). The equation then reads as follows :

"dead eloquence" (Ca 24) = "leeres, d.h. bedeutungs- und damit auch wirkungsloses
                          Wort"
+ δύναμις   = "die objektive Gotteskraft" (A-R 14)
= "mighty eloquence"
(Ea 41)   = "powerful speech" (Dr 19).

Whereas most of the commentators ascribe the πληροφορία to the figure of the preacher,
the "divine influence" (Dr 19) designated by the δύναμις they regard as above all entering
into the preaching itself. Δύναμις therefore means here "eine Beschaffenheit der ev.
Predigt" (Zö 11) and refers to the "reality, energy, and effective earnestness, with
which ..." (El 8; cf. Gl 3)—as a "conscious power" (Mas 85)—the apostle preached
and which therefore also "aus dem predigenden Apostel hervorleuchtet(e)" (A-R 14).
The alleged "contrast" in I 1, 5 is therefore summed up as follows (as in Mi 3, 9) : Paul's
words serve "to show the *strong* contrast between the Gospel's being preached merely
by learned speech and being proclaimed in power and in the Holy Spirit" (Lin 33).
This was "the most effective means of reaching the conscience, and satisfying the religious
instincts" (Mi 3, xliii). "... the contrast is between the mere presentation of a message
and an effective, dynamic proclamation" (Mo 27), it is a "contrast between mere speaking
and effective preaching" (Mo 28).

  2 Ca 241.
  3 vH 157.
  4 Ea 41.
  5 Rö 26.
  6 Cf. Mi 3, xliii.
  7 Ew 39.

effected in Jesus.[8] And the penalty for this follows hard on its heels
in that the arguments of the human λόγος, "der eben weiter nichts
ist als ein Wort",[9] "als solche leicht verhallen".[10]

What interests us here is the fact that the basic understanding of
this passage is controlled, not primarily by this passage itself, but by
the contrast of "word" and "power" presupposed and imported from
I C. That has, as we saw, the result that Paul is understood to have
been able to speak of the "objektive(n) Gottesmacht" only at the
cost of the human λόγος and argumentation in recalling his own
missionary activity; in the light of the positive experience of "three
kind of Divine influences" [11] he could only regard the "human influence", namely the λόγος, as their exact opposite, and so as a
"negative influence".[12] Thus, it is held, Paul here contrasts word and
power as opposites and defines the positive power by the negative
word; he could only speak of God's power by speaking at the same
time of the powerlessness of the human λόγος.

But one cannot avoid the impression that it is principally the
commentators who deliberately play down the λόγος more than Paul
in order to make room for the "strongest" possible statements about
the δύναμις; for the "emptier" one makes that which is "eben weiter
nichts (ist) als ein Wort", the more powerful and "overwhelming" the
"objektive Gotteskraft" must be which fills this "emptiness".

II)   That this is a problem of far-reaching importance, which also
touches the heart of our own question, can be clearly seen from the
effects of this point of departure on our problem of the relation of
"faith" and "human reason". For, to judge from the commentators,
a corresponding evaluation or devaluation of the human λόγος goes
hand in hand for Paul with his depreciation of the understanding
attained by λόγος. For by the "contrast" referred to in I 1, 5 Paul,
or so at any rate the argument goes, wants to emphasize "that his
preaching was (not) effective on account of some skill with words;
2, 3ff. seems to denounce the sort of pleasing speech".[13] But this
shows clearly that the problem of the relation of faith and human

---

[8] Mo 16.
[9] Ko 93.
[10] Lü 26.
[11] Dr 19.
[12] Cf. Mi 3, 9.
[13] Mo 27.

reason is already posed by the question of the role and significance assigned by Paul to "speech" in his missionary activity. If we want to follow the commentators, then Paul solved this problem in that he, quite logically in the light of the relative contempt which he felt for his own λόγος, tended to withdraw the human "understanding" from the sphere of this "negative influence", i.e. λόγος, and to transplant it into that of the divine δύναμις. Thus all the "understanding" of the gospel which was produced in men is credited to the δύναμις indwelling the "word" while the λόγος itself really contributes nothing to real understanding of the gospel—and rather impedes it as a temptation and hindrance. For since Paul in 1, 5 is trying to say "that his preaching was (not) effective on account of some skill with words" [14] one can infer that "the effectiveness of the Gospel is not dependent upon human learning (= learned discourse)".[15] For "words alone, however eloquent, cannot (influence men's hearts)" [16] and can have no "Einwirkung auf die Gemüther".[17] Only the δύναμις can do that; it alone is "wirkungsvoll",[18] it alone, "in contrast to 'word' ", makes an "impression ... on the hearers",[19] it works "als Macht über die Seelen",[20] so "as to convert the soul",[21] it signifies that "with which our gospel ... came home to the minds and hearts of the hearers".[22]

But if "understanding" is credited to the "Kraft, welche das Wort, dem sie einwohnte, gewaltig ... machte" [23] and so to such an "over-whelming force",[24] then the manner of such "understanding" can only be likened to divine "rape" which "den Verstand für sich ge-fangen nimmt ..." [25] rather than persuade it. And anyone who in the face of such naked "objektiven Gotteskraft" still wants to come to an understanding of the gospel through "Sinn und Gedanken" [26] is

---

[14] Mo 27.
[15] Lin 33.
[16] Pl 1, 10.
[17] Schm 15.
[18] vH 157.
[19] Gl 3.
[20] A-R 14.
[21] Barn 15.
[22] Bi 6.
[23] vH 157.
[24] Ea 41.
[25] Rö 26.
[26] Schü 38.

unmasked as one who will surrender himself to the "Zwang von Beweisen der Weltweisheit",[27] in short is unmasked as one who wants "Weltweisheit suchen".[28] Such should heed the warning that "(we must not) expect to meet among the converts 'many wise after the flesh, many mighty, and many noble' ";[29] that too we can learn from I C about the situation obtaining then in Thessalonica.

What seems to have infiltrated into most commentaries is nothing less than the representation of Paul as the typical exponent of a docetism both of the human "word" and of the resultant human "understanding"; this is achieved by a blending of I C and 1 Th 1, 5. For inasmuch as one sees the "human influence", i.e. λόγος as ultimately swallowed up by the "three kind of Divine influence", so one sees the understanding of the gospel which is apparently the product of "Sinn und Gedanken" as swallowed up by the "over-whelming force", which "den Verstand für sich gefangen nimmt". What is completely lacking here is a positive attempt based on 1 Th 1, 5 and its context to grasp that even an event like the preaching of the gospel need not be ashamed of the constructive contribution provided by the human λόγος and the understanding resulting *from it*—without thereby needing to surrender to the "Zwang von Beweisen der Welt-weisheit".

III) The *problem* that this raises can be delineated by means of the following questions :[30]

(1) *Preliminary question* : the fact that our passage has continually been dealt with on the analogy of I C 1 and 2 under the category "contrast" poses the question whether in this dependence on I C one has remained sufficiently dependent on 1 Th itself. Has one tried hard enough to understand this passage first in the context of 1 Th

---

[27] Ko 96.

[28] Schü 38.

[29] Fra 5.

[30] Here we must give in advance a qualification which may help to to put the sharp-ness of the following questions in its true perspective. For it seems to me that the chief difficulty is that much that is said is *in itself* correct. Who could raise any objection against the deep insight of Schü (38) when he writes : "Mehr als alle Gründe überzeugt die lebendige geistliche Erfahrung des gegenwärtigen Herrn, der in dem Wort seines Sendlings wirkt und hinter ihm erkennbar ist" ? But our question is first raised when we seem to detect that God's activity can only be spoken of positively by simultaneously counting human speech as worthless.

itself? Or can this statement in 1 Th really be grasped if we primarily understand it on the basis of I C ? Could it not even be that in listening to I C we have stopped our ears to 1 Th ?

(2) Main questions :

i) Does 1 Th 1, 5 really contain the same *contrast* as that in I C or even a similar one ? What role and significance does Paul assign to "speech" in his missionary activity as a whole ?—If Paul in our verse really devalues his own λόγος (to recollect only Mi 3 : "negatively") how is this related to his "eloquence" to which "Paul's own reported discourses and many parts of his extant letters testify" ? [31] If the commentators are right and the δύναμις as it were replaces the power of persuasion within the "word" and is thus the sole factor that produces understanding, then we must ask

a) where it is said in the text that the λόγος has had *no* "Ein-wirkung auf die Gemüther" ?

b) whether "persuasion" is really only "the result of the activity of the Holy Spirit working within believers" [32] or not *also* the result of the activity of the natural human reason working within believers,[33] and thus

c) what significance is attached to persuasive speech and exposition, to the power of argument and scriptural proof ? Is this all an ἀδιάφορον ? —Does Paul know at all of the idea of the "empty" word which is then "filled" by the entrance of the δύναμις—when he speaks of his own preaching ? Could Paul have called his own λόγος "a mere display of rhetoric",[34] "mere human eloquence",[35] in short "empty words" ? [36]

---

[31] H-V 35.

[32] Mor 1, 57.

[33] Mor (2, 37) seems to indicate something like this when he formulates it more carefully as follows : "but Paul insists that eloquence is not a complete explanation of its (= the gospel's) effectiveness". This at least recognizes the relative importance of the idea of eloquence in the presentation of the gospel.

[34] Ga 55.

[35] Ne 17.

[36] Schü 38.

[37] A-R and Do are, to my knowledge, the only ones who give any sign of recognizing this important distinction (although they do not employ it as usefully as they might have in the exegesis of I 1, 5) when they write "nur dass dort das μόνον fehlt, weil vom λόγος τῶν πεφυσιωμένων, hier aber von der Predigt des Apostles die Rede ist" (A-R 14; cf. Do 70).

ii)   Is there after all any contrast involved in 1 Th 1, 5 ? [37]

iii)   What then is the *theme* of 1, 5—the manner of Paul's former preaching or the election of the Thessalonians ? Is Paul speaking *here* at all of whether or not his preaching was then "effective" "on account of some skill with words" ? [38] Must not the correct answer to this question be put to use in our exegesis of this passage ?

(3)   *Guiding questions* for the following investigation :

i)   What help can a consideration of the grammatical formula οὐ μόνον ... ἀλλὰ καί provide for our understanding of this passage ?

ii)   How should we understand δι'ὑμᾶς ?

iii)   How does Paul speak of his relation to the Thessalonians elsewhere in 1 Th—and this with regard to his own missionary activity ? [39]

B. *Attempted solution*

Since our passage itself contains no further information as to the contents of the λόγος, we can expect no more in the following attempted

---

[38] Quite apart from the question whether "some skill with words" can so easily be identified with "pleasing speech" (Mo 27).

[39] We do not want to enter into the question here whether power, the Holy Spirit and assurance have appeared in the apostles only as they preached or in the church or in both. The commentators cannot agree on this question. We merely want to allude here to an interesting fact. Previously one often interpreted ἐν δυνάμει as if Paul were referring to his miraculous actions. In doing so one was clearly moving towards a division of Paul's missionary activity into preaching on the one hand (λόγος), and healing and miracles on the other. But it is the more recent commentators, in particular those mentioned up till now, who have mostly rejected this interpretation and have as it were projected this ἐν δυνάμει into the act of preaching itself : what is subtracted from the miraculous side is credited to the preaching side.

What has happened here is that once the word δύναμις was understood of another testimony existing alongside the preaching. For this concept one could undoubtedly appeal to Jesus himself, his commissioning of his disciples and the activity of the apostles in A. But whether this old interpretation is false or not, the fact remains that in the more recent interpretation of this passage a possibly correct insight within the old allegedly false understanding has *not* been adopted and put to positive use in the newer interpretation, namely that ἐν δυνάμει need not necessarily be swallowed up in the act of preaching itself, even if one remains sceptical of the old interpretation.

solution than to open our eyes to a new evaluation, based on Paul himself, of the position (and so implicitly of the significance) of the λόγος in the "gospel-event" as a whole. But on the other hand we can hope to glean from that a more or less substantial correction of the usual interpretation. The results, i.e. such an eye-opening and the consequent correction, will, despite its seemingly modest nature, be of fundamental importance, firstly with regard to our whole subsequent investigation of the problem of the relation of "faith" and "human reason" through an examination of Paul's methods of preaching, but secondly also with regard to the influence which such a correction can possibly have on our understanding of a large part of Pauline theology. In order to come nearer to as correct an understanding of this passage, 1, 5,[40] as possible we must make three observations, one on form and two on content.

I) Observation on form

As our survey up till now has shown, this passage has generally been understood

— as if Paul's *theme* here was primarily the manner of his former preaching, and
— as if Paul expressed this theme here in terms of a *contrast* between λόγος and δύναμις.

We must first ask how Paul uses the grammatical formula οὐ μόνον...[41] ἀλλά [42] καί,[43] which according to De is "too familiar" in classical

---

[40] Cf. in general on 1, 5 Rob 566, 731, 1045; M III 50, 175; Si 158; Gr 2, 170; M II 275.

[41] On the question of negations (with a bibliography) cf. S II 590-99; K-G II 178-223; Ma II 2, 543-67; M III 281-7; Ra 210-2.

[42] Cf. on this particle in general S II 553-90; K-G II 116-339, 515f.; J 1700-28; Ma II 3, 114-74, especially 116ff.; M III 329-41; De 1-32.

[43] I) Lehmann has collected examples of ἀλλά alone and ἀλλά καί after οὐ μόνον in his commentary on Luc. dial. mort. 12, 1. II) De (3) states that in classical Greek "we occasionally find οὐ μόνον ... ἀλλά without καί ...". That is also the case in the New Testament (cf. Bu 317; Rob 1166). Ps gives an explanation of this (I 104): "Enthält das zweite Glied eine Steigerung, so tritt nach οὐ μόνον zu ἀλλά noch καί". B-D-F 448, 1 define more closely this climax expressed in the addition of καί: *the second member is a separate entity and thus does not include the first*, whereas in the case of οὐ μόνον ... ἀλλά without καί "the second member includes the first" (so also A-G 529, where X., Cyr. 1, 6, 16; Diod. S. 4, 15, 1 are cited as evidence; but Bu 317 thinks otherwise:

Greek "to need illustration",[44] elsewhere in his letters. Does he really use it [45] to take us to the heart of a given passage ? And does he really use it to express a contrast of negative and positive ? [46]

This formula appears in all 21 times in Paul's writings. Let us restrict ourselves first to 1 Th. Apart from 1, 5 Paul uses this formula also in 1, 8 and 2, 8. The interpretation [47] of these two passages shows two things :

the omission of the καί places the "Nachdruck auf den zweiten Theil"; similarly G-T 28 : "When καί is omitted ... the gradation is strengthened"). If this view is correct then this aspect alone would lead us to suppose that in the λόγος on the one hand and the δύναμις, πνεῦμα ἅγιον and πληροφορία on the other we are dealing with *different* manifestations of the gospel.

[44] De 3.

[45] Instead of οὐ μόνον we also find in non-biblical Greek οὐχ ὅτι (μὴ ὅτι) or οὐχ ὅπως (μὴ ὅπως) in the first part, followed by ἀλλά or ἀλλὰ καί.

[46] The interpretation of this bipartite formula in grammars and lexicons :

I) B-D-F and Rob, neither of whom discuss this formula itself more fully, above all emphasize here the *adversative* character of ἀλλά and correspondingly speak of the "contrary" expressed by this formula (B-D-F 488, 1) and even of the "sharp antithesis" (Rob 1165f.). Whereas A-S (21) briefly describes this formula as "opposing a previous negation" P and G-T are more explicit : the former holds that ἀλλά in this formula expresses the "Gegenteil, so dass das Vorhergehende ganz aufgehoben wird ..." (101) and the latter correspondingly treats this formula as introducing a "disjunctive statement(s) where one thing is denied that another may be established" (461; taken up by Rob 1165; cf. also L-S s.v. ἀλλά). II) M III (329f.) thinks otherwise : although he too does not examine this formula more closely, he yet states that the otherwise strongly adversative particle ἀλλά is at least "weakened" when combined with a preceding οὐ μόνον (no examples are given). III) The *climatic* significance of this formula instead of the adversative is to be emphasized; this is the view of S (II 578) who expressly takes this "parataktische Verbindung" (οὐ μόνον ... ἀλλὰ καί), not as adversative, but as climactic (633) : in this formula there is "nicht ... ein ... Gegensatz anzunehmen". Similarly Ma (II 3, 118) calls the ἀλλὰ καί "steigernd ... besonders nach οὐ (μὴ) μόνον ...". Bu (317) sees the addition πολὺ μᾶλλον (Phil 2, 12) as a perfect New Testament-expression of this "gesteigerte Vorstellung" in the second clause (W 442), or this "Steigerung" (Ps I 104)—"aber es versteht sich auch ohne (diesen) Zusatz" (Bu 317). IV) Cf. also the examples of our formula cited in M-M (417), both stemming from the 2nd cent. AD (P. Ryl. II 116, 14 and 243, 4), and the example cited by A-G, also from the 2nd cent. (P. Mich. 209, 12); also Jos. *Bell.* 3, 102. Cf. also Bey 104; 135ff., 141; Bur 481; N 83; Si 184; Tu 113f.; Ra does not deal with this formula.

[47] In both cases a climax is involved, which finds expression in this formula : "not only ... in Macedonia and Achaea, but everywhere" (1, 8); "not only the gospel of God but also our own selves" (2, 8). In both cases the point of this formula is to emphasize the especial significance, the greatness and the scope of the reality to which this formula refers. The main points are the "sounding forth of the word of God from you" and "our affection for you" respectively. Paul attests "your sounding forth" and "our affection" by means of this grammatical structure.

(1) The objects mentioned within this grammatical formula (Macedonia, Achaea—every place; the gospel—our souls) are subordinate to the realities attested by these objects (your sounding forth; our affection). Thus the *theme* of these passages is clear. Paul's purpose is in no way to say anything about the mutual relations of "Macedonia" and "Achaea" to "every place" in the one case or of "the gospel" to "our souls" in the other. The theme is rather the importance and strength of "your faith in God" and "our affection for you"—and nothing else.

(2) Since the objects mentioned within this grammatical formula are not themselves the theme, Paul cannot want to compare them with one another, let alone to contrast them. The formula is therefore not meant to express a value judgment.[48] For a contrast can only be expressed through appropriate value judgments which in general can be classified as "negative" and "positive". But how could that be the case in 1, 8 and 2, 8? This formula is rather only used in these two cases to attest by the *intensification* which it expresses (not only ... but also) the truth, the significance and the scope of the reality which is thematically prior to and above this formula. The emphasis and stress in these statements must be completely changed if it is transferred from the theme itself to the individual objects within this grammatical formula. For then the intensification expressed by the secondary objects and perfectly intelligible within the framework of the given theme, is changed into a contrast of a negative and positive.

When we turn to the other passages in Paul's writings [49] we find that this discovery is confirmed.[50]

---

[48] The only "value judgments" which appear at all here are in fact the quality of "your faith" and the quality of "our affection".

[49] II C 7, 7; 8, 10.19.21; 9, 12; R 1, 32; 3, 29; 4, 12.16.23f.; 5, 3.11; 8, 23; 9, 10.24; 13, 5; Phil 1, 29; 2, 12.27.

[50] They all show clearly that the grammatical formula οὐ μόνον ... ἀλλὰ καί primarily expresses a climax (II C 7, 7; 8, 21; R 1, 32; 3, 29; 4, 12.23f.; 8, 23; 9, 10.24; 13, 5), a climax of positive things as well as of negative (e.g. R 1, 32). But never does the formula appear combining a negative and a positive object. All the passages clearly show that the climax is related to a quite definite situation within which such an emphasis (cf. especially II C 8, 10; 9, 12) is meaningful and even necessary. This is often a climax in the sense of a concentration on a particular problem about which Paul is writing. Paul uses this formula to give his words a definite application (e.g. II C 7, 7; 8, 10, 21). Naturally a distinction is thereby made, e.g. between Titus' "presence" and his "message" (II C 7, 7), between "wanting" and "doing" (II C 8, 10) and between the evangelist and the additional chosen messenger (II C 8, 18f.) etc. But

Conclusion of the observation on form with regard to 1, 4f. :

a) Paul cannot mean to express a contrast with the formula οὐ
μόνον ... ἀλλὰ καί but only an *intensification*;[51]

b) this intensification serves to attest (or give concrete form to)
a *theme* which can be a particular condition or circumstance either of
the church or of the apostles.

But what is this theme? Only the answer to this question may
finally remove from our eyes the "Corinthian spectacles" laid upon
us above all by Baur and may thus open our eyes to a correct, unpre-
judiced judgment as to the real position which Paul assigned here to
his λόγος—and so also to the understanding of the gospel which he
hoped would result from it—within the framework of the other
testimonies of the gospel which we have seen from the previous
observation on form to be distinguished from this λόγος.[52] Thus we
come to two

II) Observations on content

(1) The objects introduced as an intensification by ἀλλὰ καί are

---

this distinction is never to be taken as a contrast but always as an addition, something
additional. Thereby this addition is often emphasized because it either expresses something astonishing (cf. R 3, 29; 4, 12.16) or contains the more important point (R 13, 5).

[51] Thus Pauline evidence leads me to treat this bipartite formula as climactic rather
than adversative following those mentioned in n. 46 (III). We must then take the ἀλλά
here in what is also its original sense : " 'not only this, but also', used to introduce
an additional point in an emphatic way" (B-D-F 448, 6), "something new, but not
essentially in contrast" (Rob 1185; cf. K-G II 286)—which in fact militates against the
negative tone of the translation "merely as so much talking" (M 78; an idea like that
clearly expressed in the words οὐ μόνον βουλεύματα ἀλλὰ ἔργα S. *Ph.* 556; cf.
f. 885; E. *f.* 642 etc. clearly lies behind such a translation). Better and more positive
is "nicht nur, sondern noch viel mehr" (*ThBl* 217), "ja selbst, ja sogar" (so Ps I 104 :
"Auch ohne vorausgehendes μόνον findet sich ἀλλὰ καί nach negat. Wörtern wie nach
οὐδέ ... οὐδείς ... in dieser Bedeutung), whereas "nicht nur ... sondern auch" (P-C 1,
280), "not only ... but also" (A-G 529; G-T 28) does not express clearly enough the
"continuative-, consecutive-steigernden" meaning of this formula. In our opinion then
1 Th 1, 5 is closer to a passage like, e.g., II C 7, 7 than to I C 2, 4 and 4, 20 and thus
the description of the former as "climacteric, not contradictory" (Rob 1185f.) better
fits our passage. Ellicott (in *A Critical and Grammatical Commentary on St. Paul's
Epistles to the Philippians, Colossians, and to Philemon*, London 1861, p. 35) describes
this formula well : "... a clause ... that serves materially to heighten the assertion
and add to its significance".

[52] Cf. also n. 43 (II).

to be closely related to the apostle's knowledge of the *election* of the Thessalonian Christians.[53] That is undoubtedly the leading idea in Paul's thought here, and it is to this idea that the other ideas are subordinated. Accordingly the *theme* of this verse is the connection, really mentioned only to encourage them, between the reality of the Thessalonian Christians' election and the additional testimonies of the gospel brought by the apostles which are clearly to be distinguished from the λόγος. This connection seems according to Paul to be twofold, yet each element depends on the other :

i)   The additional testimonies of the gospel—and not the Thessalonians' faith and conduct—are the *basis of the knowledge* (Erkenntnisgrund) of the Thessalonians' election :[54] the particular way in which the gospel "happened" then in connection with the apostles' preaching demonstrated and demonstrates the election of the Thessalonian Christians.

ii)   But presumably the Thessalonians' election is then also the *true basis* (Realgrund) for the additional testimonies : for since these would not have been possible without the Thessalonians' election, the election must have been like the efficient cause of these particular testimonies of the gospel. If Paul really had the concept of such a causal relationship between the Thessalonians' election and the event of the gospel, then we must assume that other traces of it are preserved in his letters.

(2)   The meaning of δι'ὑμᾶς in 1, 5

i)   The grammatical evidence [55]

The "commonest sense" of διά + acc. in the New Testament is

---

[53] v. 4 εἰδότες … τὴν ἐκλογὴν ὑμῶν

    v. 5 ὅτι … ἀλλὰ καί …

[54] V. 5 thus does not tell us "worin das Erwähltsein der Thess.-Christen besteht" (as Zö 10 thinks) but with the ὅτι "gibt Paulus den *Grund* an, worauf seine Überzeugung … von der Auswahl der Thessalonicher sich stütze" (Bis 1, 316; so most comms.).

[55] διά + acc. (cf. B-D-F 222; He 212f.; H 201; K-G I 484f.; Lj 32-8; Ma II 2, 368f.; H. G. Meecham, The meaning of διά c. acc. in *ET* L, 1939, 564; Joh 240-5; M 54f.; M I 105f.; Art. διά in *TDNT* II 65-70; Ra 142-5; Rob 580-4; Ross 39, 1-3; S II 448-54; Si 141; Thu 104f.; M III 267f.; W 355f.; I did not have access to B. Blackwelder, *Causal use of prep. in the Greek NT*, Diss., S.-W. Bapt. Sem. 1951).

I) διά + acc., apart its occasional use with a local sense in classical and Hellenistic Greek (cf. especially Meecham), has primarily a *causal* sense in that "der Gedanke gewissermassen den Grund durchdringt" (H); thus it is used "because of",[56] i.e. it gives both the reason and the effective cause (mediation and causation), and so the δι'ὑμᾶς here could express the causal (giving the reason : owing to you) and so [57] the instrumental

1) *to give the reason or cause* : for the reason, because of, on account of. But since the causal sense can easily pass over into the *instrumental* (cf. Ra 142; Si) and since therefore "Grund oder Motiv und Mittel an sich sehr nah verwandt sind" (W 355) it can very easily come to mean "durch (jemds. Verdienst)", "kraft", "vermittels", "dank", "infolge", "wegen" (so already in classical Greek) : διὰ ταῦτα = therefore; δι'ἡμᾶς = through our cooperation. Thus Ma holds that διά τινα when used of persons refers to

i) "*instrumental eine Vermittlung, Veranlassung*" (II 2, 426), where therefore "durch das aktive Eingreifen ... einer Person eine Wohltat erwiesen wird ..." (II 2, 368; this is followed by many examples, including some of δι'ὑμᾶς)—and not as with διά + gen. "lediglich als äusserliches Werkzeug (Medium)" (*ibid.*), "nicht im Sinn der (verhältnismässig nebensächlichen) Vermittlungsstelle", but "im Sinn des für die Ermöglichung Entscheidenden ..., das was die Ausführung ermöglicht" (S II 453; plenty of material is cited, including διὰ σὲ γίγνεσθαι etc.). Ross 39, 2 : "quo auctore quid fiat".

ii) "kausal Schuld oder Verdienst", thus "to denote the author" (*TDNT* 69). Ross 39, 1 : "cuius merito aut culpa quid fiat". A-G (180) distinguishes too between

i) "to indicate the reason why someth. happens, results, exists"

ii) "to denote the efficient cause" (with many examples; a similar distinction is drawn by G-T 134; L-S; P 571; Ps. 628; cf. also M-M 146; L 344). "Von einem Grunde aber, der zugleich einen *Zweck* oder eine *Absicht* in sich schliesst, wird gewöhnlich ἕνεκα und nicht διά gebraucht" (Lj 32; some exceptions in Th.; see K-G I 485). "Dieser Unterschied wird in der Koine nicht mehr aufrechterhalten, διά wird hier oft gesetzt, um den Zweck anzugeben" (Lj 32; cf. P 571). On the other hand W (*ibid.*) states that in the New Testament "διά mit dem Acc. ist die Präposition des *Grundes* (ratio), nicht der Absicht". M, however, takes up a mediating position when he writes of the New Testament usage "... while the commonest sense is *because of* (consecutive), some steps are traceable towards the final or prospective sense, *for the sake of* or *with a view to*" (55). So also M III (*ibid.*) : "... there are indications of a later final sense, denoting purpose ...". Both partly rely on Meecham's good summary (*ibid.*) which speaks of the "overwhelming use of διά c. acc. in a *causal* and retrospective sense in the classical and Hellenistic language". But since he (cf. also Si) holds that "the notion of ground ('because of') easily blends with aim ('for the sake of')" διά + acc. already appears (according to Meisterhans) in Attic inscriptions (yet cf. also II Macc 8, 15; Gen. 18, 24-26 LXX) with a sense approaching that of ἕνεκα and thus is used

2) *to give the purpose* (classical = ἕνεκα; cf. B-D-F 216, 1 : "hardly distinguished from διά with acc.) = "prospective" for the purpose or aim, for the sake of, with a view to, um willen, jemanden zuliebe, zu Gefallen. Ross 39, 3 : "cuius gratia quid fiat". Thus we can find that "when the personal acc. is used in the NT, it generally denotes 'for the sake of' with a certain final element" (*TDNT* 70). This leads already to the modern Greek meaning "for" (Thu 104f. : γιὰ νά = in order that).

II) Cf. also A 2294-2300, 2428c, 2705; Bur 408; Bu 287f.; D 121, 16; 192, 1; H 41; Ma II 3, 99; M II 300-3; Ra 138, 140f.; S II 167; W 376.

[56] Cf. M, M III, Meecham, *ibid.*

[57] Cf. Ra, Si, W, *ibid.*

character of the Christians (giving the effective cause : through you), namely "im Sinn des für die Ermöglichung Entscheidenden ... das was die Ausführung ermöglicht";[58] thus by and through them these additional testimonies of the gospel could come about; one would then be reminded of the connection between faith and the realization of the gospel, perhaps particularly clearly expressed in Mt 13, 58. Yet at least the possibility (cf. "some steps", "indications") cannot be excluded that in 1, 5 we have an example of the "prospective" meaning of the preposition. At any rate this much is plain, that from the point of view of the purely grammatical evidence there is absolutely no reason automatically to presuppose and introduce here in this passage the "prospective" meaning—as is universally done;[59] rather this evidence gives us every reason to expect first and above all the "retrospective", causal meaning. The decision that we reach concerning 1, 5 over and above the grammatical evidence must be reached by means of additional observations, e.g. of the occurrence of $\delta\iota\acute{a}$ + acc. in the rest of the Thessalonian correspondence, but also by means of theological reflection on the whole text.

ii)   The linguistic evidence : the other occurrences of $\delta\iota\acute{a}$ + acc. in 1 Th

$\delta\iota\acute{a}$ + acc. (excepting $\delta\iota\grave{a}\ \tau o\hat{v}\tau o$) also occurs, apart from our passage, in 3, 9 [60] and 5, 13. In both passages Paul uses $\delta\iota\acute{a}$ + acc., in 3, 9 even $\delta\iota'\acute{v}\mu\hat{a}s$,[61] to indicate a *cause*.[62]

iii)   The theological evidence : the wider context.

We could only obtain a test-case and so confirmation for our provisional thesis of the causal connection between "election" and the "gospel-event" if we found within 1/2 Th a situation which was related to and thus similar to that presupposed in 1, 5. Accordingly the situation that we have to find must, at least ideally, be characterized by Paul's speaking in it of another encounter with the Thessalonian Christians and its importance for him as a preacher of the gospel. What he said in such a context could perhaps contribute to

---

[58] Cf. S, *ibid.*

[59] Cf. comms., *ad loc.*

[60] Cf. Rob 716; M II 419.

[61] Although almost all commentators also decide on the meaning "because of you" here, yet there are a few who here too read "for your sake". Mo (58) is undecided.

[62] Cf. comms. on 5, 13.

a better understanding of what transpired at his first encounter with them.

A really ideal commentary on 1, 5 is the passage in 3, 6 [63]—9 where Paul speaks of his encounter with the Thessalonians—not his personally, but one mediated through Timothy : "Mit dem scheinbar überflüssigen πρὸς ἡμᾶς ἀφ'ὑμῶν ... will P zur Geltung bringen, worauf es ihm bei dieser Sendung angekommen war : Herstellung einer direkten Verbindung zwischen sich und der Gemeinde".[64]

Two essential points can be learnt from this passage :

a) The rightness of the Thessalonians' faith is causally related to Paul's existence. The significance of this "link" for his whole life as a preacher of the gospel is most strikingly expressed by the fact that "sein Leben ... durch ihren Christenstand bedingt (ist)".[65] Therefore the idea presupposed here by Paul is that "as a result of your faith" (διὰ τῆς ὑμῶν πίστεως : v. 7), which is the means, and, i.e. "because of you" (δι'ὑμᾶς : v. 9), who are here the authors, the effective cause and reason, "aus dem etwas geschieht, erfolgt, existiert", the following "effects" are produced in the apostle :

— παράκλησις (consolation) - ἐπὶ πάσῃ τῇ θλίψει καὶ ἀνάγκῃ ἡμῶν
— χαρά
— νῦν ζῶμεν

These "effects" have their "cause" in the rightness of the Thessalonians' faith.

b) The rightness of the Thessalonians' faith is thus also causally related to the "gospel-event" itself. For, if the faith of the Thessalonian church plays such a part as a cause of the apostle's existence and if, on the other hand, Paul's existence is inseparably joined to that of the gospel,[66] the only consequence can be that in Paul's eyes the church's reaction, its standing and the state of its faith, are part of the "gospel", i.e. they play a constitutive or causal role in the "gospel-event".[67] That this thesis is not over-venturous but that

---

[63] Cf. Rob 579, 1139; W 332; Si 79.

[64] Do 140.

[65] Do 143; A-R 50 : "es liegt an euch, dass ihr mir Tod oder Leben bereiten helft".

[66] Friedrich (in *TDNT* II 733) : "The apostolate and the Gospel are most closely related ... : What happens to him cannot be considered apart from his task as a preacher of the Gospel".

[67] Cf. Schla 2, 17.

Paul really means that here becomes clear from an additional observation : in v. 6 Paul speaks of the "good news of your (the Thessalonians') faith". Since the church's participation in the gospel-event
has also been expressed in other ways, the use of εὐαγγελίζεσθαι [68] in
this passage must (although this use of the word is a Pauline *hapax
legomenon*) be understood more as a specific or technical Pauline usage.
For we must not forget that nothing less than the apostle's "life"
depends on this "good news".

Apart from the fact of the parallel circumstances alluded to, we
should note that apart from 3, 2-10 it is only in 1, 5-9 that Paul speaks
so strikingly and in such really extravagant terms of the Thessalonians' faith; this is an additional indication that in 3, 6-9 we are in
the same position as in 1, 4f. theologically though not geographically

---

[68] εὐαγγελίζεσθαι is here interpreted either

I) "nicht-technisch" and so in a secular sense (A-G 317; C 33; Z 226), "in its wider"
and not its "distinctive Christian sense" (Mi 3, 40; cf. his excursus E 141-4), "in der
gewöhnlichsten" (B-C 154) and so "nicht sakralen Bedeutung" (Di 15) : "eine freudige
Mitteilung bringen" (Do 140 etc.; so apparently also Vulg., which reads here not
evangelizare, but annuntiare; yet this is not conclusive in the light of A 10, 36; 11, 20;
13, 32; 14, 15; 17, 18); or

II) "nicht gerade profan" (*ThWB* II 718; cf. the unprecise translation in *TDNT* II
720), "not entirely secular" (Wh 53; "... the news was *like* a Gospel ..." Pl 1, 48; "was
as it were a gospel ..." Gl 55; "ist ihm *gleichsam* ein Evangelium" A-R 49); or

III) it is made to conform to Paul's specific technical use of this word : it refers to
the Thessalonians' faith itself, "the Gospel in action" (Ne 67), "the 'gospel' ... in return"
(Fin 70; Bor 90; but cf. Do 140 for a contrary view), "a veritable εὐαγγέλιον" (Fin xxxiii);
i.e. the "tota pietatis summa" (Ca) is part of the "evangelium", is really a gospel for
Paul—through "consolation" we live now (so presumably G-T 256, who deals with the
εὐαγγελίζεσθαι of 1 Th 3, 6 together with the rest of the εὐαγγελίζεσθαι passages; Bi 34:
"The news was in itself a gospel"; Fra 131; cf. also A-R 49. But only explicitly in
J. Jervell, Zur Frage der Traditionsgrundlage der Apostelgeschichte, *StTh* 16,
1962, p. 35; this is quoted with approval by Bjerkelund, *op. cit.* 213, n. 30); it is
therefore not only a "term (used) as being the most expressive open to Paul" (Mor 1,
105), to show "how remarkably Paul was affected by Timothy's news" (Mor 2, 56), "how
deeply Paul was moved" (Mo 55).

IV) Cf. also Bens 327; E 178f.; M-M 259; Pa 233; R 300; Ba 101-6; D 267, 1; Lu
44-6; Wu 1, 42f.

V) How Paul meant this word to be understood here can only be stated once (i)
the precise situation in which Paul then wrote and had to write is known (could A 18,
5f., especially the experience of βλασφημεῖν which Paul suffered representatively for
Christ and which is most closely connected with the account of the arrival of S and
T from Macedonia, serve as an indication of this ?), and (ii) the inner connection between
the apostle's preaching and the church's faith (cf. only as an example I 1, 7f. : λόγος
τοῦ κυρίου = ἡ πίστις ὑμῶν and also 1, 5) is taken into account.

or chronologically. And if correspondingly it is true that in Paul's
"link" with the Thessalonian church described in 3, 6-9 there was
repeated for Paul—who was now in Corinth—what was normative
then during his presence when he was in Thessalonica and if the same
basic laws of encounter were now operative here, mediated through
Timothy, then this sheds light on what was characteristic in 1, 5 of
Paul's first encounter with the Thessalonians : just as in 3, 7-9
"consolation" and "joy", even the apostle's "life", result from the
state of the Thessalonians' faith and this faith can somehow be
designated also as an element, a part of the gospel itself (εὐαγγελίζεσθαι),
so presumably "power, the Holy Spirit and full conviction" in 1, 5
are the result of the Thessalonians' faith, which is here understood
as somehow being an element and part of the gospel (ὁ λόγος τοῦ
κυρίου = ἡ πίστις ὑμῶν : v. 8). So, if in 3, 7-9 the fruits of the Holy
Spirit (consolation, joy) and even the apostle's life is causally related
to the state of the Thessalonians' faith, then there is nothing to
prevent the same being true of phenomena like "power" (perhaps
overcoming "weakness"), "the Holy Spirit" and "full conviction".
Thus this also gives us good grounds for understanding δι'ὑμᾶς in
1, 5 in a causal sense.[69]

Results of the observations on the contents of 1, 4f. :

a) as regards Paul's point in 1, 4ff., his *theme* here is the Thessalonians' election—and in particular the relation of this election to
the specific testimonies of the gospel. This relation is, as Paul himself
states to encourage them, that of the basis of knowledge (Erkenntnisgrund) and consequently, as we may *infer*, that of the true basis
(Realgrund) : as the special testimonies of the gospel are the clear
basis of both Paul's and the Thessalonians' knowledge of their election,

---

[69] i) In this conclusion we are at variance with Di (4) who takes "das auffüllende
δι'ὑμᾶς" as only "aus formalen Gründen dem ἐν ὑμῖν hinzugefügt" and thus regards it
as "sachlich nicht notwendig".

ii) How precisely we are to understand the content of the terms "power, Holy
Spirit and much assurance" does not concern our study. Perhaps we can just say in
passing that these additional testimonies, if they do not refer to Paul's miraculous
activity, can perhaps be understood in the context of the θλίψις of Paul's situation
and can thus refer to the power with which Paul met the external difficulties amidst
which he had to preach in Thessalonica. That would be supported by 3, 6ff., where
the workings of the Holy Spirit evoked in the apostles by the Thessalonians' faith
(consolation, joy) come to them ἐπὶ πάσῃ τῇ ἀνάγκῃ καὶ θλίψει ἡμῶν.

so conversely the Thessalonians' election is the true basis of these particular testimonies of the gospel.

b) This last point, at first only an "inference", has shown itself more and more probable in our investigation of δι'ὑμᾶς in 1, 5 by

aa) grammatical considerations,

bb) linguistic considerations, namely the occurrence of διά + acc. in the rest of the Thessalonian correspondence, and

cc) theological considerations, namely the wider context of this passage, and in particular 1 Th 3, 6-9, where we found ourselves in a similar position to 1, 5 theologically though not chronologically or geographically.

C. *Conclusions*

The theme of 1, 4ff. *is* "our gospel" in its relation to the election of the Thessalonians and *not* the manner of Paul's preaching as such. 1, 4f. expresses a climax, but not a contrast. By this climax Paul emphasizes the additional testimonies of the gospel as clear proofs of the Thessalonians' election. This is meant to console them.

These additional testimonies were brought about through the Thessalonians' election and their reaction of faith. In all probability therefore the "three Divine influences" were brought about following upon the apostles' preaching, by the Thessalonians' acceptance of the gospel. These influences cannot therefore be meant simply to describe more precisely the manner of Paul's preaching. Our observation on form pointed in the same direction : the second phrase within the formula οὐ μόνον ... ἀλλὰ καί refers to a separate entity and thus it does not include the first phrase, not even in the sense that it defines it more accurately. Thus one cannot so combine the two entities as to say, "he proclaimed not argumentatively, but 'in power and in the Holy Spirit and in much assurance' ".[70] That means that the "understanding" of the gospel cannot have been produced so exclusively by the δύναμις as is generally assumed. Rather the "understanding" must also have come about in the context of what is referred to as the λόγος.

On the basis of these verses we can therefore infer the idea which Paul had of the connection between the "gospel-event" and "election" :

---

[70] Mi 3, xliii, etc.

God testifies to the apostles' preaching not through signs and wonders (A 14, 3), but by the fact that the church receives this preaching—despite afflictions—with the joy of the Holy Spirit. But God also testifies to the Thessalonians' election by the fact that through their acceptance of Paul's preaching there are produced the additional testimonies of the gospel, i.e. "power, Holy Spirit and great assurance".

But we cannot infer from these verses the negative or positive concept which Paul had of the function and significance of the λόγος in the whole event of the "coming of the gospel" and especially of its significance for the understanding of this gospel. Paul says nothing about that. Thus far the result of our investigation must be a negative one. But the result is yet a positive one in so far as we have shown the negative judgment of almost all commentators to be false, the judgment which held that we have here a "disjunctive statement", "where one thing is denied (= λόγος) that another may be established (= δύναμις, etc.)". This passage should not be interpreted as if Paul were pleading for an "objektive Gottesmacht" *at the expense* of the human λόγος and argument or *at the expense* of human capabilities, both in Paul's presentation and in the Thessalonians' rational acceptance of the λόγος. But the recognition that there is not here "some kind of adversative relation between the two clauses" and furthermore the recognition that Paul is not meaning to say that in the matters of the understanding of the gospel his λόγος counts for nothing, leads to some important conclusions :

— In 1, 5 there is a little depreciation of the λόγος in comparison with the δύναμις, etc., as there is in 2, 8 of τὸ εὐαγγέλιον in comparison with τὰς ἑαυτῶν ψυχάς. For 1, 4f. conveys with regard to the function and significance of the λόγος in the whole of the "coming of the gospel" as little as 2, 8 does with regard to the function and significance of the εὐαγγέλιον with "our love for you".

— But if the λόγος is no longer the "negative influence" that it has always been regarded as on the basis of this passage, there is then no more cause to remove the "Verstaendlichmachen" of the gospel from this λόγος and its possible influence and to assign it exclusively to the δύναμις.[71] We can ask anew—and now without prejudice—

---

[71] Thereby we take issue with those who on the one hand indeed recognize "die bewusst gewählten menschlichen Worte(,) als notwendig(e) ..." (Do 71) and "unumgänglich(es) ..." (Bor 58) for the apostolic preaching, but yet on the other hand regard these as only "Mittel" (Bor 58) or even only as the "Form" (Do 71). But if one has so

what significance Paul ascribed to the λόγος besides its being an "unumgängliches Mittel" and "notwendige Form", that is besides its informative function, for the understanding of the gospel and what qualities, besides the statement of the bare facts, ought to belong to such a λόγος. This clears the way for possible positive statements concerning the role and the consequent influence of the λόγος on the understanding of the gospel.

Section 2 : 1 Th 2, 2f.

A) The Problem

A short examination of 1 Th 2, 2f. is justified and even necessary because the juxtaposition of τὸ εὐαγγέλιον and ἡ παράκλησις has been and still is explained in the most varied ways. Some of these explanations directly affect our question of the relation of faith and human reason in Paul's preaching; for some of these explanations of ἡ παράκλησις are overshadowed by the attempt to understand the meaning of this word *in this context* by disregarding this context (2, 1-6; ch. 1 and 1/2 Th) and to formulate it in contrast to concepts which are alien at least to this context, like διδαχή, διδασκαλία & κήρυγμα. This leads to qualifications which seek to define the epistemological or non-epistemological character of ἡ παράκλησις. Instead of using its natural context as one's primary hermeneutic key to the understanding of this concept, one tries to understand ἡ παράκλησις in contrast and distinction to the "borrowed" concepts that we have mentioned.[72]

The various interpretations are as follows :

I) ἡ παράκλησις is understood as *one* part of Paul's missionary activity, the third part, designated as "exhortation",[73] "that follows

---

low a view of λόγος then it follows that there must "noch etwas hinzukommen, soll die Wirkung (= Verstehen und Annahme des Ev.) entstehen ..." (Do 71). This, as these commentators interpret this passage, is "ausgeführt und getragen" (Bor 58) by the "Kraft, welche das Wort, dem sie einwohnt(e), gewaltig und wirkungsvoll macht(e)" (vH 157).

[72] The comms. generally treat this passage as if the problem confronting Paul here were that of, e.g., I C 14, 3 or R 12, 7f.

[73] Translated thus in AV; *The Holy Bible*, by B. Boothroyd, 1853; etc.

the 'preaching' and 'teaching' " [74] or, alternatively, "reasoning" and "proclaiming",[75] and thus has more the character of an "appeal",[76] an "urging", which is only directed to those "who were persuaded of the truth". This involves "certain practical considerations";[77] it is thus an exhortation to those already won. But this explanation is shown to be false by vv. 2 (... λαλῆσαι πρὸς ὑμᾶς τὸ εὐαγγέλιον), 3 (...γάρ...) and 4 (ἀλλά ... πιστευθῆναι τὸ εὐαγγέλιον ... οὕτως ...).

II) In the light of this, ἡ παράκλησις in this passage is interpreted, with some measure of truth, as a comprehensive term,[78] as "the missionary proclamation" [79] or "von der Predigt des Evangeliums überhaupt".[80] But how can one explain why, if "the telling of the Gospel of God" is here described "as ἡ παράκλησις ἡμῶν",[81] this particular phrase is used, unless one simply takes it as a case of "a part being put for the whole" ? [82] In other words, in what sense does one understand παράκλησις comprehensively—and this in relation to τὸ εὐαγγέλιον ?

(1) It is explained in relation to τὸ εὐαγγέλιον in terms of a distinction of form and content : in contrast to εὐαγγέλιον which expresses the "matter",[83] the "content of the message",[84] and so the "Inhalt oder Gegenstand der Predigt",[85] the παράκλησις is used to describe

---

[74] Ad 166.

[75] H-V 52.

[76] Translated thus in RSV; NEB; *The Complete Bible. An American Translation*, by Smith/Goodspeed, 1946; *The Berkeley Version in Modern English*, 1959; etc.

[77] H-V *op. cit.*

[78] So in the translations "our preaching" (*The Jerusalem Bible*, 1966; *The NT in Modern Speech* by Weymouth, 1908; *Living Letters*, by K. N. Taylor, 1965; etc.), "our message" (Phillips; *The New Testament*, by C. K. Williams, 1952; etc.), "our witness" (*The Bible in Basic English*, CUP, 1949; etc.), "unsere Predigt" (Schue 45).

[79] *TDNT* V 795; without further qualification : e.g. Ne 36 "the appeal we make— i.e. the Gospel we preach"; Alford III 254 "our whole course of preaching"; Barn 24 "preaching in general"; Be "totum praeconium evangelicum"; Di 6 "Predigt"; Zoe 14 "Predigt"; so also Bjerkelund 25; C 555 "So bezeichnet Paulus seine Predigt des Evangeliums als παράκλησις".

[80] Bis 1, 322.

[81] *TDNT* V 795.

[82] *The Holy Bible*, by J. Benson, VI 1336.

[83] Mor 2, 44.

[84] Mor 1, 70; Fra 94.

[85] Lü 43.

the "manner of preaching",[86] the "outward approach",[87] the "address itself",[88] the "Predigen selbst".[89] Understood thus, παράκλησις can be translated as "persuasive discourse"[90] and is in fact "aehnlich mit dem πείθειν II Kor 5, 11; Gal 1, 10".[91]

(2)   Mo on the other hand rightly casts doubt on all these views when he maintains that παράκλησις here neither means "his manner of preaching" alone, nor is directed only to those "who are persuaded of the truth".[92] Rather παράκλησις means "the whole enterprise of preaching as it was directed towards winning converts to faith".[93] "Paul uses this expression and not εὐαγγέλιον, λόγος, κήρυγμα, or such like terms, because here the question is about preaching, not in so far as it is a proclamation, but as it wins and transforms the hearers ..."[94] Understood in this way, as gospel preaching, the meaning of παράκλησις in contrast to τὸ εὐαγγέλιον τοῦ θεοῦ (regarded in terms of its content and no longer of its form) embraces either "exhortation" *and* "consolation",[95]—"blended together"[96] or meaning now the one, now the other, "according to circumstances"[97] or it is "die erste evangelische Verkündigung ihrem Wesen nach *mahnende* Ansprache",[98] which "sich gegen sittliche oder intellektuelle Mängel richtete",[99] and thus "pleaded with the hearers to forsake their wicked ways ..."[100]

---

[86] Mor 2, 44.

[87] Mor 1, 70.

[88] Fra 94 : "In this connection however, as λαλῆσαι (v 2) and λαλοῦμεν (v 4) make evident, the address itself ... is meant". Is that really evident ?

[89] Lü 43; so also A-R 24; Roe 38.

[90] G-T 483; Ro IV 16; Lin 44; cf. also Ea 58.

[91] Do 87.

[92] Cf. n. 78.

[93] Mo 34; so also Fin 36f. : "here it is not 'exhortation' to those already Christians, but 'the appeal' of the Gospel to those who hear it ..."

[94] *A Commentary on the Holy Scripture*, by J. P. Lange 1872, 360.

[95] Gl 26; Mi 3, 17.

[96] Gl 26; "the same Gospel exhorts comforts" (*A commentary on the Old and New Testament*, by A. R. Fausset, 459).

[97] Mi 3, 17; "je nach den verschiedenen Umständen" (Lü 43).

[98] So also *Das Neue Testament*, ed. A. Dächsel; Kel 16; Wo 42; Luther; Bjerkelund (27) objects that "Wir sind ... der Meinung, die Übersetzung 'Ermahnung' bindet den Begriff zu sehr an das Ethische".

[99] Lü 43.

[100] Hen 62.

(3)   A third possibility, which avoids the difficulties posed by the other solutions, is to designate παράκλησις simply as a t.t. for a particular sort of preaching.[101] And yet this answer seems to me to get us no further. To say that παρακαλεῖν and παράκλησις are to be understood more comprehensively as only ethical preaching does not help us with regard to 1 Th 2, 3, but is in fact self-evident in this context. In what sense is it more comprehensive?—that is the question. It is therefore significant that Bjerkelund cannot say "wie ἡ παράκλησις von den anderen Begriffen der Verkündigung abzugrenzen ist".[102]

(4)   The most popular answer to the question as to how παράκλησις can be comprehensively described is to hold fast on the one hand to the "whole" concept of παράκλησις and yet at the same time on the other to adopt a horizontal interpretation of the chronological or vertical trichotomy of preaching, teaching and exhortation, which is rightly rejected in *this* latter form, in order to provide the "material" through which one hopes to give expression to the particular characteristic of παράκλησις here. The criterion for our understanding of this παράκλησις rightly understood as in some way a comprehensive term, is thus not the context of this passage but primarily the artificial comparison with διδαχή/διδασκαλία and κήρυγμα, as if the text itself encouraged or even compelled us thus to do. The particular comprehensive character of παράκλησις in our passage is nothing but its being determined by its relation to διδαχή/διδασκαλία on the one hand to κήρυγμα on the other. The range of interpretation thus made possible stretches from the identification of παράκλησις and διδαχή to the distinguishing between them :

παράκλησις is "gleichgestellt"[103] with διδαχή, διδασκαλία,[104] is "in effect"[105] like them or a "Lehrweise",[106] "Christian teaching",[107] and thus "practically equals instruction"[108]—that is one end of the

<hr/>

101 Bjerkelund 25, n. 11, cites with approval a work of R. Asting's (still in preparation) as representing this opinion.

102 Bjerkelund 27.

103 Schmi 28.

104 So already in Chrys., Theod.; then also in Ko 145; Wet 98.

105 Ea 58.

106 B-C 137.

107 Ol 410.

108 *A Catholic Commentary* 1960, 1139; G-T 483 is ambiguous : "used of the apostles' instruction or preaching".

scale. At the other end is the statement : "Doch ist es irrig, παράκλησις
geradezu mit διδαχή oder διδασκαλία gleich zu setzen",[109] for the
meaning of παράκλησις thus becomes "ungehörig verflacht".[110]

Between these two poles are statements like those to the effect that
παράκλησις "approaches in meaning",[111] "corresponds to διδαχή or
διδασκαλία on one side ... and on another side to κήρυγμα"[112] is
"closely allied with διδαχή ... or διδασκαλία ..."[113] Or the identification
of παράκλησις and διδαχή is accepted but qualified with the statement
that it is "nicht nur theoretische Unterweisung",[114] and is "nie
schlechthin lehren";[115] it is "rather persuasive than didactic
instruction".[116]

The result of all this is that the understanding of παράκλησις
reached by such co-ordination and definition is primarily seen "im
Unterschied von διδαχή und διδασκαλία",[117] as speech directed "an
Gefühl und Willen",[118] at "Gemüt und Willen" [119] and so as determin-
ing "Willen und Entschlusskraft eines anderen Menschen" [120] and
thus "einen Eindruck zu machen, eine bestimmende Wirkung zu
üben";[121] therefore it is understood as an "Appell", "being directed
more to the feelings",[122] which "immer schon ein Vorwissen voraus-
setzt, an das erinnert wird mit dem Ziel ..." [123] namely "to make
men take a particular line of action. 'Our efforts to get men to act
as we wish', St. Paul says ..." [124] In παράκλησις therefore there is a
"besondere Betonung der eindringlichen, praktischen, anwendenden
Art",[125] an "Erweckung zur Befolgung und Anwendung des

---

[109] Lü 43; also Pl 1, 20 contrasts ἡ παράκλησις with the διδαχή/διδασκαλία; Mi 3,
17 : "... not to be identified".

[110] Zoe 14.

[111] El 17.

[112] Fin 37.

[113] Mil 3, 17.

[114] Bor 77.

[115] Schmi 28.

[116] Ea 58.

[117] Ko 145.

[118] Hol 2, 460.

[119] Do 87.

[120] *ThBl* 272; vH 168.

[121] vH 168; Zoe 14.

[122] El 17 (adopted by Fin 37); Pl. 1, 20.

[123] *ThBl* 272.

[124] Mas 87.

[125] Bor 77.

Gesagten".[126] In contrast, διδαχή or διδασκαλία is primarily an "appeal to the intellect",[127] "to the understanding",[128] and is so directed "vorwiegend an die intellektuelle Einsicht und Erkenntnis".[129] It is imagined that we can get all this out of this passage. But has it also been mentioned what παράκλησις means here set against its context, apart from what it can mean when set against διδαχή etc. (if we must argue in terms of these contrasts !) ? The specific element of the general meaning of παράκλησις that is meant in our passage is at any rate—if one tackles the problem *thus*—a "certain touch of passion";[130] the "Sagen des Evangeliums Gottes als ἡ παράκλησις ἡμῶν" is "permeated by ... an atmosphere of gentle, soothing affection ...", is "a system 'tinctured by emotion' ..." [131] and is above all a "practical 'appeal' ".[132]

B) *An attempted solution*

So much for the different and varied interpretations. What, after all, does ἡ παράκλησις[133] mean in 2, 3 ? We must confine ourselves to a few remarks—but, we hope, fundamental ones.

---

126 Ko 145.

127 Pl 1, *op. cit.*

128 El *op. cit.*

129 *ThBl op. cit.*

130 *The Jerome Biblical Commentary* 230.

131 *The Holy Bible Commentary*, ed. F. C. Cook, III 710 (cf. Bengel's addition "passionum dulcedine tinctum").

132 Fin 63.

133 παρακαλεῖν in 1/2 Th (cf. A-S 340; A-G 622f.; C 552-6; G-T 483; Z 426f.; Ba 217; H 146; Wu 1, 81; D 153, 4; 187, 14; 222, 4; 307f.; Mi 2, 93; Mi 1, 12, 6; Me 55, 123, 143; Rob 66; M II 319f.).

I) Often it refers to behaviour (περιπατεῖν I 2, 12; 4, 1.11), action (ποιεῖν I 4, 10), activity (πράσσειν, ἐργάζεσθαι I 4, 11; II 3, 12). Its meaning is then mostly the same as that of "appeal" : μὴ ἐγκακήσητε (II 3, 13) : one encourages (παρακαλεῖν) another to increase and continue (περισσεύειν μᾶλλον : I 4, 1.10) in conduct (περιπατεῖν 4, 1) and action (ποιεῖν 4, 10) already practised before now which corresponds to the παραγγελίαι (I 4, 11) earlier given (διδόναι : I 4, 2) and received (παραλαμβάνειν : I 4, 2). Here nothing is argued, reasoned, in order to make something more intelligible. Here we are not starting at square one. In this usage παρακαλεῖν is not so much explanation, instruction aimed at intellectual understanding, as encouragement to continue, appeal to the will and to decision, to steadfastness and perseverance.

II) Often it also implies the element of instruction, not so much in questions of ethics as in those of doctrine : I 3, 2; 4, 18; 5, 11 with the purpose of "consoling" (in afflictions and sufferings). Παρακαλεῖν is not meant to "encourage" one to continue as

One thing at any rate has become clear : we must first start from the immediate context in which ἡ παράκλησις occurs,[134] and ask whether an examination of this context cannot by itself provide us with a satisfactory understanding of παράκλησις.

I) παράκλησις must firstly be related to λαλεῖν τὸ εὐαγγέλιον τοῦ Θεοῦ ἐν πολλῷ ἀγῶνι. Here then Paul is speaking of "telling of the gospel" in the face of "conflict". It has met with a hostile reaction which both the preacher (2, 2; cf. also 3, 7) and the hearers (1, 6; cf. also 2, 14) could detect. That is one theme underlying both letters : αὐτοὶ ... οἴδατε ὅτι εἰς τοῦτο (= θλῖψιν) κείμεθα (I 3, 3). And a decisive reason both for Timothy's visit to Thessalonica and for the writing of the Thessalonian epistles is also the danger that they σαίνεσθαι ἐν ταῖς θλίψεσιν ταύταις (3, 3)—in those very θλίψεσιν which they had taken upon them in their "receiving of the word" μετὰ χαρᾶς πνεύματος ἁγίου (1, 6). But what had changed since then and what reasons could there be for this "wavering in these afflictions" ?

II) For that we must understand this παράκλησις also on the basis of the ἐκ πλάνης [135] and from the other accusations levelled against Paul which followed from this basic accusation. In the "speaking of the gospel" which Paul here alludes to with the word παράκλησις what made possible or provoked the accusation (justified or unjustified) that it was done in "deception" and therefore deceived others too (ἐν δόλῳ [136])—that he "spoke to please" men and "flattered" them ? Could his "manner of preaching" (if παράκλησις means that here) perhaps be meaningfully accused of being based on "deception" ? Hardly. Could an "exhortatory address", "which had pleaded with

---

before in things already supposedly understood, but here παρακαλεῖν is meant to correct what is not understood or is misunderstood and make it intelligible. In this sense παρακαλεῖν makes a fresh start. So here παρακαλεῖν is the attempt to convey consolation and encouragement by means of good, intelligible reasons and arguments.

III) In the passive "be consoled" (I 3, 6)—so also II 2, 16.

[134] Hen 2 is right at least in principle : "The exact meaning depends on the context in each instance".

[135] ἐκ designates the origin, the source (cf. Rob 598); to be interpreted passively as = πλανᾶσθαι : error, delusion, erroneous religious views (cf. lexicons and comms).

[136] This designates the manner, the method (cf. W 437; Bu 315); to be interpreted actively as = cunningly, in an artful way, with craftiness or deception, with guile (cf. lexicons and comms.).

the hearers to forsake their wicked ways …", an "exhortatory address" which contained exhortations like "He who will not work should not eat either" (2 Th 3, 10), an "exhortatory address" which ended with 1 Th 4, 6—could such an address (if παράκλησις means that here) meaningfully provoke the accusation that one "was speaking to please", that one "flattered" them with a παράκλησις understood in this way ? Could the accusation have been levelled in all seriousness at Paul because of all this, which contained so little of "flattery", namely that he had "deceived" his hearers ? Hardly. But what was it in the gospel, which is here described as παράκλησις, that made all these accusations possible ?

(1) The accusation of "deception"—if it has not simply been produced out of thin air—can first be made meaningful only *after* an already-held view or hope for the future has either shown itself to be illusory or apparently been shown to be so by someone else. The change from the aorist in v. 2 to the present in v. 3 is striking. Is Paul perhaps saying thereby that the παράκλησις which consisted in and was expressed in his former "speaking of the gospel" *is* not "deception" and does not come from it—*even if that may seem to be the case today* ? That would then be the point here. But in what are the apostles themselves and also their hearers supposed to have been deceived in the "telling of the gospel" ?

(2) The second central problem which Paul has to tackle in the two Thessalonian epistles is the theme of the "return of Christ". Apparently the Christians expected Christ's return and thus their ἀπάντησιν τοῦ κυρίου (4, 17) while they still lived and thus could not conceive of the πάντοτε σύν κυρίῳ εἶναι (4, 17) as being reached by passing through dying and death. To die was synonymous with the loss of eternal life. Thus the idea of Christ's return was bound up with the idea that thereby one would avoid the fateful necessity of death.

And certainly, we may assume, they took on, even μετά χαρᾶς, all the θλίψεις which were inseparably bound up with the preaching of the gospel and the acceptance of it because this promise and expectation seemed to be given them.[137] And now Christ's return had not

---

[137] Lü 44: "der Apostel und seine Gehülfen scheuen darum bei der Verkündigung des Evangeliums selbst Leiden und Trübsale nicht, weil ihre Predigt nicht auf einer Fiction, einem Hirngespinst, einer Träumerei, einem Irrwahn beruht …"

taken place, but the Christians were dying. Could their former consolation which they had received in and for their sufferings be today
described as "deception" ? Had they been the victims of "fair speakers",
of those who knew how to "make Christians' mouths water" with
their "assurances" for the future ? And if the consolation which lay
in the idea of Christ's return was thus shown to be a deception, were
not also the sufferings in vain which they undertook for the sake of
this supposed consolation ? Their "wavering in these sufferings" is
not for nothing related to their "being deceived" in the question of
Christ's "return" (2 Th 2, 2f.).[138] Therefore it was first necessary, in
the face of the fact of the delay in his return, to refute the accusation
that this doctrine was based on deception. And so we find Paul in
1 Th occupied in defending the "consolation" of Christ's return with
good reasons, i.e. with arguments designed to remove ἀγνοεῖν, in the
face of the grief that had already come upon them (1 Th 4, 13). By
the sort of argument practised here (4, 13-5, 11) they ought to be
"consoling" themselves by teaching (4, 18; 5, 11).[139] And in 2 Th
Paul picks up the same theme again (2, 1-12), though here in somewhat
different circumstances. At any rate in both passages in which Paul
deals at length with the problem of Christ's return we find this
promise and hope described at the close as "consolation", and
significantly even as *eternal* consolation (2 Th 2, 16), as the subject
of "consoling" (1 Th 4, 18; 5, 11).

3) It seems to me that we must understand the παράκλησις in
1 Th 2, 3 in the same way : here the "speaking of the gospel of God"
is described comprehensively as consolation [140] (just as it can also be
described as power), consolation which consists above all [141] in the

---

[138] "σαλευθῆναι ... scheint dem σαίνεσθαι in I 3, 3 zu entsprechen, fast möchte man
sagen, es erklären zu wollen" (Do 164). Cf. also C 728 : "Am nächsten liegt es wegen
der Verbindung mit θροεῖσθαι, das σαλευθῆναι ἀπὸ τοῦ νοός (II Th 2, 2) nach Analogie
von νοῦν ἔχω, mentis compos sum, νοῦν ἀποβαλεῖν zu erklären, also synom. πλανᾶσθαι".

[139] Correctly translated as "console, encourage, comfort" (cf. comms. *ad loc.*).

[140] To my knowledge only Scha 54 has a similar view.

[141] The accusation of "deception" which seems to be levelled here primarily with
regard to the expectation of Christ's return only forms a logical companion to the series
of other accusations of πλάνη which the Jews used to level against Jesus' Messiahship
as well as his resurrection (as πρώτη and ἐσχάτη πλάνη—Mt 27, 63f. : although here
πλάνη is to be taken in an active sense). Even from the point of view of this alone but
also in the light of the ὃν ἤγειρεν (1 Th 1, 10) and the εἰ γὰρ πιστεύομεν ὅτι ... (4, 14),
the emphasis on the theme of Christ's return in both Thessalonian epistles should
not cause us to overbook the fundamental connection existing between Jesus' Messiahship (= ῥυόμενον ἡμᾶς ἐκ ... 1, 10), his resurrection (*ibid.*) and his return (*ibid.*).

"expectation of his Son from the heavens" and the associated "salvation from the wrath to come" (1, 10);[142] this consolation shows itself to be effective in the steadfast endurance of sufferings and springs from no "deception", but rather can be defended with good arguments and therefore has no need of "cunning speech", let alone of "flattery", that it should require one to "speak to please men".

C) *Conclusions*

ἡ παράκλησις is not here either

I)   the ethical exhortation that follows after preaching and teaching,
II)   the manner of the preaching of the gospel,
III) a t.t. for a particular kind of gospel preaching, or
IV)   an exhortatory address directed only towards "feelings" and the "will" as opposed to the "intellect" and "understanding".

Rather the gospel is here more precisely described by a word which is suggested by the particular situation in which the gospel has been preached. Accordingly, the παράκλησις is the gospel described as consolation—because of the "struggle" in which the preaching of the gospel takes place for both preacher and hearer. The point of this passage seems to me to be missed if one reads into it statements which place the gospel primarily in the realm of the "feelings" because of the παράκλησις mentioned here and which do not see it also directed towards the "intellect" and "understanding". But if one reads here primarily what is actually written, then the appeal in ἡ παράκλησις, as in 1 Th 4, 18; 5, 11 and II 2, 16, is directed just as much to the "feelings" (that is as consolation and consoling) as to the "understanding" and the "intellect" : "consolation" can only come by way of the "understanding". The "feeling" of λυπεῖσθαι can only be removed by the removal of ἀγνοεῖν. And that is what παράκλησις was meant to achieve then and is meant to achieve again in the two Thessalonian epistles.

---

[142] Quite apart from the fact that the whole of ch. 1 is designed to "console" (the mention of "election" in 1, 4 also serves this purpose), the idea of "saving" which is bound up with Christ's return is above all an indication that παράκλησις here means "consolation" and not "admonition" (as one could perhaps interpret παράκλησις following a passage like Mt 3, 7b, to cite but one example).

§ 4. 2 Thessalonians 2 [1]

Introduction

Our starting-point is two facts : on the one hand Paul in this chapter comes to the "Hauptsache",[2] to the "eigentlich geschäft-liche(n)" [3] of his letter, "nämlich die Thess. über die Erwartung der Zukunft Christi zu verständigen".[4]

On the other, this chapter is probably for us today one of the *hardest to understand* in the whole Pauline corpus.[5] Yet even in this jungle of ideas Paul is apparently carrying out his declared purpose, "to save his readers by leading them to more sober ways of thinking".[6] But is that not a contradiction ? We think not. Rather this fact makes two things clear. Firstly, we are dealing with a letter and not a treatise.[7] And secondly, our difficulties in understanding Paul are not the same as those of the Thessalonians.[8]

---

[1] The Pauline authorship of 2 Th is contested and both the fact of his composition of this document and the denial of it alike raise difficult questions which cannot be answered here. Yet since we are only concerned with ch. 2, it is worth noting that two of the main points of those who criticize its Pauline origin, namely the different eschatological scheme in II-2, 1-12 compared with 1 Th and the language peculiar to the letter, are not adequate evidence that it is not genuine (cf. Kuemmel, W. G., *Introduction to the New Testament*, London, 1966, 188f.).

[2] B-C 183.

[3] Ew 25.

[4] Wet 123. Therefore all that Paul says here is of fundamental importance and can, so far as the principle is concerned, be taken as representative.

[5] Cf. Fin 162; Gl 23; Mor 1, 213. A reference to II Pet 3, 16 is completely justified.

[6] Fin 49.

[7] That means that Paul presupposes in his readers a certain amount of knowledge which he and they shared but we do not. Hence we are also unable to understand fully a large part of what Paul writes here. For, whereas mere allusions to Paul's first missionary activity were enough for the Thessalonians to "put them in the picture" and to make Paul's correction "meaningful" for them, for us on the other hand it is "very difficult to fill in the gaps, and to catch his allusions" (Mor 1, 213)—"without which indeed he does not expect what is here written to be understood" (Fin 162). Thus it is partly correct to say that "the more familiar the subjects with which they deal were to their first readers, the more veiled they are from us ..." (Mi 3, xlii).

[8] It is important to bear this in mind when investigating the problem of faith and human reason with regard to the *content* of Paul's preaching. For this means that :

i) it is difficult for us today to check up whether Paul really fulfilled his own claim (i.e. "to lead them to more sober ways of thinking"), and that

ii) our deficiencies in knowledge and thus in understanding cannot strictly speaking

Thus we must reckon it all the more fortunate that, quite apart from its contents, this chapter quite clearly describes

1) the malady affecting the Thessalonians (2, 2),[9] and
2) the means that Paul uses to cure this malady (2, 13-15).[10]

Since the study of both can help us "to find out what was Paul's method in proclaiming the good news ...",[11] we will here too investigate the "intellectual element" in Paul's preaching. Yet in restricting ourselves only to the structure of this chapter we have to take it to heart "that we do not possess the key to everything that is here said, and accordingly to maintain some reserve in our interpretations".[12]

Section 1 : 2, 2

The Thessalonians are evidently in danger of taking leave of their senses.

A. σαλεύειν σαλεύεσθαι

I) In classical Greek

The figurative meaning of σαλεύειν/σαλεύεσθαι [13] referring to

---

be a part of such an investigation. For "if these points were known to us, *as they were to the Thessalonians*, most of the obscurity ... would disappear" (Gl 23).

[9] In general on this verse, cf. B-D-F 396; 425, 4; Rob 582, 895, 964, 1033, 1140, 1189; M III 137, 158; W 437, 544; Bu 307; Si 174; G 179f.; F 202; Mi 1, 32; Me 105; on εἰς τό + the infinitive cf. Rob 1072; Bur 412.

[10] The structure of ch. 2 is this :
the ταχέως σαλευθῆναι ἀπὸ τοῦ νοός is to be prevented by the στήκετε, κρατεῖτε τὰς παραδόσεις, ἃς ἐδιδάχθητε (so also A-R 129; Bor 381), through the reminder of what Paul has said to them time and again (v. 5; on this v. cf. Rob 1139; M 53; M II 467).

[11] Har 56—but not just with regard to its content "concerning Christ the Lord and His Parousia" (*ibid.*), but with regard to Paul's whole preaching and in particular his methods.

[12] Mor 1, 213.

[13] σαλεύειν :

I) *Etymology* : Buck 675f.; W-P 1, 709f.; Po I 1081; Bo 850; Pr 454; Mey IV 55f.; Ho 303f.; Fr II 673; Ka I 339; cf. also ἀπο-, ἐπι-, διασαλεύειν.

II) *Meaning* : σαλεύειν, which is akin in meaning to σείειν (cf., e.g., Job 9, 6; Nah 1, 5; Hab 2, 16; Is 33, 20; I Macc 9, 13), κινεῖν and its derivatives and also ταράσσειν (cf. A 17, 13 etc.), comes from σάλος (L 21, 25). "σάλος ist die flutende Bewegung des Meeres ... σαλεύειν heisst an dieser Bewegung, z.B. auf dem Schiffe teilnehmen, ihr

"schwankenden, unsichern Zuständen" is often in classical Greek "transferred to conditions of mind",[14] in a general sense, but sometimes is used specifically of intellectual shocks and confusion :[15] ὀλίγοι γάρ εἰσιν οἷς (=φυσωμένοις καὶ σαλευομένοις) παραγίγνεται τὸ φρονεῖν.[16] This condition is caused either ὑπὸ τῆς ἐντὸς ἀγνωμοσύνης [17] or διὰ σοφισμάτων of others.[18] But if the σαλεύων (intransitive) qua σαλεύων is no longer near to φρονεῖν but has rather moved away [19] from τὸν οἰκεῖον λογισμόν,[20] then the consequences must be correspondingly catastrophic :
the σαλεύων (intransitive)

---

unterworfen sein ..." (Sch III 143). Both words thus describe "the restless movement of the sea with its rise and fall, whether from the standpt. of inconstancy suggesting transitoriness or of peril suggesting destruction" (TDNT VII 65; Bertram here gives on pp. 65-70 a thorough description of the words' meaning, but does not pay more attention to 2 Th 2, 2). This means that σαλεύειν has both a literal and a figurative meaning, a transitive meaning and an intransitive.

1) σαλεύειν is used literally of the "Bewegung, sowohl von Pers. als von Sachen" (Ps II 2, 1369; so also A-S 400; G-T 567; M-M 568) produced "durch die Wellen des Meeres" (Ps II 2, 1369), "durch Wind, Wellen usw." (H 185), but also "beim Erdbeben" (Sch III 138).

Transitive : "schwankend oder wankend machen, erschüttern; Pass. hin- und herbewegt werden, erschüttert werden, hin- und herschwanken, wanken" (Bens 756), "to agitate or shake" (G-T 567; M-M 568), i.e. "to render insecure" (A-S 400).

Intransitive : "in schwankender, unruhiger Bewegung seyn, schwanken" (Ps II 2, 1369; P II 859), "hin- und herschwanken" (P-K II 449), "to be in motion as waves are" (Ol 473).

2) σαλεύειν is used figuratively (in A 2, 25; Hb 12, 26f.; cf. also in LXX) of "ähnliche unsichere oder auf und ab wogende Bewegungen" (Sch III 143), and thus generally "von schwankenden, unsichern Zuständen" (Ps II 2, 1369), "all violent passions of joy, grief, or fear" (Ol 473).

Transitive : "to unsettle or drive away" (A-S 401) etc.

Intransitive : "unruhig, unglücklich sein ... in unruhiger Gemüthsstimmung sein, sich fürchten" (P II 859) etc.

[14] Ol 473.

[15] Thus it is in no way "foreign to prof. auth". (G-T 567).

[16] Plu Mor 68F; τὸ φρονεῖν παραγίγνεταί τινι = the understanding is near to somebody, is somebody at hand.

[17] Plu Mor 780B = ignorance.

[18] Epict Arr III 26, 16.

[19] The σαλεύεσθαι that is akin to κινεῖν (cf. n. 13) is always movement away from something (ἀπό Epict Arr III 26, 16) and correspondingly towards something else (e.g. πρὸς τὸ ... Plu Mor 651B; 714D; etc.).

[20] Plu Mor 454A = his own reasoning power.

— τὴν γνώμην ἐπισφαλῆ ποιεῖ καὶ ἀκατάστατον [21]
— causes... τὸ βέβαιον καὶ νενομισμένον ἐπισφαλὴς γίνεσθαι [22]
— βεβαίου τὸ παράπαν οὐδεμίας γνώμης ἑταῖρος ὤν [23]
— σαλεύει every δόξαν.[24]

And since μὴ παρεσκευασμένον ἔχῃ τὸν οἰκεῖον λογισμόν [25] he cannot even προσδέχεσθαι λόγον ἀλλότριον,[26] which would be his sole resource in a condition of such intellectual confusion. Hence it comes about that the σαλεύων (intransitive) is not only always κλονούμενος,[27] but often thus meets his destruction [28] or downfall,[29] even if this is often concealed by his being φυσώμενος.[30] Such can only be saved if they φρενῶν ἐπεισάκτων δέονται καὶ λογισμῶν πιεζόντων ἔξωθεν αὐτοὺς ... φυσωμένους καὶ σαλευμένους.[31]

II) Application to 2, 2

Correspondingly, the σαλευόμενοι [32] of Thessalonica were no longer *near* to φρονεῖν, but had *moved away* from it. They were therefore also the sort of people who φρονῶν ἐπεισάκτων δέονται καὶ λογισμῶν which πιεζόντων ... αὐτούς (= which press or weigh them *down*); for they

(1)   through their σαλευθῆναι ἀπὸ τοῦ νοός wanted to precipitate the *heavenly ascent* first promised for the future (I 4, 17): ἁρπαγῆναι ἐν νεφέλαις εἰς ἀπάντησιν τοῦ κυρίου εἰς ἀέρα; thus they

(2)   had hurried [33] away from the *clarity* of the νοῦς into the

---

[21] Plu *Mor* 714E.

[22] Plu *Mor* 756B; cf. here the contrast in Phld *Rh* I 260, 10ff., βεβαίως ἀλλ'οὐ σαλευομένως.

[23] Ph *Leg all* III, 53.

[24] Plu *Mor* 1123F.

[25] Plu *Mor* 454A.

[26] *Ibid.* = to admit the reasoning of another.

[27] Ph *Leg all* III, 53.

[28] E.g. περιτρέπεσθαι = to be capsized, collapse (Plu *Mor* 780B).

[29] σφάλλεσθαι (e.g. Plu *Mor* 337C), ἐπισφαλής.

[30] Plu *Mor* 68F.

[31] *Ibid.*

[32] = "mentally agitated or disturbed" (Ea 255), "shaken mentally" (Pa 555).

[33] I) Along with the majority of comms we take this adverb as "refer(ring) to manner rather than time, 'soon and with small reason' (Alford). It implies certainly a mental disturbance, quickly, easily, and unthinkingly brought about ..." (Ea 255f.).

II) Cf. the close relationship to Gal 1, 6; 3, 1.

clouds, where they supposed that they were already σύν κυρίῳ and free of the tears of θλίψις (Rev 21, 4).

And apparently it was so important to fetch these Christians back from their flight to heaven because it was realized that ἐὰν ἐφ'ἑνὸς ταράττηται καὶ σαλεύηται τὸ βέβαιον ... ἐπισφαλὴς γίνεται πᾶσα καὶ ὕποπτος.[34] This can apparently only be avoided by helping the Thessalonian Christians—and this would then be the purpose of this chapter—to παρεσκευασμένον ἔχειν τὸν οἰκεῖον λογισμόν, in order, on the one hand, (positively) to προσδέχεσθαι λόγον ἀλλότριον [35] and, on the other, (negatively) to be on their guard ἵνα μή τις ὑμᾶς ἐξαπατήσῃ κατὰ μηδένα τρόπον (2 Th 2, 3). The essence of this chapter would then be the warning, μελετᾶτε μὴ (ἀπο)σαλεύεσθαι (διὰ σοφ ... ; ὑπὸ τῆς ἐντὸς ...) ἀπὸ τοῦ νοός [36] = You ought to practise to avoid being shaken away from the νοῦς.

B) νοῦς [37]

I) The problem

The word νοῦς has a whole wealth of possible meanings [38] but

---

[34] Plu *Mor* 756B.

[35] I.e. Paul's λόγος : cf. I 1, 6; II 3, 14; 2, 15, etc.

[36] Epict *Arr* III 26, 16 : μελετᾷς μὴ ἀποσαλεύεσθαι διὰ σοφισμάτων· ἀπὸ τίνων; (here : ἀπὸ γνώμης).

[37] The New Testament never uses the regular 2nd decl. form but the secondary hellenistic 3rd decl. one (cf. S I 241, 249, 252, 310 etc.; B-D-F 52; Ra 56; Rob 261; M I 48; M II 9f.; 121, 127, 142; Ma I 2, 13; II 1, 124; W 59; Bu 12; Thu 63 for the modern Greek forms which also include χάνω τὸ νοῦ μου "lose my reason" (343); cf. also He 49; Th 160).

II) On the etymology, cf. Fr II 322f.; Bo 672; Ho 219; Buck 1197ff.; Cu 135; Va 197.

III) On linguistic questions, cf. also G-T 429; M-M 431; P-K II 141 and the examples cited here; also Suppl. 1, 2. Lief. 1969, 189; Schmidt, J. H. H., *Handbuch der lat. und griech. Synonymik*, 1889, 637f.; Sch I 283; Z 378.

IV) Literature on the meaning of νοῦς :

Sch III νοῦς 621-55

TDNT IV Art. νοέω Behm (948-59)

ThBl Art. Vernunft (νοῦς) Harder (1288-94).

[38] "Seit Kant versteht man unter *Vernunft* (lat. ratio) das zusammenfassende Erkenntnisvermögen des Menschen, das die Einzelerkenntnisse des Denkens, Wissens und Verstehens zu einer Einheit verbindet" (*ThBl* 1288). How is this view related to the history of the meaning of νοῦς ?

I) The *original* meaning of νοῦς has its *Sitz im Leben* in "popular usage" (*TDNT* 954),

which meaning does it actually have when used in the New Testament and in particular in 2 Th 2, 2 ?

(1)   It can be formulated in quite general terms : νοῦς "denotes the faculty of physical and intellectual perception, then also the power to arrive at moral judgments",[39] it is "the ruling faculty, mind, understanding, reason",[40] "the intelligent or intellectual principle, the mind".[41]

(2)   But if one, for whatever reasons, posits too rigid a distinction

in the "Sprache des Lebens", and thus the "lebendigen Sprache ... des Volkes" (Sch III 622f.); as regards its *Sitz im Menschen* it "gehört als Denkvermögen neben Gefühl und Willen zu den inneren Kräften des Menschen" (*ThBl* 1289). Here νοῦς means "*Sinn ..., der an sich selbst erfahrend die Gegenstände erkennt*" (Sch III 627) and is "das geistige Wahrnehmen" (P II 262), the "(inner) sense directed on an object" (*TDNT* 952; *ThBl* 1288; Ps II 1, 361), and thus "das innere oder geistige Wahrnehmungsvermögen" (Ps *ibid.*); hence we can say that "Erkenntnis" is the "eigentliches Wesen des νοῦς". Thus νοῦς means quite "allgemein die Sinnesart" (Sch III 627) and does not (like, e.g., διάνοια, σύνεσις and γνώμη) belong "in den engeren intellektuellen Bereich des diskursiven Verstehens" (*ThBl* 1288; Sch III 627), but is basically a *wider* term in keeping "seinem Umfange nach ... dem deutschen *Sinn* (entsprechender)" (Ps II 1, 361), which can "alle Instrumente des sinnlichen und geistigen Wahrnehmens umfassen" (*ThBl* 1288); in other words (as *TDNT* 951 says) it embraces " 'sensation', 'power of spiritual perception', 'capacity for intellectual apprehension' ... also 'mode of thought', 'moral nature' ", or (according to *ThBl* 1289) "Sinn, dann Gesinnung, Verstand, Einsicht, Vernunft und Geist ... ist aber auch die sittliche Haltung und Gesinnung, die durch den nachdenkenden Verstand bestimmt wird ... bedeutet ferner Entschluss und Absicht ..."; similarly also P II 263. Therefore νοῦς can refer to "je nachdem den Sinn, Verstand, Gedanken oder die Vernunft" (*ThBl* 1288).

II) Inasmuch as νοῦς was "theoretisch ausgebildet" (*ThBl* 1289) "in der griech. Philosophie und Religion" (*ibid.*) and thus "in der philosophischen Sprache", whose main requirement "scharfe Sonderung und Trennung der Begriffe ist" (Sch III 622), i.e. "sich zum Begriffe des denkenden Geistes emporgeschwungen (hat)" (Sch III 634), it had necessarily thereby "weit entfernt" (Sch III 622) itself from everyday language. "The transition of the word from popular usage to the vocabulary of philosophy gives it greater pregnancy and in so doing restricts its meaning. It comes to denote the organ of knowledge, and from the more general sense of 'mind' it becomes equivalent to 'reason' or 'spirit' " (*TDNT* 954). The result of that was that on the one hand "das Moment des Gefüles" (Sch III 622), "the practical relation (of feeling, willing and acting) to an object" (*TDNT* 954) "ganz in den Hintergrund" (Sch III 622) or simply "retreats" (*TDNT* 954), while, on the other hand, "the theoretical relation (of thinking and perceiving) comes to the fore" (*TDNT* 952). As a part of man, νοῦς is then "der Verstand, der die Gegenstände richtig abwägt, sie in ihrem waren Wesen erkennt ..." (Sch III 634), "bedeutet dann als Vernunft und Geist das Organ des Denkens, das Welt und Dasein erfasst" (*ThBl* 1289).

[39] A-G 546.
[40] A-S 305.
[41] R 484.

between the "popular" and "philosophical" meanings of νοῦς in the
New Testament and especially in 2 Th 2, 2, then distortions are
produced, so it seems :

i) Not as part of any fixed terminology :
Should one understand νοῦς here exclusively as part of "everyday
speech" and "as in the popular usage of the Greeks ... (with) no
precise meaning", while "there is no connection with the philosophical...
use" ? [42] And should one correspondingly understand νοῦς in the New
Testament along the lines of an "Empfindungsvermögen",[43] i.e. of
"mind, attitude, way of thinking as the sum total of the whole mental
and moral state of being" [44] and therefore less as "Denkkraft",[45] i.e.
as "understanding, thinking" ? [46]

ii) As part of a fixed terminology :
On the other hand, many take νοῦς in the New Testament and
particularly in our passage as having a special, indeed "Christian"
character.
a) Belonging to the realm of morality
νοῦς is taken as the "organ of moral thinking and knowing, the
intellectual organ of moral sentiment ...", "organ of moral thought,
knowledge and judgment, in fact as moral consciousness", in contrast
to the (philosophical, non-New Testament) sense of the "ability to
think and to reflect".[47] The latter is belittled since "the reasoning
faculty esp. on its moral side, (is) the highest part of man's own
nature, through which he is most open to Divine influences." [48]
b) Belonging to the realm of will
Or it is said, with regard to the Greek and Hellenistic ideas that
Paul took over with the word νοῦς, that "so sehr er einerseits" had
also taken over "Kategorien und Fragestellungen aus dem Hellenis-
mus", yet he had in no way "die griech. Lösungsversuche über-
nommen".[49] This is combined with the assertion that this group of

---

[42] *TDNT* IV 958.
[43] Ps II 1, 362.
[44] A-G 546.
[45] Ps *op. cit.*
[46] A-G *op. cit.*
[47] C 436.
[48] Mi 3, 96; cf. also Ol 474 : "the higher powers of the soul in man".
[49] *ThBl* 1292.

words took on their own special character in the New Testament ("eine bestimmt entwickelte Vorstellung"([50]) because they were "stärker in voluntaristischem Sinn profiliert" and no longer moralistic; thus "das Verstehen (wird) selbst zu einer Gesinnung, einem Gesinntsein und damit zu einer Glaubenshaltung".[51]

The consequences for our passage of such a "Christian" understanding of νοῦς must then be that, as often happens, one here takes [52] νοῦς, contrary to its usual meaning, to mean γνώμη, "settled faith",[53] "your settled convictions",[54] "your hitherto settled persuasion of your minds",[55] "your earlier and more correct view",[56] "mental views of the Thessalonians".[57]

II)   An attempted solution

But can that be said of 2 Th 2, 2 where the word νοῦς is used as little problematically (it is rather meant to be obvious) as it is meant to be a moralistic or voluntaristic concept meaning a "way of thinking"? Rather it is used in the context of "accepting the love of the truth". Here it is a case not of a νοῦς that is either a moralistic or voluntaristic concept being in danger of losing its moralistic or voluntaristic character, but rather of the Thessalonians being in danger of just losing their senses. Here the Thessalonians find themselves in a situation which, slightly altering Schmidt's [58] words, we may describe thus : "... es gibt keinen Hottentotten, der nicht eben so gut wüsste als wir, dass die überspannte Parusieerwartung den Verstand allmälig verdunkeln muss ..."

Thus, subject to the findings of a thorough investigation,[59] νοῦς presumably means here

---

[50] Cf. C 727.

[51] *ThBl ibid.*

[52] Do (264) rightly objects to this : "Aber es handelt sich hier ... nicht um Unsicherwerden in der Glaubensüberzeugung" (so also A-R 110; B-C 194; Bis 2, 22; Bor 360; Fra 245; Wet 130). It is simply a variation of this when one understands the νοῦς not as the Thessalonians' state of faith, but Paul's : νοῦς = the meaning of Paul's earlier statements (cf. here Ea 256; B-C 194; Lü 193; Bor 360).

[53] Ca 323; cf. also Eg 85 (sound doctrine); B-C 194; Ol 474.

[54] Ad 234; H-V 243.

[55] Blo 488.

[56] Cf. here Ea 256.

[57] Ad 234.

[58] Sch III 623.

[59] Only a more thorough investigation could establish what aspect of the wide range

(1) in general the "state of sensibleness, composure" [60] and "Ver-
nünftigkeit",[61] and that "in contrast to the disturbance of soul",[62]
and thus that which is "über den Gemütsbewegungen [63] stehend(en)" [64]
and therefore the "Verstand" [65] which is marked by "Klarheit",[66]
"Besonnenheit",[67] "Nüchternheit" [68] and "Ruhe" [69] and also by
"Prüfung" [70] and "Kritik",[71] in short by "Gesundheit",[72] and which
is appropriately accompanied by an "überlegender" [73] "Denkweise" [74]
and "Urteilskraft";[75] it is the "frame or state of mind",[76] "their
ordinary, sober, and normal state of mind",[77] "right mind",[78] such
as expresses "sober ways of thinking",[79] and thinks "as you ought
to think";[80] in short, it is the "mental aspect of man".[81]

(2) But in particular, in view of the idea of σαλευθῆναι, it means

---

of meaning of νοῦς is meant in our passage. Even the *TDNT* art. "deals only with the
linguistic and historical presuppositions for an understanding of the word νοῦς" (952);
a further exposition of the New Testament's theological understanding of this word
(which apart from L 24, 45; Apk 13, 18; 17, 9 only occurs in Paul, and here 21 times)
is promised in the article on ψυχή (not yet published) (952).

Such an investigation would, among other things, have to examine the relation of
νοῦς and πνεῦμα both in I 5, 19-21 (νοῦς-δοκιμάζειν ; πνεῦμα ; προφητεία) and in 1 C (e.g.
14, 14f..19), as well as the possible parallels in R 7, 23.25; 14, 5 (φρονεῖν—νοῦς : compare
our discovery that φρονεῖν is the opposite of σαλεύεσθαι); cf. already Li 109, 152; Fin 164;
Mor 1, 215).

[60] A-G 546.

[61] Do 264; A-R 109f.

[62] A-G 546.

[63] Consequently, to understand νοῦς as "Gemüthsverfassung" (Bis 2, 22; Lü 193;
Wet 130) and translate it as "Ruhe des Gemüths" (Bis 2, 15) is not very appropriate.

[64] Scha 145.

[65] Wo 137; Schla 2, 42.

[66] Bor 360.

[67] Wo 137; Bor 360; Zoe 35; A-R 110; Lü 193; Bis 2, 22.

[68] Wo 137; Bor 360; Lü 193.

[69] Do 264.

[70] A-R 110.

[71] Do 264.

[72] Zoe 35.

[73] Scha 145; Do 264; A-R 110.

[74] Zoe 35.

[75] Wo 137; Bor 360; Do 264.

[76] Li 152.

[77] El 106; Ad 234; Fra 245; Ea 256; Hen 33; Pl 2, 41.

[78] Ea 256.

[79] Fin 49.

[80] Den 306.

[81] Mor 2, 124.

here "the intellectual element in νοῦς",[82] "the mind considered as the reason",[83] but this considered not so much as just an "organ" [84] or "mechanism of thought",[85] but rather as a "state of reasonableness",[86] i.e. a "reasoning faculty",[87] "man's ability to reason",[88] in short, "the power of considering and judging soberly, calmly and impartially";[89] but it is not just judgment, opinion or sentiment themselves. These are primarily the product of this "reasoning faculty".[90]

In contrast to the description of the Thessalonians as those "who have let their imagination rather than their reason dictate their understanding of the Parousia",[91] the νοῦς referred to here must therefore be understood [92] as "the regulative intellectual faculty".[93]

C) σαλευθῆναι ἀπὸ τοῦ νοός

But if we have here in the background the "Bild(e) des wogenden, in Aufregung gebrachten Meeres" and if, accordingly, the Thessalonians are comparable to a "Wasserspiegel, der nicht erst durch länger anhaltenden Sturm, sondern 'schnell' in Unruhe ... versetzt wird",[94] then we can describe their malady thus :

I) the "Schiff der thessalonischen Christen" should really lie ἐπ'ἀγκύρας τοῦ νοός.[95] That is, they should remain near to φρονεῖν,[96]

---

[82] Li 109.

[83] Mor 2, 124.

[84] Fra 245.

[85] Mor 2, 124.

[86] Fra 245.

[87] Mor 1, 215; Mo 99.

[88] Mo 99.

[89] G-T 429; cf. also Mo 99.

[90] Cf. here Li 152.

[91] Mor 1, 214; cf. also Li 109; similarly H-V 243 : "Believers are not to be controlled by the motions ... but by the mind".

[92] We could not incorporate the secondary literature here. Yet, in addition to the works mentioned in TDNT and ThBl, cf. the following : Büchsel, F., Der Geist Gottes im Neuen Testament, 1926, 415; Conzelmann, G., Grundriss der Theologie des Neuen Testaments, 1968, 202; Jewett, R., Paul's Anthropological Terms, Leiden, 1971, 358-90 (1/2 Th 367-73); Kümmel, W. G., Die Theologie des Neuen Testaments, Göttingen, 1969, 156-9.

[93] Fin 164; followed by Mor 1, 215.

[94] Scha 145.

[95] Cf. Plu Mor 493D.

[96] Cf. Plu Mor 68F.

hold on to their *"presence* of mind" [97] and so "keep their heads".[98]
For only thus could they continue to use their reasoning powers
which must "das Steuer behalten, auf dass die Richtung nicht verloren
wird".[99]

II) But now the "Schiff" has been tossed about and thus has been
"weggerissen" [100] ἀπὸ [101] τῆς ἀγκύρας τοῦ νοός and consequently has
been [102] "abgetrieben".[103] In other words, they have now moved
away from φρονεῖν, they are *"out* of their mind" [104] and have thus
"lost their heads".[105] They are "driven off their intellectual moor-
ings" [106] and "shaken from their reason".[107]

---

[97] R 484.

[98] Rob IV 47.

[99] Scha 145.

[100] Schla 2, 42.

[101] I) ἀπό the "Präposition des Scheidens und Ablassens" (W 331) with its "notion
of separation" (M II 297), serves here too "to designate separation, alienation" (B-D-F
211), of "Abstand" (S II 444), and consequently has the meaning "ab, von, weg ...
'fern von sein' " (S II 444f.), " 'of' or 'away from' " (Rob 575; M II 297). Cf. also B-T
506; K-G I 456ff.; K-B 71-4; M III 258f.

II) Bu 277 comments : "Die Grundbedeutung derselben (= ἀπό), nehmlich das
Ausgehn von *dem Äussern* eines Gegenstandes her, ist natürlich auch im NT die vor-
herrschende. Indem jedoch ... wir ... diejenigen *einzelnen* Fälle, wo die Präp. zwar in
besonders eigenthümlicher oder prägnanter, aber auf den Grundbegriff derselben
zurückführenden Bedeutung gebraucht wird, der Hermeneutik überlassen ..."; in a
note he cites as an example of such an "eigenthümlich" use 2 Th 2, 2.

III) See also other such pregnant ἀπό-constructions : 2 Th 1, 9; R 6, 7; 7, 2.6; 9, 3;
Gal 5, 4; II C 11, 3; Col 2, 20; A 8, 22; Hebr 10, 22; II Tim 2, 26 etc.

IV) It is therefore incorrect to translate it "moved, shaken in mind" as A.V., Bar 81,
Har 56, Eg 120, Mo 99.

V) Even if σαλεύεσθαι ἀπό does not occur often (yet cf. ἀποσαλεύεσθαι ... ἀπό Epict
Arr III 26, 16; Plu *Mor* 493D; OGIS 515, 47-3rd century A.D.), yet this construction
can best be explained by contrasting it with σαλεύειν ἐπί τινός ... "sich worauf verlassen
oder stützen, wie ein Schiff auf seine Anker".

[102] A-R 110; Lü 193 : they were "abgebracht von ..." (so also Bis 2, 22).

[103] "Durch den Zusatz ἀπὸ τοῦ νοός verbindet sich das Bild der Unsicherheit mit
dem Bilde der Entfernung vom rechten Standpunkt" (Bor 360; so also A-G 546 : "be
shaken, and thereby lose your calmness of mind"; also A-R 110; Zoe 36; Schm 37).

[104] Ea 256; "out of their wits" (Mas 136).

[105] Hen 168; Gra 97.

[106] Wh 97; so also Blo 488; Fra 245; Li 109; Mi 3, 96; Mor 1, 215; 2, 124; Ne 157.

[107] Mas 126; Mi 3, 96.

III) Thus they are "verschlagen" [108] and "abgelenkt" [109] from the "gesunden Sinne" which is so important if one is to live in "Hoffnung" [110] and they have "turned aside from using their faculty of reasoning";[111] consequently they wallow around in restless billows of enthusiasm and "heisse Leidenschaft" [112] without a κυβερνήτην [113] to take the "Steuer" in his hand and to show them δείκνυσι τὴν εὐθείαν (sc. ὁδόν).[114]

IV) Thus far outside and removed from φρονεῖν, "the νοῦς loses its power",[115] even "versagt" [116] completely and thus "gelangt (so) nicht (mehr) zu seiner Funktion".[117] Therefore a "mental ... weakness" [118] must come over the Thessalonians as a result of which they lose their "whole mental balance".[119] Then they reach the point where the "condition of the ἄνοια commences".[120]

Consequently, since "ihr Nachdenken unterdrueckt wird", they "nicht mehr der Wahrheit untertan bleiben".[121] And, in concrete terms, that means there is a danger that

(1)   because of the "alarms, distress, horror" [122] caused by their σαλευθῆναι ἀπὸ τοῦ νοός they will no longer be ready "to listen any longer to calm and reasonable words" [123] and will therefore

(2)   be the victims of "deception".

---

[108] B-C 194.

[109] Zoe 35.

[110] Schla 2, 42.

[111] Mo 99.

[112] Schla 2, 42.

[113] Cf. Plu *Mor* 454A.

[114] *Ibid.*

[115] Ol 474; and, correspondingly, they *lose* their "Besinnung" (Bu 277; vH 308), their "sobriety" (Eg 121), "Kommen um die Vernunft" (Wo 137), and are thus "um ihr nüchternes Urteil gebracht" (Lue 24).

[116] Wo 137.

[117] Lü 193.

[118] Mor 1, 214.

[119] Mor 1, 215 and 2, 124; Pl 2, 41.

[120] Ol *op. cit.*

[121] Schla 2, 42.

[122] θροεῖσθαι (cf. Ke 126), which is also used in Mt 24, 6 and Mk 13, 7 in the context of the parousia and which in our passage expresses the durative effect (pres.) of the sudden (ταχέως and aor.) σαλευθῆναι which signifies above all movement (cf. Mor 1, 215, n. 4), is a "neues, die Rede steigerndes Moment" (Lü 193 and most comms).

[123] Eg 121.

Section 2 : 2, 13-15

Paul wants the Thessalonians to meet this danger by holding fast to the traditions which they have been taught.

A) *The connection with I 1, 4f.*

I)   Only in I 1, 4 and II 2, 13 do we find the Thessalonian Christians addressed as ἀδελφοὶ ἠγαπημένοι ὑπὸ τοῦ θεοῦ (κυρίου)—moreover, on both occasions this is very closely connected with their "election".

II)   Only in these two passages does Paul also speak of this election of the Thessalonians (I 1, 4 : ἐκλογὴ ὑμῶν; II 2, 13f. : αἱρεῖσθαι, καλεῖν) in the closest possible connection to "our gospel" (τὸ εὐαγγέλιον ἡμῶν is only used in 1/2 Th in these two passages) :

   i)   1, 4f. : "we know ... that he has chosen you; for our gospel ..."
   ii)   2, 13f. : "To this he called you through our gospel ...".

If in the one instance the call is seen as having taken place through "our gospel", then in the other, the first passage, the fact of their call and election can be inferred from the manner of the coming of "our gospel".

III)   In both passages "our gospel" is very closely connected with the λόγος :

   i)   1, 5 : "for our gospel came ... not only ἐν λόγῳ, but also ..."
   ii)   2, 14f. : "... through our gospel ... So then, brethren, stand firm and hold to the traditions which you were taught ..., either διὰ λόγου or by letter".

In I 1, 5 the λόγος recedes somewhat into the background in comparison with the other testimonies of the gospel. In II 2, 14f. its importance is clearly emphasized and the other testimonies of the gospel are not even mentioned. How can we explain this fact ? We ascertained that the playing down of the λόγος in I 1, 5 was deliberate and was meant to emphasize the criteria by which one could recognize the Thessalonians' election. A corollary of this was that Paul chiefly spoke of the other, "word-less" testimonies of the gospel. In II 2,

13-15, on the other hand, the nature of the gospel as word is in the foreground because Paul is no longer giving the criteria by which we may know the Thessalonians' election. He speaks rather of the consequences (ἄρα οὖν v. 15) which follow for the Thessalonians from such an election. In short, the λόγος is played down in I 1, 5 because here their election is mentioned to *console* them. It is emphasized in II 2, 13-15 because their election is here referred to in order to *exhort* them. If the λόγος is emphasized more here than in I 1, 5 then this gives us reason to hope that we can here obtain information concerning something about which we could discover nothing precise in our investigation of I 1, 5, namely the function and the significance of the λόγος in the whole event of the "coming of the gospel".

B. *The relation of λόγος/διδάσκειν to the "coming of the gospel"*

I) The concepts

(1) λόγος

i) λόγος and ἐπιστολή belong together.

a) λόγος refers to the apostle's former preaching activity in Thessalonica, ἐπιστολή to "letters" in general, but above all here to 1 Th. Accordingly, the former oral λόγος is continued in the ἐπιστολή; both merge with one another so that he can simply speak of his λόγος διὰ τῆς ἐπιστολῆς (3, 14).[124] For "Wort und Brief bezeichnen nur zweierlei Form für den gleichen Inhalt".[125] But that means that the meaning, purpose and character of the present letter is basically no different from Paul's former λόγος-activity : "Als solcher ist er Wort Gottes".[126]
    b) λόγος therefore describes

---

[124] The expression λόγος ἡμῶν διὰ τῆς ἐπιστολῆς belongs to the final section of the letter beginning in v. 13 and refers to 2 Th (i. The art. τῆς is equivalent to a demonstrative pronoun : cf. I 5, 27; also R 16, 22; Col 4, 16. ii. The article does not need to be repeated after ἡμῶν since only *one* idea is involved; cf. M III 187; B-D-F 269, 2; Ra 117; Bu 80; W 128. Good survey and discussion of the different interpretations in Lü 238f.); it refers to the whole of 2 Th (so A-R 138; B-C 257; Bor 397; Fin 167; Mor 1, 148; others however think the λόγος is only v. 12—Lü 239—or find it "especially" in this verse—Fra 308f.) and this includes both "dogmatics" and "ethics".

[125] A-R 129.
[126] Schue 7.

aa) the original preaching (I 1, 5f.; II 2, 15)
bb) Timothy's visit (I 3, 1-5)
cc) 1 Th (II 2, 15)
dd) 2 Th (II 3, 14)

But what does λόγος *mean* here?

ii) When it is said in our passages that the Thessalonians have been taught the traditions either through the λόγος or through the ἐπιστολή then that means that the λόγος is nothing but the teaching of the traditions.[127] This is its basic function and significance in the context of the "coming of the gospel". But that already shows that the "intellectual element" in Christian preaching cannot be handled separately from the relation which the "teaching of the traditions" and the "coming of the gospel" have to one another.

(2) διδάσκειν [128]

i) Its basic meaning [129] is "lehren, klar und vollständig auseinandersetzen, darstellen, zeigen, beweisen, darthun, unterweisen".[130] "Die Verdrägung von δα—durch die Formen von διδάσκω bedeutet den Ersatz der einfachen Vorstellung des Lernens und Könnens durch die der mühseligen Schulung".[131] Thus διδάσκω, which describes "das stückweise, stufenweise Vorrücken des Unterrichts mit seinen immer neuen Versuchen und Anläufen" [132] can be paraphrased as follows:

---

[127] παραδόσεις is here to be understood, with most comms, as "teaching and conduct" and not just, as, e.g., in 3, 6, as rules of conduct.

[128] I) Etymology : Ben II 346; Bo 185; Buck 1223f. (cf. also 1721-3); Ch 278; Fr I 387; Ho 58; Ka I 173; Mey III 205f.; Po 202; Pr 115; Va 117; W-P I 784.793; cf. also a full treatment of etymology and the history of its various forms in A. Debrunner, διδάσκω in : Mélanges E. Boisacq, Institut de Philologie et d'Histoire Orientales ... Annuaire, Brussels, Université, vol. 5, 1937, 251-66 (with bibliography).

II) Cf. also H. Güntert, *Indogermanische Ablautprobleme*, Strassburg, 1916, 45; P. Kretschmer, Literaturbericht für das Jahr 1910, in : *Glotta* 4, 349; S I 307; Bjoerck, G., 'Ην διδάσκων. *Die periphrastischen Konstruktionen im Griechischen*, 1940.

[129] On διδάσκω in general cf. B-T 342; H 159; K-B I 2, 400; Ma I 3, 151; II 3, 45 (διδαχθήτω = der Nachweis soll erbracht werden); M II 383; Pal 149; S I 707, n. 1, 710.

[130] Ps I 1, 676; P I 615; So 377; P-K I 371; vanH 211.

[131] Debrunner, *loc. cit.*, 265.

[132] Debrunner, *loc. cit.*, 264.

"ich suche jemanden durch immer wieder in einzelnen Absätzen wiederholte Belehrung eine Kenntnis beizubringen".[133]

ii) So too in our passage. Since the διδάσκων has to have "die Gabe des Unterrichts in ... verstandesmässiger Lehrentwicklung",[134] διδάσκειν therefore "in Gespräch und Unterweisung verläuft" [135] and thus is "directed particularly to the understanding",[136] the "Mühsal des Lehrens" [137] is here the "auf die Sache eingehende, beleuchtende und begründende, auf Bewirkung des Verständnisses berechnete Lehrtätigkeit".[138] παραδόσεις ἃς [139] ἐδιδάχθητε therefore means "d. Überlieferungen, über die ihr belehrt worden seid" [140] and "die ihr gelernt habet",[141] in the form of "discourse with others in order to instruct them".[142]

iii)   But that has three consequences :

a)   The "auf Bewirkung des Verständnisses berechnete" διδάσκειν τὰς παραδόσεις is matched on the Thessalonians' part in I 1, 6 by their δεξάμενοι τὸν λόγον [143] which is characterized by "verstehende Aneignung". But if in II 2, 15 ἐδιδάχθητε ... διὰ λόγου refers to their "Gelehrtwerden von Überlieferungen" and if this is echoed by their

---

[133] Debrunner, loc. cit., 262, following a definition by W. Porzig in : IF 45, 1927, 159.

[134] H. A. W. Meyer, Kritisch Exegetisches Handbuch über den Brief des Paulus an die Römer, Göttingen, in KEK IV, 6th ed. revised by B. Weiss, 1881, 570f.

[135] J. Schniewind, Das Evangelium des Matthäus, in : NTD 2, 1956, 36.

[136] J. Murray, The Epistle to the Romans, vol. II, 1965, 125.

[137] Debrunner, loc. cit., 264.

[138] C 300; A-S 113f.

[139] Διδάσκειν in the passive retains the accusative of the thing taught : "Man muss sich den Begriff des Verbs mit dem des Akkusativs zu einer Einheit verschmolzen denken" (K-G II 1, 326); cf. B-D-F 159, 1; B-T 436, 438; Bu 163; M III 247; Rob 485f.; W 204.

[140] Cf. also Bens 186; E 102f.; M-M 159; R 179; Sch I 608; Z 132; cf. also Westcott, B. F., The Epistle to the Hebrews, London, 1920, 402.

[141] Bis 2, 41.

[142] G-T 144.

[143] I) It is the characteristic of intelligent acceptance which distinguishes δέχεσθαι from παραλαμβάνειν (cf. 1 Th 2, 13).

II) The correspondence of ἐδιδάχθητε and δεξάμενοι is, interestingly enough, also attested in A. In 17, 11, which is closely related to the Thessalonian pericope, it is said of the hearers' reaction that ἐδέξαντο τὸν λόγον. But this implies the καθ' ἡμέραν ἀνακρίνοντες, which in turn corresponds to Paul's form of "teaching", διαλέγεσθαι (cf. Discuss. § 1, Section 1).

δεξάμενοι τὸν λόγον in I 1, 6, then there is nothing to prevent our
taking the ἐν λόγῳ in I 1, 5 as also meaning "through the teaching
of traditions". Accordingly, the gospel would "nicht nur durch die
Belehrung über die Überlieferungen zu ihnen gekommen, sondern
eben auch ..."

b) We can find "traditions" not only in Paul's former λόγος but
also in 1/2 Th. But neither the former λόγος nor the present ἐπιστολαί
are simply the sum of many different "traditions". Rather the
traditions in the λόγος and in 1/2 Th have been handed down to us
and to the Thessalonians only as "processed" by continually being
taught. For in the λόγος and the ἐπιστολαί the Thessalonians are not
so much taught the traditions as taught about them. One could never
grasp the "pure" traditions, but only traditions in the form of being
taught. They have thus already passed through the stage of being
comprehended and assimilated. They are only preserved in a form
that is suitable for assimilation.[144] It squares with this that in 2, 2
the νοῦς is the place where these "traditions" have been anchored
and should be anchored again.

c) When it is said: "Its use (= παραδόσεις) by the Apostle of
Christian doctrine is at once a denial that what he preached originated
with himself, and a claim for its divine authority",[145] then we must
ask whether this statement is correct when applied to our passage.
For the question has been ignored whether Paul was *here* really
concerned with this "denial" and this "claim" and not rather with
διδάσκειν. For he mentions that here too. Paul's declared intention
in v. 2 of restoring the Thessalonian Christians to their νοῦς would
point to that. But then "divine authority" must be *understood*—and
that against the background of Paul's efforts then to make the
traditions intelligible, against the background of his disappointment
at the Christians' refusal to understand (v. 5) and against the background of his renewed attempt to anchor the gospel in their νοῦς.
Then we have to say that such a *teaching* of traditions largely "origi-

---

144 Although Fra (285) speaks on the one hand of the source "of these words, deliv-
erances, teaching, commands, etc.", being "for Paul the indwelling Christ", yet on the
other he sees that "still they are historically mediated by the OT, sayings of Jesus,
and the traditions of primitive Christianity". It seems to me that we must go a step
further and in the light of the νοῦς in v. 2 and the διδάσκειν in v. 15 say that these
"traditions" are not only "historically mediated", but also "mentally mediated". These
traditions have not only found their way down through history but must be taught in
order to "come" to men.

145 H-V 275.

nated with himself". H-V refer to the words "through revelation of Jesus Christ" in Gal 1, 12 to support their contentions that we can but say that Paul there speaks of something that is
aa) *not* taught, but bb) given through revelation. But that is not what he is talking about here; rather he says "you *have* been taught". And in that case the question of "divine authority" within Paul's preaching is no longer so "unambiguous" a matter. The introduction of a different context here as well as in I 1, 5 results in the preaching of Paul being understood by those commentators in such a way as to suggest that ultimately the λόγος and the διδάσκειν is of no importance to Paul. But the whole context here indicates that Paul does not base his call to the Thessalonians to hold fast the traditions on the fact that they had "divine authority", but on the fact that he has then and again now tried to make them intelligible.[146]

If we recognize that tradition in general must always be "packaged" in an intelligible form then it follows that the true significance of human reason in preaching can only be seen, and seen in its true perspective, when we discern the relation between the "teaching of the traditions" and this "coming of the gospel".

We will now cite two representative answers to this question.

II) The "relation" itself according to

(1)   C. H. Dodd [147]

Dodd's starting-point is "a clear distinction between preaching and teaching" (3) in the New Testament. "Preaching ... is the public proclamation of Christianity to the non-Christian world" (4), whereas διδάσκειν, which is identified with παράκλησις, is "addressed to a congregation already established in the faith" (5). He describes the kerygma as follows : "(it) signifies not the action of the preacher, but that which he preaches ..." (3). To discover more about that "that" Dodd reconstructs the different, generally known themes of the original apostolic preaching. These themes are the "data of faith". How then are they related to the problem of the understanding ? "It

---

[146] Statements like, e.g., "By τὰς παραδόσ. are meant 'doctrines and precepts delivered to the world by the Apostles'... *as* a revelation from God" (Blo 493) certainly need qualification if they are really to say something about the situation referred to in our passage.

[147] Dodd, C. H., *Apostolic Preaching and its developments*, London, 1936.

(which is here one datum of faith, namely the coming judgment, but
that stands for all the other data) is not something for which Paul
argues, but something from which he argues; something therefore
which we may legitimately assume to have been part of his fundamental
preaching" (16). In other words, the kerygma is epistemologically
characterized by the exclusion of "arguing for". This "arguing for"
first appears in the διδάσκειν. This is described more fully : "διδάσκειν
is in a large majority of cases ethical instruction. Occasionally it
seems to include what we should call apologetic, that is, the reasoned
commendation of Christianity to persons interested but not yet convinced" (4f.). These "teachings" are "all addressed to readers already
Christian, and they deal with theological and ethical problems arising
out of the attempt to follow the Christian way of life and thought in
a non-Christian world ... They presuppose the Preaching. They expound and defend the implications of the Gospel rather than proclaim it" (8). Διδάσκειν, he says elsewhere, represents "the theological
superstructure of this thought", "which can be clearly distinguished
from"... "what Paul was accustomed to preach as Gospel" (12). By
means of these phrases, "clearly distinguished from" and "clear
distinction" (3), Dodd is in a position to exclude the intellectual
element entirely from the original preaching and to give a place
only in the διδάσκειν as "... instruction ... reasoned commendation ..."
(4), "... theological superstructure of his thought ..." (12), "... arguing
for ..." (16). Dodd considers that this distinction coincides with that
between the earlier oral preaching and the letters written later. Conclusions : the intellectual element in διδάσκειν is thus retained. But
at the same time this διδάσκειν is separated from κηρύσσειν, from the
real "coming of the gospel", and has a place only in the life of those
already converted.

(2)   K. H. Rengstorf [148]

He shows how the purpose of the διδάσκων in secular Greek is
"the highest possible development of the talents of the pupil" (135).
The διδάσκειν "mediates instruction which by way of perception
exercises a formative influence on the men concerned" (141). "The
word calls attention to two aspects, being applied on the one side to

---

[148] Art. διδάσκω in *TDNT* II 135-165. K. Wegenast's article in *ThBl* 852ff. does not
add to this.

the insight of the one who is to be instructed and on the other to the knowledge presupposed in the teacher" (135). "How strong the intellectual ... element in διδάσκειν is" (136) is then shown by means of its usage in colloquial language as attested by papyri and ostraca, where διδάσκειν means "to demonstrate, to prove, to show" (136). His basic point in all this is, positively, that διδάσκειν has only "an intellectual reference" (137) both in classical and postclassical writers and also in the writings of Philo, that διδάσκειν has "a strongly intellectual use" (141) and "von Haus aus die Wendung an den Intellekt vollzieht" (ThWB 144), and that "everything lies in the sphere of the intellect" (141). Negatively, he shows that "the idea of total claim is not to be detected in secular Greek" (137).

This clearly shows the difference from the LXX : "The διδάσκειν of the LXX always lays claim to the whole man and not merely to certain parts of him" (137). For "in secular Greek ... the aim is to develop talents and potentialities. In the LXX (OT) ... the concern is with the whole man ..." (137). The "concern with the whole man" here is used quite specifically of "vor allem ... den Willen" (139);[149] the "Wendung an den Intellekt", to the "Einsicht", is subordinated to this.[150]

If the appeal to the intellect has already clearly been assigned a place after and below that of the appeal to the will, then it is only a short step further to discover what is supposed to be characteristic of the New Testament : the "novel feature in this use by the Evangelists is the complete suppression (= radikale Überwindung) of the intellectual element present in non-biblical usage" (141). That is made clear by a comparison with Philo, who linguistically is an heir of the sophists (he uses διδάσκειν in the sense of the intellectual and rational communication of knowledge and understanding) : for him διδάσκειν "is a function of the thinker in which he addresses himself primarily to the thinking powers of his fellows. That is the exact

---

[149] Wegenast, loc. cit., 852 : "Ziel allen Lehrens ist die Vermittlung von Wissen und Können und darin die Entwicklung der Anlagen des Schülers, nicht aber die Anbahnung von Willensentscheidungen".

[150] In rabbinic usage למד is "in the strict sense, however, ... a specialised term for the translation of the Torah into concrete directions for the life of the individual" (TDNT 138). Wegenast (loc. cit., 853) adds : "Dass das Rabbinat mit diesem Verständnis von limmed dem hell. Verständnis von διδάσκειν ... näher stehe als dem z.B. der LXX, wie zuweilen behauptet wird, ist wenig wahrscheinlich, denn bei aller intellektuellen Anstrengung des Auslegers ... geht es dem Rabbinat doch zweifellos nicht um die Ausbildung von Anlagen, sondern ... um den Gehorsam gegenüber dem Willen Gottes ..."

opposite of the διδάσκειν of Jesus with its demands on the will" (142). Thus the subordination to be seen in the LXX becomes in the New Testament a thorough defeat. The "intellectual element" is blotted out (radix, radical) of the meaning of the word διδάσκειν. To use Rengstorf's language : if διδάσκειν in non-biblical usage "von Haus aus die Wendung an den Intellekt (vollzog)" (144) then this word and its meaning have lost their place in the "biblischer Raum" and have become homeless and "alienated".

It clearly follows that the meaning of the word has been so much "domesticated" that one can use it without much danger as a synonym for κηρύσσειν. In other words, διδάσκειν no longer means what it has "von Haus aus" and "wurzelhaft" meant, but is a parasite clinging to the meaning of κηρύσσειν.

Conclusions : here διδάσκειν is seen in the closest possible connection with κηρύσσειν, with the "coming of the gospel". But at the same time this διδάσκειν is more or less completely denied its "intellectual element".

(3)   Thus both of these scholars, and also countless others,[151] appear to be striving to keep the activity of preaching and the act of coming to faith free from intellectual influences, both on the part of the preacher and on that of the hearers. We have also said above that the intellectual element in preaching can only be seen in its proper perspective when it is seen in the wider context of the question as to the relation of the "teaching of the tradition" to the "coming of the gospel". That does not seem to me to have been noticed in previous attempts to answer this question. This has produced these distortions of a fact which, seen from the right angle, need not be explained away (away from κηρύσσειν, away from the root of διδάσκειν).

Before we put forward our own attempt at a solution in our final section, we must put some questions to Dodd and Rengstorf.

---

[151] Here only a few samples : " 'teaching', didache, succeeds the 'preaching' or kerygma" (Carrington, Ph., *According to Mark*, CUP, 1960, 49) and that in the sense that "der Lehrende von dem spricht, was der Mensch zu tun hat, der Ausrufende von dem, was Gott tun wird" (Schlatter, A., *Der Evangelist Matthäus*, Stuttgart, 1959, 121). Thus it is "Teaching (moral truths), Proclaiming (the good tidings of the kingdom)" (McNeile, A. H., *The Gospel according to St. Matthew*, London, 1915, 47).

(4) Questions put to

i) C. H. Dodd

Since Paul will have had his reasons for distinguishing κηρύσσειν
and διδάσκειν, we now have to go on to ask, not about the fact of
Dodd's distinction of "preaching" and "teaching", but about its
nature; we will do this on the basis of our own previous investigations
and discoveries.

a) Must one infer from the fact that there were two things like
"kerygma" and "didache" in early Christianity that "kerygma" has
nothing to do with διδάσκειν and "didache" has nothing to do with
κηρύσσειν ?

aa) The word διδάσκειν is found both in A 17, 1ff. and in 1/2 Th
as an expression for the whole process of preaching the gospel, not just
for the "instruction" or "exhortation" following this.

bb) Since the διδάσκειν of the former preaching of the gospel
(ἐν λόγῳ I 1, 5; διὰ λόγου II 2, 15) is continued in the διὰ τῆς ἐπιστολῆς
we can also say accordingly that the letters are ultimately "of the
nature of kerygma" (8), and thus are a preaching of the gospel.[152]
That is confirmed by Timothy's mission (I 3, 1-5), which Dodd understands as "didactic" in contrast to Paul's "kerygmatic" activity. But
here we must also note in the same verse the phrase συνεργὸν τοῦ Θεοῦ
ἐν τῷ εὐαγγελίῳ. That we are on the right track here finds
additional confirmation in the other passages in which Timothy is
mentioned :

Ph 2, 22 : ἐδούλευσεν εἰς τὸ εὐαγγέλιον
I C 16, 10 : τὸ γὰρ ἔργον κυρίου ἐργάζεται ὡς κ' ἀγώ
II C 1, 19 : ... ὁ ἐν ὑμῖν δι'ἡμῶν κηρυχθείς, δι'ἐμοῦ καὶ ...
Τιμοθέου ...

b) Must one infer from the fact that Paul in his letters often
"argues from" that his former preaching was characterized by his
omitting "to argue for" ?

---

[152] "... the epistles are ... not of the nature of kerygma ... They have the character
of what the early Church called 'teaching' or 'exhortation' " (8).

An example may make this clearer. According to Dodd, the theme of "return and judgment" was also part of the original preaching of the gospel. In fact, 1/2 Th makes this plain. But to say that "It is to be observed that in these passages the fact of judgment to come is appealed to as a datum of faith. It is not something for which Paul argues, but something from which he argues" (16) and to infer from that that "reasoned commendation of Christianity", "to expound and to defend" (8), "to argue for" only belonged to the second stage, to the διδαχή, and were not characteristic of the preaching of the gospel itself is doubtful for two reasons :

aa) A itself and in particular the passage with which we dealt show that Paul's kerygma was directed towards "persons interested but not yet convinced". And διανοίγων and παρατιθέμενος in A 17, 3, both expressions used for Paul's preaching, can only mean "to expound and to defend".

bb) Paul can only argue in his letters *from* his earlier preaching because he had then argued *for* a new concept of the Messiah, *for* his return, etc. Then he wanted to anchor these "data of faith" (16) in the νοῦς (cf. διαλέγεσθαι-ἀνακρίνειν in A 17, 3). That is indeed the point of his repeated "you yourselves know very well", "do you not remember ?".

Thus we find the "clear distinction "between "to argue from" and "to argue for", between "simple proclamation" and "reasoned commendation", between "to proclaim" and "to expound and defend" problematic and not very helpful. On the contrary, we suppose that the so-called "facts", the "data of faith", in Paul's preaching were very far from being *bruta facta* characterized by the absence of "reasoned commendation". Rather they seem to have been much more closely related to the "theological superstructure of his thought", that is, to be part of the process of διδάσκειν.[153]

ii)   K. H. Rengstorf

In order to assess Rengstorf's exposition and resultant interpretation aright we would have to investigate more closely the word διδάσκειν and its actual use in non-biblical and biblical Greek. Yet some questions

---

[153] Cf. the discussion in Furnish, V. P., *Theology and Ethics in Paul*, New York, 1968, 106-11.

already arise from our previous investigation which should be put to Rengstorf.

a)   Is it correct that the difference between the meanings of διδάσκειν in secular Greek and in the New Testament is determined on the basis of relatively extreme examples?

Our starting-point in our critique of Dodd was his sharp separation of preaching from teaching. Though Rengstorf's ideas are different, he can also be criticized for a sharp either-or. For he understands teaching, with all that it involves, so much from the point of view of preaching that teaching has really lost *its* own character in his treatment. Let us recall his words : the "novel feature in this use by the Evangelists is the complete suppression (= radikale Überwindung) of the intellectual element present in non-biblical usage" (141). Comparing this with Philo's use of διδάσκειν as "a function of the thinker in which he addresses himself primarily to the thinking powers of his fellows" (142), he says that "This is the exact opposite of the διδάσκειν of Jesus ..." (142). But we have, as in Dodd's case, to ask whether this sharp contrast is really correct. Is one closer to the real issue when one uses the category "exact opposite"? How does that category apply while the usages have unquestionably at least one thing in common, namely that they use the same word? Is it really true that Philo's διδάσκειν has nothing at all to do with the human will? Is it really true that Jesus' διδάσκειν "with its demands on the will" can make them without any appeal "to the thinking powers" of his hearers? For *that* would then be "the exact opposite", the "radikale Überwindung des intellektuellen Moments".

If the "intellectual element" is "von Haus aus" proper to the meaning of διδάσκειν, i.e. if the "intellectual element" is a *constitutive* part of διδάσκειν, but this "Stammeigenschaft" has been completely destroyed, i.e. extinguished, devalued, what are we left with but a word which has lost *its* meaning which was proper to it alone?

But phrases like "radikale Überwindung" and "the exact opposite" are formulations which follow logically from a quite definite idea which Rengstorf expresses thus : on the one hand there are the Greeks who, whenever they speak of διδάσκειν, refer only to "certain parts" of man but never to "the whole man" (137). But this statement follows from a very definite concept of the "whole man", for the LXX "always lays claim to the whole man" when it speaks of διδάσκειν. The "whole man" is here seen as involving the "intellect" and above all the "will"; consequently it is the lack of the element of the will which so impoverishes the Greek idea of διδάσκειν. Yet we must ask

aa) whether the meaning of διδάσκειν for the Greeks has really been understood independently and so whether enough thought has been given to the possibility that the Greek concept of διδάσκειν is fundamentally more comprehensive than a comparison with the Hebrew idea leads us to believe, and

bb) whether "intellect" and "will" together make up "*the* whole man"; or does one not have to speak here of Hebrew and biblical nuances being given to this Greek word? Certainly Rengstorf would have been more judicious in his inference if he had compared διδάσκειν and νουθετεῖν with one another. For if διδάσκειν is a matter of "die Entwicklung und Führung des Intellekts", then "wird durch νουθετεῖν auf den Willen und das Gefühl ... eingewirkt".[154]

We must emphasize again that we are not in a position to decide whether this distinction which Rengstorf makes in the meanings of διδάσκειν is accurate and really characteristic. But we cannot avoid the impression that the non-biblical idea is being deliberately played down in order to make more of the biblical one. Both the non-biblical and the biblical usage seem to me to militate against this:

aa) the non-biblical usage of διδάσκειν: on the negative side we suspect that Rengstorf can only speak of a "radikalen Überwindung des intellektuellen Moments" in διδάσκειν because he always selects relatively extreme examples from both the Greek side and from the biblical side to contrast them with one another. But then it is easy to talk of "radikaler Überwindung" without seeing that this "radikale Überwindung" had already taken place within the more basic semantic field of διδάσκειν—even before the idea of διδάσκειν was taken over by the LXX usage. At any rate the significance and value of the intellect in the sophisitic movement can in no way serve as the yardstick by which one measures how much store the Greeks in general set by the "intellectual element" in the life of men.[155]

Positively we must say that

---

[154] F. Selter in *ThBl* 273.

[155] We can illustrate what is meant here from a completely different context: no one who wants to describe the nature of Christianity will start from its off-shoots (e.g. the Crusades) and describe them as "characteristic". Just as little does it help to try to understand communism from Stalinism.

a) διδάσκειν in Greek includes not only the handing on of theoretical knowledge, but also teaching through one's own example.

β) Essentially διδάσκειν had the aim, not of passing on neutral and insignificant scraps of information, but of making man "capable of living".

These observations alone show that it is going too far to say that there is "*not* (= nichts!) to be detected ..." when one asserts that "The idea of a total claim is not to be detected in secular Greek" (137). A clear distinction between "only intellect" and "will", between "not a whole man" and "whole man" is at least more problematic than Rengstorf would have us believe.

bb) 1/2 Thessalonians: if the blotting out of the intellectual element is characteristic of the biblical understanding of διδάσκειν then we can only rate Paul as anachronistic. For his concern is still to emphasize the positive function of the νοῦς as the "state of sensibleness" in the life of a Christian. Paul's charge against the Thessalonian Christians is precisely this, that they have let the "intellectual element" which was contained in the previous apostolic preaching be blotted out and have abandoned it. They have torn loose from their *anchor* of understanding and have thus rendered their νοῦς *hors de combat*. Now Rengstorf holds that in the biblical use of διδάσκειν we do not find that "διδάσκειν mediates instruction which by way of perception exercises a formative influence on the man concerned" (141). Since Rengstorf has emptied the idea of διδάσκειν of all intellectual meaning, we cannot be surprised when he finds himself in basically the same position as the erring Christians in Thessalonica who "let their imagination rather than their reason dictate their understanding of the Parousia".[156] But that means that one has to refuse to let oneself be influenced "by way of perception". What Paul criticizes in them Rengstorf praises.

To be sure, this is to exaggerate the consequences. But it may show where Rengstorf's postulated distinction between secular Greek and the biblical use of διδάσκειν can lead us if we do not work with greater subtlety and circumspection. For what Rengstorf wants to show through the history of the meaning of διδάσκειν is that in the biblical sphere the intellect itself has been utterly blotted out along with this "intellectual element". The example of the word διδάσκειν

---

[156] Mor 2, 214.

shows that the division between the Greeks and the Bible lies in the fact that the first are "intellekthörig" and the latter is "intellekt-feindlich".

Hence, we suppose, Rengstorf's exegesis is the result of his already-held view that faith can only come into play, can only appear, when every intellectual element has first been swept away, i.e. has been completely blotted out.

b) Cannot parallels to Paul's understanding of διδάσκειν be found in the more basic range of meanings of διδάσκειν?

aa) The long process of learning : the imperfect in II 2, 5 together with διδάσκειν in v. 15 points to the fact that here something is happening which is similar to what Rengstorf, referring to the non-biblical use of διδάσκειν, describes thus : "Thus διδάσκειν is the word used more especially for the impartation of ... knowledge when there is continued activity with a view to gradual, systematic and therefore all the more fundamental assimilation" (135).

bb) The example of the teacher as a "bridge" : Rengstorf, again referring to the non-biblical use of διδάσκειν, shows that "especially when it is a question of practical arts and crafts, the example of the teacher forms a bridge to the knowledge and ability of the pupil" (135). " 'Pupil' " he continues (135, n. 2) "is not to be understood here as though the scholar were merely passive". Both seem to me to have a parallel in Paul's thinking.

α) When Paul in II 2, 15 says in general terms that the Thessa-lonians "were *taught* the traditions" and when in 3, 6 he then describes his *own* conduct as tradition in the sense of a τύπος (v. 9), which thus also falls under the heading of "being taught", then Paul is using διδάσκειν in a sense which is in striking agreement with the "non-biblical secular" meaning of διδάσκειν—the practical conduct (περι-πατεῖν) corresponding to the "practical arts and crafts" of secular usage. And doubtless "the example of the teacher" is here "a bridge to the knowledge and ability of the pupil". From this viewpoint the connection of life and instruction as both being "teaching of the traditions" is quite intelligible against the background of the use and meaning of this word in secular Greek. But this is not to deny that here rabbinic influence is quite possible.[157] But this much is clear,

---

[157] Cf. Wegenast, K., Das Verständnis der Tradition bei Paulus und in den Deutero-paulinen, *WMANT* 8, 1962, 118, n. 3.

that Paul's appearance and conduct had a didactic function. He can therefore "argue" with his exemplary life.

β) In connection with our investigation of διαλέγεσθαι and ἀνακρίνειν the idea also suggested itself that the learner actively participates in the learning process.

CONCLUSIONS :

THE REASONS FOR AND THE SIGNIFICANCE AND FUNCTION
OF HUMAN REASON IN PREACHING

§ 3

Here it was simply shown that Paul in no way depreciated his
λόγος, contrary to the belief of most. But nothing further could be
said about the actual function and resultant significance of this λόγος
in the gospel-event as a whole and in particular for the understanding
of this gospel.

§ 4

From the investigation of both sections we can infer that Paul in
his preaching was concerned to anchor the "gospel" in the νοῦς of the
Thessalonians. This can also be regarded as characteristic of Paul's
preaching in general. And it is in the teaching of the παραδόσεις,
whether by the λόγος or by the ἐπιστολή, that this "intellectual
anchoring" took place. That is the function and significance of the
λόγος.

Concluding observations and summary

I)   Whatever the content of Paul's preaching may be, it is characterized by φρονεῖν which is diametrically opposed to all σαλεύεσθαι.[1]
Paul's purpose was to recall them to that φρονεῖν. By means of this
φρονεῖν the so "extraordinary" and in every respect "abnormal"
gospel was to be "trans-lated into" (ueber-setzt) them, translated into
the internal thinking and external practice of the "ordinary" and also
otherwise "normal". It had to become rooted and established on this
ground. But if it was to be rooted there it had to be "intellectually

---

[1] i) We have recognized in A 28, 22 this φρονεῖν to be the basic character of Paul's
καταγγέλλειν.

ii) Is it not significant that φυσᾶσθαι and σαλεύεσθαι σαλευ./φυσιον. in the New Testament), which according to Plu *Mor* 68F are parallel terms for the description of those
who have moved away from φρονεῖν, are used in the New Testament (1 C and here)
about people who either understood themselves to be already resurrected or understood
Christ to have already come again ?

anchored". For only this being anchored can lead the hearer to clear thinking—especially in view of this "extraordinary" gospel. So Paul would not allow either himself or his hearers to omit thinking and thinking through.

The following point will confirm that this rightly reflects Paul's basic purpose and concern as expressed in his λόγος and his ἐπιστολή : in I 1, 5 Paul emphasizes the word-less and more spectacular phenomena that attest the gospel, as opposed to "speaking". But Paul does not maintain this evaluation in these two letters. In other words, when Paul speaks at all of more spectacular manifestations, he does so within the framework of his own appearance and ordinary behaviour in which he tried to avoid drawing attention to himself. The ἐν δυνάμει seems to be "bridled" in the rest of the letter within the form of ordinary everyday life and in no respect in the form of miraculous demonstrations of power. That means that if such things did happen during Paul's stay in Thessalonica they have no particular significance for the exposition and justification of his thinking or for the understanding of the gospel. Already here we can see his inclination towards "intelligibility", not in inconceivable, inimitable miracles, but in conduct which is utterly intelligible and therefore can be imitated. Paul rather justifies all his statements, exhortations, etc., by referring back to his former λόγος and his διδάσκειν. That is what the Thessalonians should recall, and not special manifestations of the Spirit in charismatic signs of power.

Therein lay a great temptation, to match and to answer the "extraordinariness" of the gospel with extraordinary reactions, perhaps with the abandoning both of outward ways of proper behaviour and of inward ways of sensible thought.

So it is significant that it is the very fact of their having been chosen and called which they used to justify their desire to precipitate the "heavenly rapture", which was in Paul's eyes the strongest reason for holding on to the traditions that they had been taught (II 2, 14f.). "Being called" means no „being called away" from their natural capacities of thought and judgment. So, just as they *could* trace their "election" from the "coming of the gospel", so they *should* now draw the consequences from their "election" with regard to their responsibility towards the world. For only through the στήκετε, κρατεῖτε τὰς παραδόσεις can there be a true στήκετε ἐν κυρίῳ (I 3, 8). For how could one "stand" when one had lost one's "mental balance", one's "intellektuelle Gleichgewicht" ? How could one be "*in* the

Lord" when one was at the same time "*out* of one's mind"? How could one be *close* to the Lord when one was *far* from one's νοῦς? No, only if one "bei der Vernunft bleibt" can one also "bei der Wahrheit bleiben". This is "der einzig sichere Weg, sie bei dem Grunde ihres Heils, dem Evangelium selbst, zu halten".[2]

This raises the final question, what exactly the human reason has to do with this "basis of their salvation" and with this abiding "in the truth"?

II) We must start by recognizing that it is in the *teaching of the traditions* that the "intellectual anchoring" of the *gospel* takes place. It follows that ultimately we can only see the reason and the necessity for employing the human reason in preaching from the relationship in which the "teaching of the traditions" stands to the "coming of the gospel". Thus there is a *relationship* between the "gospel" and the "teaching of the traditions", and not a contrast. Consequently the question that we must ask is: How closely are they related to one another?

With regard to 1/2 Th there seem to be basically two things to be said:

(1) Paul, the witness, presupposes other witnesses; he takes up a tradition and thus is a link in a chain of tradition, although that is only really *discernible* in a very few cases. But 2 Th, in particular ch. 2, does recall this fact.

(2) But at the same time Paul is *more* than a mouthpiece for historical traditions that have been handed down to him in a fixed form. For Paul παραδόσεις are not so much something "handed down, but something handed over".[3]

But how can we explain this apparent contradiction? It seems to me that we must fix our attention on two things:

(1) The hearer of the "message"

Paul is *called upon to be a "witness for" by virtue of his own historical situation* and is therefore called to be a *teacher* of the tradition, i.e.

---

[2] Bor 381.
[3] Ea 297.

constantly to *translate* the traditions that he has received and that have been passed on to him.

That was already true of the so-called "missionary preaching" and it is true also of Paul's dealings with the already-existing Christian church in Thessalonica, shaken as it was by crises. So in 1/2 Th we constantly come across Paul reminding his readers of the traditions that they have already been taught, namely of the λόγος. These letters are characterized throughout by the technique of "reminding" : Paul reminds them of the foundations, i.e. the "traditions", which he once "intellectually anchored" amongst them, and from which this Christian community derived. With these Christians he reflects on the church's beginnings, and often does so the more emphatically because they themselves neglected to do so. Paul's indignant aposiopesis in II 2, 3f. betrays Paul's underlying idea : "If only *you* had thought through aright what we taught you earlier, then you would not have let yourselves be driven so quickly and needlessly from your senses". This is Paul's concern : to urge his "message" again in the face of their crises —but only in that he again *spells out* and interprets anew this tradition of his *in its implications* for the present situation. This makes it plain that a mere quoting of "traditions" is inadequate both here and on the occasion of his first visit. Obviously Paul would not have executed his commission in that way. Thus the formative influence of "traditions" or of "tradition" in general on Paul is *limited*, since he sees himself called upon to exercise *freedom* with respect to the actual wording of the tradition in the face of the situation in which he stands, and especially he together with his hearers, the Church. Thus through the διδάσκειν that he practised then and again now (cf. also διαλέγεσθαι, διανοίγειν, παρατίθεσθαι, φρονεῖν) he comes to the point of *remodelling* the tradition—so much so that sometimes even the consistency of Paul's statements seems to be in question.

But that poses the question why Paul felt *bound* to continue with this "labour of teaching" and ever new translations of the tradition, apart from the demands of these various circumstances.

(2) The "subject" of the message

The reason lies in the *"witness to"*, lies in the tradition itself, in this tradition.

   i) This "tradition" was "preaching" and
   ii) was meant to be handed on *as preaching*.

i) *This* tradition only came to *exist* as witness, as witness to the known and encountered presence of the risen Christ.

So this tradition always came *to* Paul and his fellow witnesses as *preaching*, i.e. as the profoundly existential attestation of the presence and rule of Jesus Christ. In such "traditions" Paul apparently encountered the same present Lord as he encountered before Damascus. From this point of view tradition was never, could never be for Paul just "tradition", but was always witness.

ii) But if he who is Lord of the *present* was encountered by the witnesses in and through the "traditions", then their further dealings with these traditions must have from then on been determined and influenced by their knowledge of this presence. That *must* have left its traces on the "traditions".

We will point out here two such traces :

a) *this* tradition allowed of nothing else than a *witnessing* transmission. The very character of this tradition predetermined the need to transmit it *as* witness. For the point of its existence lay in the fact that the Lord whose unique history is attested in it, wants to be attested anew in every present.

b) But that means that the presence of the risen Christ is primary and the tradition itself which testifies to him is secondary. Accordingly, Paul only *uses* these traditions; he uses them *in the service* of his preaching. He does so in order to *point* to the action of God in Jesus Christ that is attested in them. Thus he uses them in order to appeal by them to the *substance* of the traditions. And here the human reason clearly has its function and significance too : it should help the substance of the tradition to find expression. *That* means *teaching* of the tradition. So, just as Paul's "conduct", which is also "tradition", should *point* to the substance lying behind such a "tradition", so Paul was concerned to let the traditions say what they had to say in a particular situation by means of διδάσκειν.

It is therefore the presence of the risen Christ attested in the "traditions" and the lordship of Jesus Christ expressed in them which make this "tradition" ever anew become preaching; this happens when in this "tradition" *taught* by means of human reason men *encounter* the same present Lord whom Paul encountered before Damascus. Hence Paul could only ever pass on tradition as witness which found new words and new accents. Obedient witnessing did not mean for him the mere repetition of the tradition, but preaching carried out in responsibility to the *present* situation of the hearers *and* the *presence* of the risen Christ.

(1 and 2)   The obligation to employ the human reason in preaching the gospel therefore *ultimately* arises neither from the influence of actual circumstances nor from an alleged mobility and inner logic of the tradition. Rather this obligation arises from the fact that the Lord attested in this tradition with his word and his activity is no figure only of the past but is characterized by his being *present*. Therefore this obligation arises from the fact that in *these* traditions we we meet the Lord who wants to make himself heard *today*.

III)   The role of the human reason as it is reflected in Paul's preaching methods arises from the basic premise and the centre of his theology, that is, from the Christ-event. For this reason, tradition always becomes preaching and tradition is not only repeated and recited but is being "trans-lated" (ueber-setzt) through the "labour of teaching" and thus spoken as a contemporary message for the present time.

BIBLIOGRAPHY

I. THE BIBLE

The Holy Bible: Revised Standard Version, O.T., New York, 1952; *Apocrypha*, Edinburgh, 1958; *N.T.*, New York, 1946.

The New English Bible with the Apocrypha, Oxford and Cambridge, 1970.

Biblia Hebraica, ed. R. Kittel, P. Kahle, 3rd ed. by A. Alt, O. Eissfeldt, 11th ed., Stuttgart, 1954.

Septuaginta, ed. A. Rahlf, 7th ed., Stuttgart, 1962.

The Greek New Testament, ed. by K. Aland, M. Black, B. M. Metzger, A. Wikgren, Stuttgart, 1966.

II. BIBLIOGRAPHY OF ANCIENT GREEK LITERATURE

(1) *Texts, scholiae, special lexica, concordances, indices, commentaries*

Aeschines
  Text : Blass (T) 1908
  Scholia : in F. Schultz (T) 1865
  Index : S. Preuss 1896.
Aeschylus
  Text : G. Murray (OCT) 1955[2]
  Scholia : Paley, F. A., Cambridge, 1878, repr. Amsterdam, 1967
  Lexicon : W. Dindorf, Leipzig, 1876
  Indices : G. Italie, Leiden, 1955; Editio altera curavit S. L. Radt 1964
      B. W. Beatson 1830.
Andocides
  Text : Blass-Fuhr (T) 1913
  Index : L. L. Forman 1897
Antipho
  Text : Blass-Thalheim (T) 1914
  Index : F. L. van Cleef 1895.
Aristophanes
  Text : Coulon (Budé), 5 vols, 1923-30
  Scholia : F. Dübner, Paris, 1842
  Lexicon : J. Sanxay, Oxford, 1811
  Concordance : Dunbar 1883
  Index : O. J. Todd, Cambridge/Mass., 1932.
Bacchylides
  Text : Bacchylidis carmina cum fragmentis, ed. B. Snell 1961[8]
  Index : Fatouros.
Demosthenes
  Text : Fuhr-Sykutris (T) ed. maior, 3 vols, 1914-27

Blass-Fuhr (T) ed. minor, vols 1/2 1928-32
Blass (T) vol. 3, 1923.

Dinarchus
Text : Blass (T) 1888
Index : L. L. Forman 1897.

Epictetus
Text : H. Schenkl (T) Leipzig, 1894.

Euripides
Text : G. Murray (OCT) 1910-13
Scholia : Ed. E. Schwartz 1887-91
Concordance : J. T. Allen and G. Italie, London, 1954
Index : C. D. Beck, Cambridge, 1829.

Hesiod
Text : Rzach 1902 (ed. maior)
1913³ (T; ed. minor)
Op : Coloona, 1959; U. v. Wilamowitz-Moellendorf 1828.
Fr : Merkelbach-West 1967
Scholia : Scholia vetera in Hesiodo Opera et Dies, ed. Pertusi, Mailand, 1955
Glossen und Scholien zur Hesiodischen Theogonie mit Prolegomena, ed. Flach,
Leipzig, 1876; Scholia ad Hesiodum e codd. MSS., ed. Gaisford, Leipzig, 1823;
in : Poetae Minores Graeci II
Lexicon : Ph. Buttmann, Lexilogus ... London, 1836
Index : J. Paulsen, Lund, 1890.

Homer
Text : Iliad, ed. T. W. Allen (OCT) 1931
Odyssey, ed. T. W. Allen (OCT) 1906
Scholia : Scholia Graeca in Homeri Iliadem, ed. Dindorf, Oxford, 1875-77
Scholia Graeca in Iliadem Townleyana, ed. Maass, Oxford, 1888
Scholia in Homeri Odysseam, ed. Dindorf, Oxford, 1855
Lexica : G. Authenrieth, An Homeric dictionary, London, 1923
F. Bechtel, Lexilogus zu Homer, Halle 1914,
J. Bekker (ed.), Apollonii Sophistae Lexicon Homericum, Berlin, 1883, repr.
1967
R. J. Cunliffe, A lexicon of the Homeric dialect, London, 1924
H. Ebeling, Lexicon Homericum, 2 vols (T), Leipzig, 1880-5
L. Doederlein, Homerisches Glossarium, 3 vols, Erlangen, 1850.
E. Hermann, Sprachwissenschaftlicher Kommentar zu ausgewählten Stücken
aus Homer 1914
M. Leumann, Homerische Wörter, in : Schweiz. Beiträge zur Altertumswissen-
schaft, vol. 3, Basel, 1950
Snell/Mette/Fleischer, Lexicon des frühgriechischen Epos, Göttingen, 1955
Indices : H. Dunbar, Odyssey and Hymnus of Homer 1880; new ed. 1962 (B.
Marzullo)
G. C. Prendergast, Iliad 1875; new ed. 1962 (B. Marzullo)
C. E. Schmidt, Parallel-Homer, Göttingen, 1885; repr. 1965.

214

Hyperides
   Text : Jensen (T) 1917
   Index : H. Reinhold (in T).
Isaeus
   Text : Thalheim (T) 1903
   Indices : W. A. Goligher/W. S. Maguinnness 1961
      J.-M. Denommé 1968.
Isocrates
   Text : Benseler-Blass (T) 1879, with app. crit. E. Drerup, vol. 1, 1906
   Index : S Preuss 1904.
Lycurgus
   Text : Blass (T) ed. maior 1899; ed. minor 1912
   Index : L. L. Forman 1897.

Lysias
   Text : Thalheim (T) ed. maior 1913; ed. minor 1928
   Index : D. H. Holmes 1895.
Menander
   Text : A. Körte, Menander, Reliquiae I 1938, 1957² (with supplement by A. Thier-
      felder); II 1959, ed. A. Thierfelder
   Index : C. Jensen, Menandri Reliquiae 1929 (pp. 134-84).
Orphean Literature
   Text : Orphei Hymni, ed. W. Quandt, Berlin, 1941 (Index : 64-79)
      E. Abel 1885
      O. Kern, Fragmenta Orphicorum 1922.
Philo
   Text : L. Cohn and P. Wendland, Berlin, 1896-1915.
Philodemus
   Text : Volumina Rhetorica, ed. S. Sudhaus, 2 vols. Leipzig, 1892, 1896.
Pindar
   Text : O. Schroeder, Pindari Carmina 1900
      C. M. Bowra, Pindari Carmina 1947²
      A. Turyn, Pindari Carmina 1948
      B. Snell, Pindarus, 20 vols, 1959/1964
   Lexica : J. Rumpel (T) Leipzig, 1883
      W. J. Slater, Berlin, 1969
   Commentaries : C. J. T. Mommsen, Pindari Carmina, Berlin, 1864
      A. Boeckh, Pindari Opera, Leipzig, 1811-32
Plutarch
   Text : Moralia, ed. G. N. Barnardakis, 7 vols (T) Leipzig 1888-96.
Sophocles
   Text : A. C. Pearson (OCT) 1923
   Scholia : Ed. P. Elmsley, Oxford, 1825
   Lexica : W. Dindorf, Leipzig, 1870
      F. Ellendt (Editio altera emendata curavit H. Geuthe, Berlin, 1872)
   Index : B. W. Beatson, Cambridge, 1830.
Theognis
   Text : D. Young 1961

Index : G. Fatouros, Index Verborum zur fruhgriech. Lyrik 1966.

(2) *Old Dictionaries*

Harpocration

Harpocrationis lexicon cum annotationibus interpretum
lectionibusque libri MS. Vratislaviensis, 2 vols, Leipzig, 1824
    (ed.) W. Dindorf. Harpocrationis lexicon in decem oratores Atticos, 2 vols in
1, Oxford, 1853
    (ed.) J. Bekker. Harpocration et Moeris, Berlin, 1833.

Hesychius (Alex.)

    (ed.) J. Alberti. Hesychius : Lexicon, 2 vols, Leiden, 1746-66
    (ed.) M. Schmidt. Hesychii Alexandrini lexicon, ed. minor, Jena, 1867[2]
    (ed.) K. Latte. Hesychii Alexandrini lexicon —2vols so far : I) A-Δ 1953; II) E-O
1966. Copenhagen.

Lexica Graeca Minora

Lexica Graeca Minora, selegit K. Latte disposuit et praefatus est H. Erbse,
Hildesheim, 1965.

Lexicon Rhetoricum Cantabrigiense

    (ed.) E. O. Houtsma, Leiden, 1870, now in : Lexica Graeca Minora, pp. 61-139.

Paroemiographi Graeci

    (ed.) E. V. Leutsch/F. G. Schneidewin : Corpus Paroemiographorum Graecorum,
2 vols and a supplement, Göttingen, 1839; repr. Hildesheim, 1958; (ed.) T. Gaisford : Paroemiographi Graeci quorum pars nunc primum ex codicibus manuscrip-
tus vulgatur, Oxford, 1836.

Photius

    (ed.) R. Parson. Φωτίου τοῦ πατριάρχου λέξεων συναγωγή E codice Galeano
descripsit, 2 vols, London, 1822
    (ed.) G. Hermann, Photii lexicon e duobus apographis. Accedit Io. Albertii index
suppletus et auctus, Leipzig, 1808
    (ed.) R. Reitzenstein, Der Anfang des Lexikons des Photios, Leipzig and Berlin, 1907
    (ed.) S. A. Naber, Photii Patriarchae Lexicon, 2 vols in 1, Amsterdam, 1965
(1st ed. 1864f.)
    (ed.) K. Tsandsanoglos τὸ λεξικὸ τοῦ Φωτίου. Χρονολόγηση. Χειρόγραφη παραδόση.
Θεσσαλονίκη 1967.

Pollucis Onomasticon

    (ed.) E. Bethe, Pollux : Onomastikon, 2 vols, Leipzig, 1900-31, in : Lexicographi
Graeci IX i-iii (T)
    (ed.) I. Bekker, Pollux : Onomastikon, Berlin, 1846
    (ed.) W. Dindorf, Pollux : Onomasticon cum annotationibus interpretum, 5 vols in 6,
Leipzig, 1824.

Stephanus Byzantius

    (ed.) A. Westermann, 'Εθνικῶν quae supersunt (T) Leipzig, 1839
    (ed.) A. Meineke, Stephanii Byzantii Ethnicorum quae supersunt, Graz, 1958
(1st ed. 1849).

ἡ Σοῦδα

    (ed.) L. Kuster, Suidae Lexicon, Graecae et Latine, 3 vols, Cambridge, 1705
    (ed.) T. Gaisford 1834

(ed.) G. Bernhardy, Suidae Lexicon. Graecae et Latine, 2 vols, 1853

(ed.) I. Bekker, Suidae lexicon, Berlin, 1854

(ed.) A. Adler, Suidae lexicon, 5 vols, Leipzig, in : Lexicographi Graeci I i-v (T) 1929-38.

συναγωγὴ λέξεων χρησίμων

(ed.) I. Bekker, in : Anecdota Graeca, vol. 1, pp. 1-422, Leipzig, 1828; repr. Hildesheim, 1965.

(3) *Etymological Works of the Byzantine Period*

Reitzenstein

R. Reitzenstein, Geschichte der griechischen Etymologika 1897; repr. 1964.

Etymologicum Genuinum

(ed.) E. Miller (extracts only), in : Mélanges de Littérature Grecque, Paris, 1868 (repr. Amsterdam, 1965), pp. 11-318 (cf. Reitzenstein, who edited a small part of the lexicon—the glosses beginning with ἀμ—).

Etymologicum Gudianum

(ed.) F. W. Sturz, Etymologicum Graecae linguae Gudianum ..., Leipzig, 1818

(ed.) A. de Stefani, Etymologicum Gudianum quod vocatur. Facs. 1 : A-B 1965; Facs. 2 : B-Z 1965. Amsterdam (1st ed. 1908/1920).

Etymologicum Magnum

(ed.) F. Sylburg, Etymologicon magnum, Heidelberg, 1594; improved impression by H. Schafer, Leipzig, 1819

(ed.) T. Gaisford, Amsterdam, 1962 (1st ed. Oxford, 1846).

Orion Thebanus : Etymologicon

(ed.) F. W. Sturz, Leipzig, 1820.

Etymologicum Symeonis

(ed.) H. Sell, Das Etymologicum Symeonis, (a-αἴω), Meisenheim, 1968.

(4) *Modern Dictionaries*

Kiessling, E., Wörterbuch der griechischen Papyrusurkunden, Amsterdam, 1971.

Liddell, H. G., and Scott, L. S., Greek-English Lexicon, new ed. (Stuart Jones and McKenzie) with a supplement, Oxford, 1968.

Pape, W., Griechisch-Deutsches Handwörterbuch, 2 vols, Braunschweig 1845; 1880[3]. Repr. of 3rd impr. 1914 revised by M. Sengebusch, Graz, 1954.

Passow, F., Handwörterbuch der griechischen Sprache. 5th ed. by V. C. F. Rost, F. Palm, et al. 1841-57; repr. Darmstadt, 1970.

Passow, F., Handwörterbuch der griechischen Sprache, completely revised by W. Crönert 1912-3.

Presigke, F., and Kiessling, E. Wörterbuch der griechischen Papyrusurkunden mit Einschluss der griechischen Inschriften, Aufschriften, Ostraka, Mumienschilder usw. aus Ägypten, 3 vols in 9, Berlin/Marburg, 1925-1969.

Preisigke, F., Fachwörter des öffentlichen Verwaltungsdienstes Ägyptens in den griechischen Papyrusurkunden der ptolemäisch-römischen Zeit, Göttingen, 1915.

Schmidt, J. H. H., Synonymik der griechischen Sprache, 4 vols, 1876; repr. Amsterdam, 1967-9.

Sophocles, E. A., Greek Lexicon of the Roman and Byzantine Periods from B.C. 146 to A.D. 1100, 2 vols, Cambridge/Mass., 1887; repr. New York, 1957-67.

Stephanus, H., *ΘΗΣΑΥΡΟΣ ΤΗΣ ΕΛΛΗΝΙΚΗΣ ΓΛΩΣΣΗΣ* : Thesaurus Graecae Linguae, 8 vols, Paris, 1831-65.

van Herwerden, H., Lexicon Graecum supplementarium et dialecticum, 2 vols, Leiden, 1910.

(5) Etymological Dictionaries

Benfey, T., Griechisches Wurzellexikon, Berlin, 1839-42.

Boisacq, E., Dictionnaire étymologique de la langue grecque, 4. ed. augmentée d'un Index par H. Rix, Heidelberg, 1950.

Buck, C. D., A Dictionary of Selected Synonyms in the Principal Indo-European Languages : A Contribution to the History of Ideas, London, 1949.

Buttmann, P., Lexilogus : or a critical examination of the meaning and etymology of numerous greek words and passages intended principally for Homer and Hesiod, London, 1836.

Chantraine, P., Dictionnaire Etymologique de la langue Grecque, Paris, 1968 (A-K so far).

Curtius, G., Grundzüge der griechischen Etymologie, Leipzig, 1879[5]; Engl. transl. : Principles of Greek Etymology, 2 vols, 1886[5].

Fick, A., Vergleichendes Wörterbuch der indogermanischen Sprachen, 4th ed., 3 vols, Göttingen, 1890-1909.

Frisk, H., Griechisches Etymologisches Wörterbuch, 2 vols, Heidelberg, 1960-70.

Hofmann, J. B., Etymologisches Wörterbuch des Griechischen, München, 1949.

Kaltschmidt, J. H., Sprachvergleichendes und etymologisches Wörterbuch der griechischen Sprache, 3 vols in 2, Leipzig, 1839-41.

Meyer, L., Handbuch der griechischen Etymologie, 4 vols, Leipzig, 1901-02.

Pape, W., Etymologisches Wörterbuch der griechischen Sprache, Berlin, 1836.

Pokorny, J., Indogermanisches Etymologisches Wörterbuch, 2 vols, Bern and München, 1959-69.

Prellwitz, W., Etymologisches Wörterbuch der griechischen Sprache, 2nd ed., Göttingen, 1905.

Rohlfs, G., Etymologisches Wörterbuch der unteritalienischen Gräzität, Halle, 1930.

Vanicek, A., Griechisch-Lateinisches Etymologisches Wörterbuch, 2 vols, 1881[2].

Walde, A., and Pokorny, J., Vergleichendes Wörterbuch der indo-germanischen Sprachen, vols 1-3, 1930-32.

Wharton, E. R., Etyma Graeca. An Etymological Lexicon of Classical Greek, London, 1882.

(6) On the Dictionaries (aids and word studies)

Bodoh, J. J., Index of Greek Verb Forms, Hildesheim/New York, 1970.

Buck, C. D., and Petersen, W., A reverse Index of Greek Nouns and Adjectives, Chicago, 1944.

Chantraine, P., Études sur le vocabulaire grec, Paris, 1956.

Delbrück, B., Vergleichende Syntax der indogermanischen Sprachen, Strassburg, 1893.

Fournier, H., Les verbes "dire" en grec ancien.

Goetz, G., and Gundermann, G., Glossae Latinograecae et Graecolatinae, Leipzig, 1888.

Gonda, J., δείκνυμι, 1929.

Kretschmer, P., and Locker, E., Rückläufiges Wörterbuch der griechischen Sprache, Göttingen, 1944, 1963².

Marinone, N., and Guala, F., Complete Handbook of Greek Verbs, Cambridge/Mass., 1961, 1963.

Petersson, H., Griechische und lateinische Wortstudien, Lund, 1922.

Schulz, S., Die Wurzel πειθ-(πιθ) im älteren Griechischen. Eine Formal- und Bedeutungsgeschichtliche Untersuchung, Dissertation, Bern, 1952.

Strömberg, R., Griechische Wortstudien, Göteborg, 1944.

Traut, G., Lexicon über die Formen der griechischen Verba, Darmstadt, 1868 (1st ed. 1867).

Veitch, W., Greek Verbs irregular and defective, new ed., Oxford, 1871.

Wüst, W., 'Ρῆμα Mitteilungen zur indogermanischen Wortkunde, München, 1955.

(7) *Grammars*

1) *Greek Grammars*

Brugmann, K., Griechische Grammatik, 4th ed. by A. Thumb, München, 1913, in: Handbuch der Altertumswissenschaft II:1.

Buttmann, P., Ausführliche griechische Sprachlehre, Berlin, 1819.

Calder, W. M., Index Locorum zu Kühner-Gerth, Darmstadt, 1965.

Chantraine, P., Grammaire homérique, 2 vols, Paris, 1942-53.

Goodwin, W. W., A Greek grammar, London, 1894²; repr. 1968.

Jannaris, A. N., An historical Greek Grammar, London, 1897.

Kieckers, E., Historische Griechische Grammatik, 4 vols, Berlin and Leipzig, 1925.

Kühner, R., Ausführliche Grammatik der griechischen Sprache. Erster Teil: Elementar- und Formenlehre, in neuer Bearb. hrsg. von F. Blass. Vol. I 1890, vol. II 1892. Hannover,

Kühner, R., Ausführliche Grammatik der griechischen Sprache. Zweiter Teil: Satzlehre, in neuer Bearb. hrsg. von B. Gerth. Vol. I 1898, vol. II 1904. Hannover and Leipzig (1955⁴).

Meisterhans, K., Grammatik der attischen Inschriften, Berlin, 1900³ (enlarged and revised by E. Schwyzer).

Meyer, G., Griechische Grammatik, in: Bibliothek indogermanischer Grammatiken, vol. III, Leipzig, 1896³.

Schumann, W. W., Index of Passages cited in H. W. Smyth Greek Grammar, Cambridge, 1961.

Schwyzer, E., Griechische Grammatik, auf der Grundlage von K. Brugmann's Griechischer Grammatik, 3 vols, München, 1960².

Smyth, H. W., Greek Grammar, revised ed. by G. M. Massing, HUP, 1963.

2) *On the Grammar*

Bäumlein, W., Untersuchungen über griechische Partikeln, Stuttgart, 1861.

Bernhardy, G., Wissenschaftliche Syntax der griechischen Sprache, Berlin, 1829

Curtius, G., Das Verbum der griechischen Sprache, seinem Baue nach dargestellt, 2 vols, 1873-76 (Engl. transl. 1880).

Chantraine, P., La formation des noms en grec ancien, Paris, 1933.

Debrunner, A., Griechische Wortbildungslehre, Heidelberg, 1917.

Delbrück, B., Die Grundlagen der griechischen Syntax, Halle, 1879.

Denniston, J. D., The Greek Particles, Oxford, 1954[2].

Dover, K. J., Greek Word Order, Cambridge, 1961.

Gildersleeve, B. L., and Miller, C. W. E., Syntax of classical Greek from Homer to Demosthenes, 2 vols, New York, 1901-11.

Goodwin, W. W., Syntax of the moods and tenses of the Greek verb, London, 1912.

Hirt, H., Handbuch der griechischen Laut- und Formenlehre, Heidelberg, 1912.

Humbert, J., Syntaxe grecque, Paris, 1960[3].

Johannson, K. T., Beiträge zur griechischen Sprachkunde, Upsala, 1891.

Middleton, G., An essay on analogy in syntax, London, 1892.

Mutzbauer, C., Die Grundbedeutung des Konjunktiv und Optativ, Leipzig and Berlin, 1908.

Rodenbusch, E., Beiträge zur Geschichte der griechischen Aktionsarten, in: IF 21, 116-45.

Rossberg, C., De praepositionum Graecorum in chartis Aegyptiis Ptolemaeorum aetatis usu, Dissertation, Jena, 1909.

Solmsen, F., Beiträge zur griechischen Wortforschung, 1. Teil, Strassburg, 1909.

Solmsen, F., Untersuchungen zur griechischen Laut- und Verslehre, Strassburg, 1901.

Stahl, J. M., Kritisch-historische Syntax des griechischen Verbums der klassischen Zeit, Heidelberg, 1907.

Svensson, A., Zum Gebrauch der erzählenden Tempora im Griechischen, Lund, 1930.

Viger, F., De praecipuis Graecae dictionis idiotismis liber cum animadversionibus H. Hoogevenii, J. C. Zeunii et G. Hermanni, Lipsiae, 1934[4].

Wackernagel, J., Vorlesungen über Syntax, 2 vols, Basel, 1926-8; repr. 1950.

(8) *Reference Works*

Der kleine Pauly. Lexikon der Antike 1964.

Das Lexikon der Alten Welt, 1965.

The Oxford Classical Dictionary, 1970[2].

III) BIBLIOGRAPHY OF NEW TESTAMENT AND RELATED LITERATURE

(1) *Dictionaries, Word Studies and Concordances*

Abbott-Smith, J., A Manual Greek Lexicon of the New Testament, Edinburgh and London, 1923[2].

Arndt, W., and Gingrich, F. W., A Greek-English Lexicon of the NT and Other Early Christian Literature. A translation and adaption of W. Bauer's Griechisch-Deutsches Wörterbuch zu den Schriften des NT und der übrigen urchristl. Literatur, 4th revised and augmented ed. 1952, Cambridge, 1963.

Barclay, W., New Testament Words, London, 1964.

Benseler, G. E., Griechisch-Deutsches Schul-Wörterbuch, Leipzig, 1896[10].

Coenen, L., (ed.), Theologisches Begriffslexikon zum Neuen Testament, Wuppertal, 1967.

Cremer, H., Biblisch-theologisches Wörterbuch der Neutestamentlichen Gracität, Gotha, 1902⁹; Engl. transl. by Urwick : Biblico-Theological Lexicon of the New Testament Greek, Edinburgh, 1883; repr. 1955.

Ebeling, H., Griechisch-deutsches Wörterbuch zum Neuen Testamente, Hannover and Leipzig, 1913.

Field, F., Notes on the Translation of the New Testament being the Otium Norvicense, Cambridge, 1899.

Goodspeed, E. J., Problems of New Testament Translation, Chicago, 1945.

Green, T. S., Critical Notes on the New Testament, London, 1867.

Heine, G., Synonymik des Neutestamentlichen Griechisch, Leipzig, 1898.

Hunter, A. M., Exploring the New Testament, Edinburgh, 1971.

Kennedy, H. A. H., Sources of New Testament Greek or the influence of the Septuagint on the vocabulary of the New Testament, Edinburgh, 1895.

Kittel, G., (ed.), Theological Dictionary of the New Testament. Engl. transl. by G. W. Bromiley, Grand Rapids, 1964ff.

Kittel, G., (ed.), Theologisches Wörterbuch zum Neuen Testament, Stuttgart, 1933ff.

Lampe, G. W. H., (ed.), A Patristic Greek Lexicon, Oxford, 1961-8.

Luther, R., Neutestamentliches Wörterbuch, Hamburg, 1966.[17]

Moulton, W. F., and Geden, A. S., A Concordance to the Greek Testament, Edinburgh, 1963.

Moulton, J. H., and Milligan, G., The Vocabulary of the Greek Testament illustrated from the Papyri and other non-literary sources, London, 1930.

Nägeli, T., Der Wortschatz des Apostels Paulus. Beitrag zur sprachgeschichtlichen Erforschung des Neuen Testaments, Göttingen, 1905.

Parkhurst, J., A Greek and English Lexicon to the New Testament, London, 1851.

Robertson, A. T., Word Pictures in the New Testament. vols I-VI, New York, 1930-33.

Robinson, E., A Greek and English Lexicon of the New Testament. A new edition. London, 1850.

Schleusner, J. F., Lexicon Graeco-Latinum in Novum Testamentum, London, 1826.

Thayer, J. H., A Greek-English Lexicon of the New Testament being Grimm's Wilke's Clavis Novi Testamenti, transl., revised and enlarged by J. H. Thayer, Edinburgh, 1914⁴.

Trench, R. C., Synonyms of the New Testament, new ed., London, 1915.

Vincent, M. R., Word Studies in the New Testament, vols I-IV, London, 1887.

Wuest, K. S., Studies in the Vocabulary of the Greek New Testament, Grand Rapids, 1955.

Zorell, Fr. (S. J.), Novi Testamenti Lexicon Graecum, Paris, 1911.

(2) *Grammars and Grammatical Studies*

Abott, E. A., Johannine Grammar, London, 1906.

Beyer, K., Semitische Syntax im Neuen Testament, vol. I : Satzlehre, part 1, Göttingen, 1968.

Blass, F., and Debrunner, A., A Greek Grammar of the New Testament and other Early Christian Literature with Supplementary Notes by A. Debrunner, revised and transl. by R. W. Funk, Cambridge, 1961.

Burton, E. de W., Syntax of the Moods and Tenses in New Testament Greek, Edinburgh, 1894[2]; repr. 1955.

Buttmann, A., Grammatik des neutestamentlichen Sprachgebrauchs, Berlin, 1859.

Green, T. S., A Treatise on the Grammar of the New Testament Dialect, London, 1862.

Helbing, R., Grammatik der Septuaginta. Laut und Wortlehre. Göttingen, 1907.

Johannessohn, M., Der Gebrauch der Präpositionen in der Septuaginta, Berlin, 1925.

Ljungvik, H., Beiträge zur Syntax der spätgriechischen Volkssprache, Leipzig, 1932.

Mayser, E., Grammatik der griechischen Papyri aus der Ptolemäerzeit, vols I and II, Berlin, 1906-70.

Moule, C. F. D., An Idiom Book of New Testament Greek, Cambridge, 1959[2].

Moulton, J. H., Howard, W. F., Turner, N., A Grammar of New Testament Greek, 3 vols, Edinburgh, 1908-63.

Palmer, L. R., A Grammar of the Post-Ptolemaic Papyri. Vol. I : Accidence and Word Formation, Part I : The Suffixes. Oxford, 1945.

Radermacher, L., Neutestamentliche Grammatik, Tübingen, 1925[2].

Robertson, A. T., A Grammar of the Greek New Testament in the Light of Historical Research, New York, 1947.

Simcox, W. H., The Language of the New Testament, London, 1889.

Thackeray, H. S. J., A Grammar of the Old Testament in Greek according to the Septuagint, vol. I, Cambridge, 1909.

Thrall, M. E., Greek particles in the New Testament, Leiden, 1962.

Thumb, A., Handbook of the Modern Greek Vernacular, Engl. transl. by S. Angus, Edinburgh, 1912.

Turner, N., Grammatical Insights into the New Testament, Edinburgh, 1965.

Winer, G. B., Grammatik des neutestamentlichen Sprachidioms, Leipzig, 1855[6].

Winer, G. B., Grammatik des neutestamentlichen Sprachidioms, 8th ed. revised by P. W. Schmiedel. Part I : Einleitung und Formenlehre. Göttingen, 1894.

(3) *Commentaries*

1) *Acts*

Alexander, J. A., The Acts of the Apostles, 2 vols, London, 1884.

Alford, H., The Greek Testament ... and a critical and exegetical commentary, new ed., London, 1880-81.

Bartlet, J. V., The Acts, in : The Century Bible, Edinburgh, 1901.

Bengel, J. A., Gnomon Novi Testamenti, Stuttgart, 1860.

Blaiklock, E. M., The Acts of the Apostles, in : The Tyndale New Testament Commentaries, London, 1959.

Bruce, F. F., The Acts of the Apostles, London, 1952[2].

Bruce, F. F., Commentary on the Book of the Acts, in : The New International Commentary on the New Testament, Grand Rapids, 1956.

Conzelmann, H., Die Apostelgeschichte, in : Handbuch zum Neuen Testament, Tübingen, 1963.

Foakes-Jackson, F. J., The Acts of the Apostles, in : The Moffatt New Testament Commentary, London, 1940.

Haenchen, E., Die Apostelgeschichte, in : Meyers Kritisch-Exegetischer Kommentar über das Neue Testament, Göttingen, 1968.

Hanson, R. P. C., The Acts, in : The New Clarendon Bible, Oxford, 1967.

Hervey, A. C., The Acts of the Apostles, London, 1906.

Holtzmann, H. J., Die Apostelgeschichte, in : Hand-Commentar zum Neuen Testament, Tübingen, 1901[3].

Jackson, F. J. F., and Lake, K., (eds.), The Beginnings of Christianity. Part I : The Acts of the Apostles. Vol. IV, Engl. transl. and Commentary, and vol. V, Additional Notes, by K. Lake and H. J. Cadbury. London, 1933.

Lumby, J. R., The Acts of the Apostles, in : Cambridge Greek Testament for Schools and Colleges, Cambridge, 1904.

Lumby, J. R., The Acts of the Apostles, in : The Cambridge Bible for Schools and Colleges, Cambridge, 1893.

Meyer, H. A. W., Critical and Exegetical Handbook to the Acts of the Apostles, 2 vols, Engl. transl. by Gloag and Dickson, Edinburgh, 1887.

Munck, J., The Acts of the Apostles, rev. by W. F. Albright and C. S. Mann, in : The Anchor Bible, New York, 1967.

Preuschen, E., Die Apostelgeschichte, in : Handbuch zum Neuen Testament, Tubingen, 1912.

Rackham, R. B., The Acts of the Apostles, in : Westminster Commentaries, London, 1910[5].

Schlatter, A., Die Apostelgeschichte, in : Erlauterungen zum Neuen Testament, Stuttgart, 1948.

Stählin, G., Die Apostelgeschichte, in : Neues Testament Deutsch, Göttingen, 1966[2].

Wendt, H. H., Kritisch Exegetisches Handbuch über die Apostelgeschichte, von H. A. W. Meyer. 5th ed. revised by H. H. Wendt, in : Kritisch Exegetischer Kommentar über das Neue Testament, Göttingen, 1880[5].

Williams, C. S. C., A Commentary on the Acts of the Apostles, in : Black's New Testament Commentaries, London, 1957.

2) *1/2 Thessalonians*

Adeney, W. F., Thessalonians and Galatians, in : The Century Bible, Edinburgh, n.d.

Auberlen, C. A., and Riggenbach, C. J., Die beiden Briefe Pauli an die Thessalonicher, in : Langes Theologisch-homiletisches Bibelwerk, Leipzig, 1864.

Barnes, A., Notes explanatory on the Epistle of Paul to the Thessalonians, to Timothy, to Titus, and to Philemon rev. by J. Cumming, London, 1847.

Baumgarten-Crusius, L. F. O., Commentar über die Briefe Pauli an die Philipper und die Thessalonicher, in : Exegetische Schriften zum Neuen Testament III, 2, Iena, 1848.

Bicknell, E. J., The First and Second Epistles to the Thessalonians, in : Westminster Commentary, London, 1932.

Bisping, A., Erklärung der Briefe an die ... und des ersten Briefes an die Thessalonicher, in : Exegetisches Handbuch zu den Briefen des Apostels Paulus, Münster, 1855.

Bisping, A., Erklärung des zweiten Briefes an die Thessalonicher, in : Exegetisches Handbuch zu den Briefen des Apostels Paulus, Münster, 1858.

Bloomfield, S. T., I and II Thessalonians, in The Greek Testament, with English notes, 2 vols, London, 1855.

Bornemann, V., Die Thessalonicherbriefe, in : Kritisch exegetischer Kommentar über das Neue Testament, Göttingen, 1894[6].

Calvin, J., The Epistles of Paul the Apostle to the Philippians, Colossians and Thessalonians, Engl. transl. by J. Pringle, Edinburgh, 1851.

Denney, J., The Epistles to the Thessalonians, in : The Expositor's Bible, London, 1892.

Dibelius, H., An die Thessalonicher I, II, An die Philipper, in : Handbuch zum Neuen Testament, Tübingen, 1937$^{2-3}$.

von Dobschütz, E., Die Thessalonicherbriefe, in : Kritisch exegetischer Kommentar über das Neue Testament, Göttingen, 1909.

Drummond, J., The Epistles of Paul the Apostle to the Thessalonians, in : International Handbook to the New Testament, London, 1899.

Eadie, J., A Commentary on the Greek Text of the Epistle of Paul to the Thessalonians, London, 1877.

Egenolf, H. A., The Second Epistle of the Thessalonians, Engl. transl. by W. Glen-Doepel, London, 1969.

Ellicot, C. J., St. Paul's Epistles to the Thessalonians, London, 1880[4].

Ewald, H., Die Sendschreiben des Apostels Paulus, Göttingen, 1857.

Findlay, The Epistles of Paul the Apostle to the Thessalonians, in : Cambridge Greek Testament for Schools and Colleges, Cambridge, 1904.

Frame, J. E., A Critical and Exegetical Commentary on the Epistles of St. Paul to the Thessalonians, in : International Critical Commentary, Edinburgh, 1912.

Garrod, G. W., The First Epistle to the Thessalonians, London, 1899.

Gloag, P. J., I Thessalonians. II Thessalonians, in : The Pulpit Commentary, London, 1907.

Grayston, K., The Letters of Paul to the Philippians and Thessalonians, Cambridge, 1967.

Harris, J. T., The Writings of the Apostle Paul, with Notes Critical and Explanatory, 2 vols, London, 1901-02.

Hendriksen, W., Exposition of I and II Thessalonians, in : New Testament Commentary, Grand Rapids, 1955.

Hofmann, J. C. K. von, Die Thessalonicherbriefe, in : Die Heilige Schrift neuen Testaments, Nördlingen, 1862.

Hogg, C. F., and Vine, W. E., The Epistles of Paul the Apostle to the Thessalonians, Glasgow and London, 1914.

Holtzmann, H. J., Die Thessalonicherbriefe, in : Handcommentar zum Neuen Testament, Freiburg, 1889-91.

Jowett, B., The Epistles of St. Paul to the Thessalonians, Galatians, and Romans, London, 1894[3].

Kelly, W., The Epistles of Paul the Apostle to the Thessalonians, London, 1953[3].

Koch, A., Commentar über den ersten Brief des Apostles Paulus an die Thessalonicher, Berlin, 1855[2].

Lake, K., The Earlier Epistles of St. Paul, London, 1911.

Lattey, C., and Keating, J., St. Paul's Epistles to the Churches, London, 1921.

Lightfoot, J. B., Notes on Epistles of St. Paul from unpublished commentaries, London, 1895.

Lineberry, J., Vital Word Studies in I Thessalonians, Grand Rapids, 1960.

Lueken, W., Der erste Brief an die Thessalonicher, Der zweite Brief an die Thessalonicher, in : Die Schriften des Neuen Testaments, Göttingen, 1917.

Lünemann, G., Kritisch Exegetisches Handbuch über die Briefe an die Thessalonicher, in : Kritisch Exegetischer Kommentar über das Neue Testament, Göttingen, 1878[4].

MacEvilly, J., An Exposition of the Epistles of St. Paul ... ,vol. II, London, 1856.

Mason, A. J., Thessalonians, in : Commentary for Schools, ed. C. J. Ellicott, London, 1883.

Milligan, G., St. Paul's Epistles to the Thessalonians, London, 1908.

Moore, A. L., 1 and 2 Thessalonians, in : The Century Bible, New Series, London, 1969.

Morris, L., The First and Second Epistles to the Thessalonians, in : The New London Commentary on the New Testament, London, 1959.

Morris, L., The Epistles of Paul to the Thessalonians, in : The Tyndale New Testament Commentaries, London, 1956.

Neil, W., The Epistle of Paul to the Thessalonians, in : The Moffatt New Testament Commentary, London, 1950.

Oepke, A., et al., Die kleineren Briefe des Apostels Paulus, in : Neues Testament Deutsch, Göttingen, 1965[10].

Olshausen, H., Biblical Commentary on St. Paul's Epistles to the Galatians, Ephesians, Colossians, and Thessalonians, Edinburgh, 1851.

Plummer, A., A Commentary on St. Paul's First Epistle to the Thessalonians, London, 1918.

Plummer, A., A Commentary on St. Paul's Second Epistle to the Thessalonians, London, 1918.

Röhm, J. B., Der erste Brief an die Thessalonicher, Passau, 1885.

Sadler, M. F., The Epistles of St. Paul to the Colossians, Thessalonians, and Timothy, London, 1890.

Schaefer, A., Erklärung der zwei Briefe an die Thessalonicher und des Briefes an die Galater, in : Die Bücher des Neuen Testaments, Münster, 1890.

Schlatter, A., Die Briefe an die Thessalonicher, Philipper, Timotheus und Titus, in : Erläuterungen zum Neuen Testament, Stuttgart, 1950.

Schmidt, P. W., Der erste Thessalonicherbrief neu erklärt, Berlin, 1885.

Schmiedel, P. W., Die Briefe an die Thessalonicher und an die Korinther, in : Hand-Commentar zum Neuen Testament, Freiburg, 1892[2].

Schürmann, H., Der erste Brief an die Thessalonicher, in : Geistliche Schriftlesung, Düsseldorf, 1962.

Wette, W. M. L. de, Kurze Erklärung der Briefe an die Galatar und der Briefe an die Thessalonicher, in : Kurzgefasstes exegetisches Handbuch zum Neuen Testament, Leipzig, 1845.

Whiteley, D. E., Thessalonians, in : New Clarendon Bible, Oxford, 1969.

Wohlenberg, G., Der erste und zweite Thessalonicherbrief, in : Kommentar zum Neuen Testament, Leipzig, 1903.

Zöckler, O., Die Briefe an die Thessalonicher und der Galaterbrief, in : Kurzgefasster Kommentar zum Neuen Testament, Nördlingen, 1887.

(4) *Other Literature*

Baur, F. C., Paulus, Stuttgart, 1845.

Bjerkelund, C. J., Parakalo, Oslo, n.d.

Deissmann, A., Bible Studies, Edinburgh, 1901.

Deissmann, A., Neue Bibelstudien, Marburg, 1897.

Deissmann, A., Light from the Ancient East, London, 1927.

Meecham, H. G., Light from ancient letters, London, 1923.

Meyer, E., Ursprung und Anfänge des Christentums, 3 vols, Stuttgart and Berlin, 1921-3.

Milligan, G., Here and There among the Papyri, London, 1922.

Milligan, G., Selections from the Greek Papyri, Cambridge, 1912.

Plummer, A., The Gospel according to S. Luke, in : International Critical Commentary, Edinburgh, 1905.